A Place Near Heaven
A Year in West Cork

~

Damien Enright

Gill & Macmillan

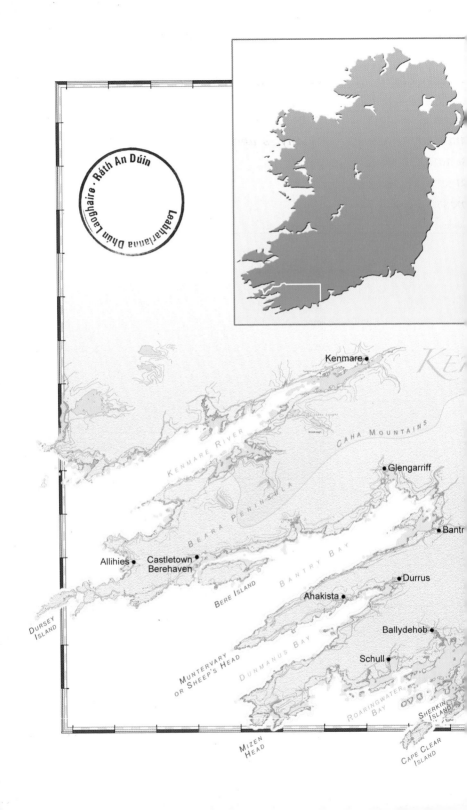

"Suer it is yett a most bewtifull
and sweete Country as any is under Heaven,
seamed thoroughout with many godlie
rivers, replenished with all sortes of fishe
most aboundantlie... "

Edmund Spenser, Poet and Planter, County Cork, 1596.

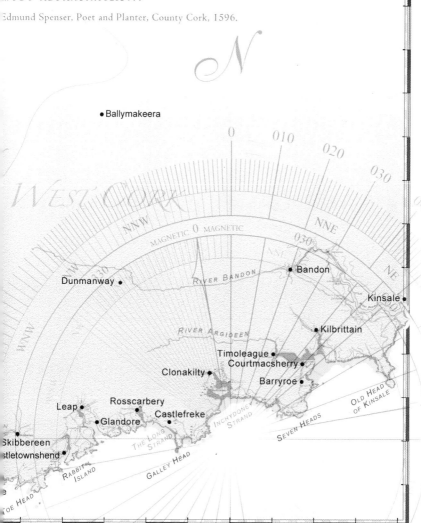

Gill & Macmillan Ltd
Hume Avenue, Park West, Dublin 12
with associated companies throughout the world
www.gillmacmillan.ie
© Damien Enright 2004
0 7171 3689 2
Illustrations by Nevil Swinchatt
Index compiled by Cover to Cover
Design by DesignLab, Dublin
Print origination by Carole Lynch
Printed by GraphyCems Ltd, Spain

This book is typeset in Venetian 301BT 11pt on 15pt.

A CIP catalogue record for this book is available
from the British Library.

1 3 5 4 2

The maps on pages iv–v and xii–xiii are reproduced from
Ordnance Survey Ireland Permit No. 7787
© Ordnance Survey Ireland and Government of Ireland

To my wife, Marie, best friend and fellow voyager; to my son, Matt Enright, for setting up the search programme invaluable in editing; to Val Sieveking and Alannah Hopkin for advice at the start; to Tim Cadogan and Penny Durell for sources; to Jonathan Williams, my agent; and to Fergal Tobin, who made this book possible.

Contents

Acknowledgments

My thanks to:
Richard Mills
Jim Graham and Mandy Kington
Nicholas Leach
Marie Enright
Mim Hill and Lily Jennings
for providing some of the photos on which Nevil Swinchatt's artwork
is based.

My thanks also to Carla Nicholson, Christopher Roche
and the rock pool children.

The following pages are extracts from my *Irish Examiner* newspaper columns, my walk books of West Cork and other writings. They owe everything to the late Seán Dunne, poet and editor, who first suggested I set down a calendar of these precious West Cork days.

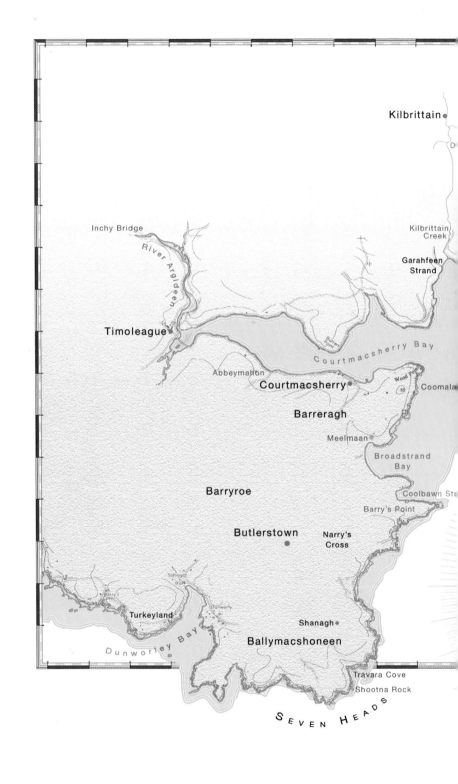

Introduction

West Cork is heaven for the amateur naturalist. The air is clean, the sea unpolluted, every spring-time hedge is a lexicon of wildflowers, every rock a confection of lichens. Summers are full of mackerel and butterflies, village festivals and horse races on the sands. Autumn brings berries and mushrooms, wild redwings and fieldfares from Scandinavia, and flocks of 5,000 golden plover spiralling over our local bay.

In November the arrival of the sprat shoals signals a wild life spectacular, with seals and gannets and every kind of diving duck. At Christmas, once every few years, there may be the magic of snow. I have written about all these things and the pleasure of living with them. With no background in botany or biology but a life-long love of nature, I have learned about them as I went, full of wonder and constantly surprised.

When we first came to West Cork, I knew neither the countryside nor the people. In fact, after thirty-two years abroad, I was a stranger everywhere in Ireland. Yes, I was born here – on the Ring of Kerry, a legendary 'beauty spot' – but my father's job moved us from small town to small town. By age eighteen I was acquainted with every 'beauty spot' in Ireland but at home in none. Nomadic by nurture, I left Ireland to travel the world. Time and again I was fortunate enough to find beautiful and unspoilt places.

From the mid-1980s, we holidayed in Ireland every few years. Skipping stones on Courtmacsherry Bay one summer evening, it came to me that here was a place as lovely and a quality of life as fine as any we'd ever found. We would never get rich but we might manage to make a living and, given the joy it would bring us and the children, wouldn't that be enough?

The first house we found was on the north side of the bay. Afterwards, we moved across to Courtmacsherry itself, a chocolate box village of 186 inhabitants, set on a wooded shore.

This part of Ireland, the west and extreme south-west, has a weather system of its own; it is never really cold and only for short spells is it ever really dry. The natural vegetation is a delight; wild palm trees, fuchsia and rhododendron thrive. Year round, humpback, fin, blue, sei and minke whales, dolphins and porpoises migrate along the coast. In summer, basking sharks, ocean sunfish and even turtles drift by on the temperate Gulf Stream sea.

Our West Cork neighbours are a passionate and convivial people, confident and independent, Catholic and pagan, Celtic and imaginative, hospitable and neighbourly. In adversity, their first resort is a sense of humour. Work is always there, woven into life, the building of houses, the harvesting of the sea, the husbandry of animals, the setting and reaping of crops; it is not a nine-to-five affair. 'When God made time, he made plenty of it ...', they say. That stone-skipping evening at Courtmac, we resolved to cherish time, to stop and do the things we had always intended to do when we were too busy bustling in the world.

When we visit city friends they look at us carefully. Has it worked, their eyes ask, are the kids happy, do we miss the city? Some would move out tomorrow but it isn't easy. They question us apprehensively, half wanting, half not wanting, to find flaws.

Sometimes, on bright mornings, as we walk the strand, I see myself back in a city, watching a couple on TV with a dog and nothing but the birds, the surf and the miles of empty sand. I think of how my heart would yearn for that, for the space and the clean air.

I think then that we've done the right thing. The children have taken values drawn from here, a sense of place and of what is real and unreal. I can't think of a better start for them, or a happier ending for ourselves.

January

In January, if we are lucky, we get rare — and thus, welcome — snow. Better at Christmas, but our children don't look a gift snow-person in the mouth and everyone enjoys the few days when the world is transformed. January is walking weather, with a bit of music afterwards by the fire. Before the 10th, primroses appear near the ruined graveyard at twelfth-century Abbeymahon, on Courtmacsherry Bay. By the month's end, the ravens at Coomalacha begin nesting.

Nothing stirs. The boats in Courtmacsherry Harbour catch the sunlight.

On New Year's Eve, flakes began to fall, few and far between, as evening darkened. Children cried out in delight. Snow may be bread-and-butter to an Eskimo; it is Dream Topping here.

The flakes thickened, falling in soft curtains, drifting past our windows. They swirled beneath the street light below the house and eddied out over the bay. They draped the woods behind us in a white gown. Before our eyes, our village underwent a snow-change. By half eleven, as we walked to the pubs for the singing in of the New Year, the main street of our one-street Gulf Stream hamlet was a slipway of compacted snow, spangled with reflections from the community Christmas tree. Through slicks of light, red-nosed children walked, staggered and slid, a fairy-tale terrace of snow-capped Georgian town houses on their left and, on their right, the dark, rippling sea.

Snow is the better enjoyed for being a novelty. In our then seven years in West Cork, we'd had only one real white-out. That was when we'd lived across the bay. In Courtmacsherry, the village of 186 souls to which we had moved, the last serious snow had fallen ten years earlier. Now, it came on a New Year's Eve, late for a white Christmas but a wonderful holiday treat. Inland there had been only a light fall. Here there was a thick carpet, a world transformed from soft, arthritic mists into a mild adjunct of the Arctic. Courtmacsherry was another country and we were citizens of a white kingdom. A spell descended. No one came or went. The flakes fell and settled in drifts and eddies, muffling the sounds of footsteps, fattening the pavements and the roofs. The dark sea washed in over snow-covered rocks, and we lived on a crinoline coast.

But did the beleaguered villagers and visitors still welcome in the New Year? Did they rise to the occasion? Snowballs flew on the way to the midnight pubs, the children excited and the adults watching their step. At twelve o'clock, muffled and mufflered, a procession of hardy souls left homes and pub firesides to wend down to the pier head, there to ring in the New Year on a hand-bell, then to return to the hostelries and the bonhomie. Later, we walked home, with the kids, crunching through fresh drifts of snow.

On New Year's Day morning, at nine o'clock, the footprints of the revellers had disappeared under a new fall and every pathway of the village was pristine. The single street was a soft, white avenue, as yet unmarked by cars. The only soul to be seen was a dedicated local photographer, snapping an unimpressed, strayed horse. With my young son Fintan, I wandered out of the half-awake house and down the drive, into a novel day. Snow, to right and left of us, turning the garden bushes into duvets you could sleep in, slow embrace of hypothermia and a warm demise.

The morning was bright and sparkling, great tracking weather. I met a woman lecturer from University College Cork who reported the footprints of a badger, two foxes and a hare. Fields across the bay were rolling slopes of white, all contours softened. How marvellous the great engine that had created, overnight, that transformation. Thank heaven for the surprises of the Great Weatherman. Thank heaven for children, to help us enjoy them in full. In summer, sand castles and rock pools; now, in winter, slides and snowballs. Down all the sloping driveways, children whizzed on dustbin liners and tea trays, and giant snow-persons adorned every second lawn. All day, the white crescent edged the beach, icing where there was always sand. After lunch, mad, heroic bathers, male and female, tiptoed into the channel, pink-cheeked and goose-pimpled, risking pneumonia to raise funds for the Courtmacsherry lifeboat.

Meanwhile, at the house, children came and went, snow in their boots and pockets and down their necks. Stuffing their wet Wellies with last week's papers, I saw great reporters and columnists disappear into the maw. Outside, blackbirds scrapped over leftovers while our robin fiercely defended the bare bird table, jealous about his feast of snow.

The following day, the snow melted and the blanketing clouds that had raised the temperature broke up and sunlight poured through. It, like the snow, was temporary, but for an afternoon the robin sang as if it was spring. Our California friends love the changeability of our Atlantic weather and say they never look out the window at the same view. Today, it is yet another contrast. Out on the bay, curtains of spray blow off the waves as they plunge like bucking broncos into the gale. Few sights in nature are more spectacular than an incoming tide meeting an offshore wind.

J. Alfred Prufrock, T.S. Eliot's sad hero, imagines mermaids singing to him and he says: 'I have seen them riding seaward on the waves/ Combing the white hair of the waves blown back/ When the wind blows the water white and black.' Looking down the estuary in the face of a storm, one can imagine the mermaids and Prufrock's conflict. Conflict is the essence of drama. The sea, with the wind, is conflict. Without it, it is often serene. The same may apply to forests, or single trees. But the ocean's clash with the elements forever draws me back to the sea.

A forest may be as large as a sea loch, and the wind charging through it quite frightening. Behind our village, we have a most beautiful forest of perhaps 500 acres, part of the old Earl of Shannon estate. It not only shelters the hamlet but makes of it a sort of Parknasilla or Killarney, an enchanted place where the waxy leaves of laurels and rhododendrons shine in their own darkness, ivy and Old Man's Beard festoon the trees, and small waterfalls gush from moss-grown cuttings. It is tragic to see these trees sometimes knocked by the wind. In the recent storms, two huge beeches and two age-old oaks came down.

But many beech and oak remain, along with an ancient cork tree, stands of red-barked myrtle, Norway spruce and Japanese cedar, indeed a botanical garden of trees, for it was the old milord's vocation to enhance the landscape with trees – natives and exotic – and to create woodlands that would be forever a pleasure to behold. The earl, long since dead, left an abiding testament to his husbandry and his deep love of this place. How valuable these woodlands are, now, to the village, in its new role as a summer retreat! Woodland walks abound. The forest floor is a wall-to-wall swathe of bluebells in one season; at another it is white with wood anemones and garlic-smelling ramsons. Locals and visitors watch the beeches redden in spring and burst into leaf at the approach of summer.

In July and August, the canopy is heavy and verdant, a world of cool shade with the sun piercing the penumbra, throwing stripes of light on the pathways, making clearings into prosceniums of sound and light, the forums of butterflies and songbirds. A clutch of long-eared owls hatches in the high trees each spring-time, and parents hoot while fledglings squeal like un-oiled hinges. Pheasants screech and warblers warble. In winter toadstools burst from the forest floor and fat beech mast gathers in drifts. Sometimes, but rarely, the woods fill with snow and then are beautiful and hushed and 'downy', as Frost, the poet, said. Long may they survive to provide the picture-book setting of this village with its toes in the sea.

The sea is omnipresent. The view from our window, depending on the weather, may be of a mirror-like millpond reflecting the brilliant colours of the small, moored boats, or of a maelstrom of flying spray and broken water. These days up to ten great northern divers fish thirty yards offshore. Their white breasts brave the choppy waves as spray flies to either side of their shoulders. Neither swept in by the incoming tide nor out by the offshore gale, held in stasis by the paddle-power of their webbed feet, they calmly dive and fish amidst the whitecaps and chaos, on the switch-back of the rock 'n' roll sea. Last week they were around the corner at Coolbawn Strand on the Seven Heads, where the sprat shoals were inshore, with thousands of birds feasting on them. A dozen grey seals wallowed so close to the shore that, had one the voice, one could have sung to them as the mermaids sang for Prufrock.

Noting the annual arrival of the sprat shoals, I had said in a newspaper article that visitors wanting to enjoy the usual wildlife extravaganza should convene outside Timoleague Abbey on the following Sunday where Wolstenholme, the Yorkshire potter and bird watcher, would introduce the Coolbawn show. Obligingly, all the performers turned up, sprats, birds and seals and, this having been confirmed, at 2pm on the Sunday a motorcade of ornithological thrill-seekers moved off, weaving through the bohreens with farm dogs yapping at their tyres and isolated bachelor-farmers rubbing incredulous eyes at the procession heading for the boiling inlet that was Coolbawn on that wild, wet, grey, spectacular afternoon.

There, the undersea world was a marine soup, larded with millions of oily sprats and crowded with divers, guillemots, razorbills, mergansers, cormorants, shags and seals. On the surface, rafts of gulls undulated like rolling carpets on the swells. Over the waves, delicate kittiwakes hovered and dipped and, beyond, big, cruciform gannets rocketed in formation into the sea. Telescopes were set up, not that there was need for them. Coolbawn Strand is hardly more than two hundred yards across and, that day, was a wildlife bottleneck. All was eminently visible with the naked eye, the curtains of screaming birds so dense that to point out a single species was impossible. 'Look, between the kittiwakes, beside the blackback, the ducks with crew-cuts — blast, they've dived!' But, what the hell, there was plenty more to see; so much one could only be silent and marvel.

But the walk-leader, Wolstenholme, did his best. Standing on the wall in the wind, he told the assembled throng all about it, illustrating his talk with a sprat produced from the oxter of his waxed overcoat, like a rabbit drawn out of a hat. With round, sad eyes, two seals, heads high above the water, watched him, as if pitying him his single fish and wondering how one small sprat could possibly impress so many earthbounders. Fifteen grey seals, in all, courted and cavorted in the waves, a mix of big, flat-headed bulls, smaller females and slight young pups. They could be observed to one's heart's content. They did not grow bored of watching us, so we could watch them at our leisure. They seemed to be there as much for the party as for the fish suppers, with time galore for backstroke and intertwining. Young Fintan thought two of them were fighting, but I'm sure he had it wrong.

In all, more than seventy hardy souls turned out to savour nature's wonders despite the inclement day. Included were West Cork's colourful natives and ex-pats, a famous author, a cabinet minister, a Japanese family, an aromatherapist, farmers, businessmen, housewives, artists, children and motley birders, all witnesses to a vigorous world in which we play no part other than as watchers and interpreters. Those who sat home watching wild life TV missed one of nature's spectaculars. Out at Coolbawn, cheeks were wind-red and hair wind-blown but there wasn't a dull expression to be seen.

Yesterday, after the weekend of half-light, the weather changed again and it was a beautiful, flashing day, as sharp as Siberia but, down by the south-facing sea, as warm as Spain. Backed into a sunny corner, I again watched the kittiwakes dance over the whitecaps. Sprats, birds and seals were still at Coolbawn strand. Television wildlife, for all its joys, cannot compare with the reality. Roll up and see the fat seals hunt the quick herrings – the Seven Heads real life annual nature show is much better than TV!

But while the birds gorge, our poor fishermen find it hard to keep going. Passing the kitchen window this morning, I peered out to see if the rain had stopped. On a sand bank, in the middle of the bay, lines of cormorants were strung out like a coal miner's washing, drying their wings in the sun. Reaching for the binoculars, I went into the garden and counted them. One hundred and seventy-four. How many fish do one hundred and seventy-four cormorants eat in a day? Boxes of herrings and dabs. Maybe our fishermen should capture them, train them, and go into the cormorant fishing business, like the Japanese.

After the rain, the day was so clear and the change so dramatic that it cried out to be enjoyed. Following a wooded path, I reached the ridge behind the village and the wide Atlantic lay out before me, glittering and dancing in the light. Downhill we walked, the dog and I, through Meelmaan, a small, once-upon-a-time fishing hamlet on a country lane sloping to the sea. Here, on summer days, chickens scratch in the dust outside Kitty O'Driscoll's cottage, cats sun themselves on gate piers and dogs lie prone in the heat. Now, in winter, there wasn't a soul to be seen. A deserted village, yes; a neighbour tells me he remembers all the houses with children; now, there are no children here. He and his friends would walk to the National School at Courtmac, summer and winter, just a mile away. But what is remarkable about this humble place above the wide expanse of Broad Strand is its architecture which, surely, is unique.

The road descends steeply. On either side are ten single-storey cottages, two or three still inhabited, a few used as holiday homes in summer, the rest in ruins. For half of these, or more, the roof ridge follows the steep slope of the road, the north gable six feet higher than the south, so that the roof sits like a cap tipped jauntily over one eye. I have never seen building like this anywhere. The design was, one assumes, the brainchild of a country builder a hundred years ago or more. It makes no sense. Water will run off the slates anyway. If, under the pressures of large families, attics were used as bedrooms, perhaps as children grew up they moved from the low end to the high, toddlers along the bottom gable, teenagers along the top?

At the end of the houses, the tarmacadam stops and gives way to a scrubby path, the track of the old road which once continued down to the shore and crossed the beach. Erosion has taken it away; one can see its other half abruptly ending on the cliff edge opposite. The beach opened up below me, deserted, like the village, most of a mile of empty sand. On the sand, it was warm as summer and presented a great temptation to stop. A haze of newly hatched insects hovered over the sun-warmed sea wrack, with pipits, wagtails and stonechats busily harvesting them. Walking is supposed to be the life-saving exercise, not sitting down but, as I sat, I excused myself with the lines of W.H. Davies, the poet-tramp, 'What is this life if, full of care,/ We have no time to stand and stare'. Far off, three miles beyond the rustle and drain of the surf, white walls of spray silently threw themselves up the ramparts of the Old Head of Kinsale, where guillemots and razorbills crowd the sea stacks in summer. What, one might ask, was the point in living longer if one hadn't time to enjoy the wayside attractions as one went?

While getting out and about to watch wildlife is, as I said, preferable to viewing it on TV, a recent addition to our household has brought wildlife indoors. We have an orphan rabbit in the house, a wild creature found abandoned and reared by a neighbour, and given as a Christmas gift to our son, Fintan. It is a very small rabbit and, when indoors, obligingly leaves its tiny currants on a sheet of newspaper. These nights, Fintan brings it in from the greenhouse where it normally resides, feasting on nasturtiums, which must make it a peppery little rabbit indeed. It would probably have an exotic flavour were we to put it in the pot. In the living room, it stretches out in front of the fire and seems to be under the illusion that it is a cat.

The dog, after an initial growl and some reassurance, ignored it but the cat – called Peter, although a female – eyed it from the back of an armchair and we were afraid she might spring upon it, emulating the Serengeti lions on the TV. For the first few evenings, however, she simply watched, sometimes curling her tail in fury. Then she jumped down and, grabbing the small bunny, gave it a good wash. Soon cat and rabbit were having unequal wrestling matches. Then when Peter stretched on the carpet, the rabbit would hop to her side, and curl up.

Rabbit and cat are now firm friends. They play tag up and down the corridor and under the chairs. The rabbit can move at a high rate of knots when pursued, but sometimes is ambushed by the cat, who drubs its long ears and then gets it in a sort of a step-over leg lock. The rabbit, perfectly docile, makes no objection, and sometimes they drop off to sleep together, furry and warm.

We have photos to attest to all this. We think it is very civilised of the cat – baby rabbits would normally be a prey species for a country feline. But then, our Peter came from London, albeit she was bought in a pet shop in a dog-eat-dog part of town. She has been a lucky cat, transported to salubrious Ireland, where every London resident with sense would want to be. She has spent her long life in the embrace of the family, whenever possible on somebody's lap. She has tolerated dogs, young pups and, now, rabbits. Perhaps she has ecological sympathies, very proper at the present time.

Otters, we know, do not play in the house or garden, except in the case of the otters in Gavin Maxwell's classic *A Ring of Bright Water*. However, recently an otter was seen gambolling on our neighbour's lawn. For a good ten minutes this large wild animal rolled about on the grass in full view of her picture windows. While Courtmac is a quiet place, with hardly a soul stirring at ten thirty on a misty January morning, nevertheless it is a village, and a car might well have passed on the road between the garden and the sea. I doubt if the otter would have been fazed in the slightest. Otters are regularly at the pier, scuttling on and off the moored boats. It's a privilege to have such trusting creatures on our doorstep. The woman who watched it thought it might have come out of the sea to wash in fresh water. A stream runs down from the woods and appears as a small cascade on the roadside below the lawn, then disappears underground again and crosses the road into the bay. She imagined the otter in the pool under the waterfall, taking a shower. True or not, I wish I'd been there to see.

A man told me he'd seen a white owl at Lislevane and another man told me of a pair at Rosscarbery. This was apropos an article I'd written lamenting the disappearance of barn owls due to habitat loss.

The Lislevane owl seemed to have arrived from elsewhere and was settling into an old barn. The team running the Barn Owl Conservation programme at the Irish Wild Bird Conservancy will be interested and may well install a tea chest in a secluded corner in order to ensure that, if it finds a mate, it will have somewhere to breed. However, these bachelor owls, young males, are a sad feature of the demise of the species in many areas. They wander from their native nests in search of a mate but no female is to be found.

The Rosscarbery man also told me of a wagtail that, last summer, nested on his ancient tractor. The tractor, little used except for driving out to his oyster frames at low tide, must have seemed a suitable nursery. He discovered the nest when he set off into the water and the wagtail parents flew around him, chirping in alarm. He stopped the vehicle and found a nest full of fledglings under a wheel strut. Deciding the oysters could wait, he left the tractor parked up until they had flown. One day, soon after, he again sat aboard ready to drive away when he saw a new nest, high on the mudguard, almost beside him. Because this time it was out of danger of flooding, he went about his business, the parent wagtails following and bringing a running buffet to the nestlings as the man tended his oysters a hundred yards from land.

Far out beyond the oyster-beds are the whales, here from June until January each year, often close inshore. Early this month, out walking, I searched the sea for ten minutes with my binoculars and saw them, five sudden plumes of white water almost on the horizon, like pillars of salt against the gun-metal sea: fin whales, amongst the biggest creatures ever to have lived on earth, migrating in stately progress along our coast. I had been standing on the headland at Dunworley. The day was clear, the sky blue, the wind sharp and knuckle-numbing, the yellow sun sinking on the horizon as I watched. A good day for walking, not a good day for standing still. I had been told by Whooley the Whale Watcher what to look for: a flock of excited birds on the sea's surface, a wave breaking unusually, a dark shape or a rill of white water, a spume or spout of spray. The face of the ocean, seen from the headland, was vast but my trusty binoculars could take me, in clear focus, from the Old Head of Kinsale on the east, to Galley Head on the west, a huge area of water. Between these headlands, many whales had been seen in the preceding days, at least fourteen seis, a large pod of fin whales and many dozen porpoises and dolphins.

I watched out for birds. Sure enough, in the sweep on my lenses I found an area two miles out on the featureless sea where white gannets soared and plummeted and gulls circled and dipped in small clouds. In that few acres of the deep, something special had to be going on. At this time of year, I knew there would be herring out there, in abundance. But while gannets are well equipped to dive on the shoals, sharp beaks splitting the surface like spears, gulls are not. As anybody who has ever gutted a catch of mackerel at sea will know, they flock and congregate where fish offal is available, swooping over the waves for scraps. Herring, out on the open ocean, are far too big and fast for gulls, unless they are half dead, or half herrings, eviscerated or chewed by larger hunters, whales or dolphins, porpoises or seals. Perfect for the gulls are herring pieces, floating *gefilte fisch*. Even so far away, as I watched I could imagine the sound of their frenzy, their shrieking and bickering over the feast. Then, out beyond them, a white pillar rising out of the sea. What else could it be but a great whale.

The fin whales that pass our coast each winter are huge, up to 65 foot long, baleen whales, without teeth, yet feeding on shoals of small fish. I had recently read Tim Severin, our neighbour's, book *The Search for Moby Dick*. This told of indigenous whale hunters in remote Polynesian and Indonesian villages who hunted the toothed, and sometimes dangerous, sperm whale with hand-thrown harpoons. To these people, the hunting of baleen whales – the blues, fins, humpbacks, etc., conventionally the prey of commercial whalers – was taboo because ancient superstition identified them as their tribal ancestors. Amongst the baleen whales, fins and seis are the least pursued because they move so quickly they are difficult to catch.

The whales seen off our coasts – fin, sei, sperm, humpback, pilot, orca, minke, bottle-nosed and beaked – roam the oceans of the world. They may be off Connecticut in October, West Cork in November,

Cochin in the New Year. Whooley, who has watched whales in Patagonia and Baja California, Canada and Australia, says that the diversity of cetacean species seen off our shores is unrivalled. Ireland's west coast is one of Europe's, if not the world's, premier whale-watching locations. On his average three-hour watch – three hours behind binoculars is quite enough – he sights an average of four species, more than double seen elsewhere. Largely owing to the efforts of the Irish Whale & Dolphin Group (IWDG), our 200-mile Economic Exclusion Zone has been Europe's first Whale and Dolphin Sanctuary since 1991. This little known national initiative is something of which the Irish can be proud.

Last year, on a sharp January day, I went to sea with a friend, an ex-commercial fisherman and amateur marine biologist who now uses his boat to take visitors out to see whales. As it happened, we saw none that day, only hundreds of dolphins. Few sights in nature can be more thrilling than a squadron of airborne dolphins in winter sunlight. Whatever about flying fish – or flying squirrels – nothing is quite as exciting as a troop of dolphins in and out of the water, keeping pace with the boat, smooth and supple as latex, black, with white sides, powerful and aerodynamic, as curious and excited as a bunch of country children seeing an exotic foreigner for the first time.

It is curiosity that makes them jump. They want to see us, as we want to see them. In and out they leap and glide, eyes fixed on the aliens in the sea craft. When they hear the trumming of the engines, they come from half a mile away, breasting the waves, urgent in their delight, converging from all points in pods and packs. Reaching the boat, they ride the slipstream. While, in these waters, we do not yet have flying fish, we have flying dolphins. Given the warming of the East Atlantic, the former may not be far away.

Last week, off the Old Head of Kinsale, common dolphins, swimming in Busby Berkeley formations, rode the bow-waves of sei whales, while harbour porpoises and bottle-nosed dolphins cavorted in Hole Open Bay. We do not usually think of Ireland as a site for exotic wildlife, yet off our coasts roam these, the largest creatures on earth, five times the size of a bull elephant. We only have to hie ourselves to the headlands to watch them.

Whales, as we know, sing, and therefore might well be attracted to the lonely fastness of Travara Cove, on the Seven Heads, which seems recently to have become a musical venue. Last August, arriving above the cove on a coastal walk with a group of academics from overseas, I was surprised to hear the strains of a concertina on the breeze. There, below us, sitting on the rocks, was a solitary woman, playing Irish airs to the seals and her heart's content. We stopped and listened. So romantic was the scene that some of the party thought I had set it up. Unfortunately, they clapped at an interval. The poor woman, aghast at being discovered, boxed her instrument and fled.

Now, Kevin Hanley, of Inishannon – a musician himself – tells me that, the other weekend, as he set off walking from the cove, a car arrived with two women of late middle years who, at this remote and isolated spot, dragged a large, oddly shaped box from the boot. As he went on his way, he suddenly heard the strains of a bagpipe and, surrendering to curiosity, returned. The two were standing on the cliff, one playing *Amazing Grace* with great conviction from a danger-ous salient, while her friend spoke into a tape recorder describing details of the scene. After a further air, they stopped and spoke to the hirsute Hanley, telling him they were retired Americans whose hobby it was to travel the world seeking wild, dramatic places, there to play and record for the pleasure of it. They were quite sane women – indeed, I would say, inspired.

Travara Cove saw a spectacular, but very tragic, shipwreck on the night of 13 January 1925. On a coast often lashed by storms, the tempest that howled ashore on 'the night of the *Cardiff Hall*' was legendary for its ferocity. Laden with maize from Argentina's River Plate, the ill-fated *Cardiff Hall* was only twenty miles from her destination, Cork harbour, when she was driven inshore and smashed on the Shoonta Rock, outside Travara. All twenty-eight aboard, Welsh and Arab sailors, lost their lives. It was a shocking event, still etched in the handed-down memories of local people. Mast lights were first seen by a cliff-top farmer alerted by a siren wailing at sea at about 8pm. Neighbours joined him with their lanterns, their eyes searching the gloom and the mountainous waves. Helpless and appalled, they could hear desperate screams and whistles from the darkness below them.

A man galloped on horseback to Barry's Point, where the Courtmacsherry lifeboat was launched, but rounding the point in such seas was impossible under oar-power; indeed it would have challenged the powerful engine-driven boats of today. For the shipwrecked, there was no salvation; even with lifebelts, the force of the sea would have dashed them on the black rocks. Two bodies, only, were found, those of the captain and an Arab seaman. The captain's son, sailing with him for the first time, was among the unrecovered.

On the following morning, at dawn, local people woke to find the wave platforms of Travara plastered in gold, the sea-bottom yellow with six thousand tons of maize and more of the bright cargo washing ashore on every wave. The bounty was enormous; many local people had never possessed more than a few shillings in their lives. They descended upon it with every container available, transporting it to their donkeys and carts on the bohreen that still leads down to the cove today. By the Friday, it seemed as if half the county was drawing maize from Travara. Local papers spoke of a 'gold rush' at Butlerstown, the nearest village, as merchants bid for the golden salvage of the sea. Ingenious trawls were devised and dragged behind boats to gather the grain from the bottom and sift it from the sand. A mill was set up. Lorries took milled grain to the towns of West Cork. In 2002 a recovered anchor of the *Cardiff Hall*, weighing three tons, was set up in Butlerstown. I told my academic companions the story that afternoon, when we walked down to Travara. Some of them threw flowers in the sea for the drowned.

Today, a couple of rooks are billing by my bird table; they should not be doing this until March. Perhaps, like the rooks in Edward Thomas's poem 'Thaw', they know something we don't and, from the high tree tops, can see winter pass. It is surprising how affectionate these mawkish, ragged-trousered crows can be – and, in full view; usually, rooks conduct their courtships high in their rookeries. There, they caw and caterwaul, and keep the farmer's guests from a morning lie-in. But unseasonable love seems to have made this pair incautious. I watch them, sitting side by side, on a very thin branch, only six feet off the ground and only twelve feet from my window. I wonder when the branch is going to bend so much under their weight that they will fall.

Meanwhile I notice a tiny spider descending on a silken thread from my forelock. It is no bigger than a full-stop on my computer screen. Taking the web, I hang it out the window, where it floats away; so do the rooks, upon seeing me. Most rural houses have their retinue of insect retainers, and ours is no exception. Recently, in the bathroom, there has been a spider hatch. Where the walls meet the ceiling, there are two fluffy, yellowish cocoons, each about the size of a pea. From these, tiny spiders emerge, and hang on transparent silk threads. They are everywhere, some days. Then they disappear. No doubt they set off to colonise other forelocks and other bathrooms. This is probably just as well because we have incidents of 'arachnophobia' amongst our loo visitors, although most know that there is little to fear from the spiders of the British and Irish Isles. Little Miss Muffet, daughter of Thomas Muffet, the sixteenth-century naturalist, was a famous arachnophobiast. Surely, in fairness to spiders, the nursery rhyme should be, 'When the harmless poor spider/ Sat down beside her/ He frightened Miss Muffet away …'

While our ragged-feathered rooks and most of our other crows are familiar to our UK visitors, the local choughs and grey crows are not. In Ireland we have seven crow species – jackdaw, jay, chough, magpie, rook, grey crow and raven, in order of size. The glossy-black chough has all but disappeared from Britain, while the grey or *scál* crow is rarely found south of the Scottish border. Here, out on the cliffs, ten minutes from the village, English birders can watch flights of screaming red-beaked, red-legged choughs tumbling and swooping over the sea. Grey crows – called hooded crows in the UK – are also common, even in the village where they frequent seaweed-covered rocks along the shore. Grey crows are neat, handsome birds, with strong, black beaks and cloaks of elegant grey. They do not flock, but I notice that when winter hardens, individuals feed heavily on the wild mussel beds. Like all crows, they are clever. Unable to open the shell even with their pick-axe bills, they take the unfortunate creature in their talons, fly to a great height and drop it onto the road. Crack! goes the shell, and there's the soft mussel. At times the road is littered with broken shells and I'm told by local garages that they sometimes puncture tyres. I was amazed at the proliferation of grey crows – and magpies – when I returned to Ireland; perhaps it is because of the increase in cars, and road-kills. I remember *scál* crows as rare and solitary birds of lonely places, the Beara and the Ring of Kerry, Connemara and Donegal.

Mist in the morning and mist in the evening, the landscape splashed with red when the sun breaks through. Mist brings magic to the world, however familiar. Only a clod or a cynic could fail to be moved by the beauty of the morning mist. Last Sunday, the day opened with white veils hanging over the bay. They lifted to give us a glorious afternoon, during which we walked the back roads of the West Cork Gaeltacht, where the natives, as the old emigrant song put it, 'speak a language [Irish] that the stranger does not know.' There, in the high lands, the veils came down again in the evening, wrapping the hills around Ballymakeera in a haze of gold.

As we topped the high point of a bohreen and looked out over West Cork to the far blue mountains of Kerry, my private celestial orchestra, as usual, filled the sky. It was playing, as always, the *Concierto de Aranjuez*, now used to sell everything from ice cream to cars; I first heard it as a trumpet solo one glorious, long-ago sunset on the Balearic island of Formentera, where there were then but eight foreigners, of whom I was one. Now, at home, so arrested am I by the glory of the West Cork evening that the jaw drops, the eyes glaze and I stand 'silent, upon a peak in Darien' (above Ballymakeera, in January) listening to Miles Davis blow the *Sketches of Spain*.

February

When we lived in the cities, February passed unremarked,
another month of winter. Nothing would change until April,
and the first warm days. Since we came to West Cork,
February is looked forward to with excitement, the prelude
to the main event, the spring of the year. February 1st,
St Bridget's Day, is the unveiling of spring in Ireland.
Everything starts to change rapidly; the headlong race for
summer's flowerings and seedings begin. The celandine
blooms; the swallows arrive. January had dog violets, daisies
and periwinkles already showing, catkins on the hazel and a
pipistrelle bat hawking in the garden. Now, February comes
in with a spring in its step, and off we go down the road to
summer, with all its burgeoning joys and heady raptures.

The light on the western sea ...

'Now, comes the spring/ The days are getting longer/ And after Féile Bríde/ I will hoist up my sail,' said blind Anthony Rafteri, wandering poet and last of the Gaelic troubadours. No doubt he smelled spring in the air and some vestige of the lengthening days flickered before his sightless eyes. He set off for County Mayo, awakening from its winter slumber; he had plans in his head and songs in his oxter, 'At Balla,' he said, 'I'll first take the floor …' We arrive back to West Cork on February 1st, after a visit to my brother in Andalucia. Not a moment too soon.

We are welcomed home by golden days, the sky as clear and cloudless as the south of Spain, and the estuary mirror-calm. Passing the National School beside the abbey at Timoleague, we see children playing football in the yard. In the creek across the road, lapwing roost, heads under wings, on gold-slicked mudbanks. Ten yards farther, below the Courtmac bridge, a heron stands stock still, its blue and white image vivid on the water. Nearby, on the muddy shore, curlews stalk and dunlin skitter. A covey of widgeon dabbles on the marsh edge; a pair of teal swim past, the drake's yellow spot very bright. Rafteri followed the spring into Connacht; after our wanderings, we find it ahead of us in West Cork.

That same first morning, two hundred golden plover roost on the mud opposite the petrol station and shop. For every bird in the water, there are twenty in the sky. Every now and then more plover descend, like leaves from heaven. Through the binoculars, one sees that there are thousands of plover aloft, swirling and dividing in great flocks, too high to see with the naked eye. Up there, what grandeur, what wildness reigns! 'Look up!' I want to shout, to flag passing cars, beard burghers, buttonhole bishops, tell the world to look at the sky. Two thousand plover pass over my head in a whisper; beyond the bridge, others rise from the roosts and join the flock. Ten thousand wings swirl and eddy over the estuary, now a great, brown flood, now turning and catching the sun like a river of stars. The massed flocks and synchronised flicking-over is said to confuse predators. A peregrine in their midst would surely lose all grasp of space, blinded by the flash of wings, the storms of sky-blown confetti.

Beneath the plover, leisurely lapwing flap back and forth before settling on the sand spits, painted faces and long top-notches shining. But though the plover always thrill, and the sallies of the lapwing delight the watcher, it is the tiny dunlin, rocketing in small, dense squadrons only inches over the water, that take the prize. The flock, anything from tens to hundreds, spreads and bunches, widens from arrowhead to discus, contracts from wave front to diamond, brown to white in an instant, now-you-see-them-now-you-don't, a dazzling, hurtling checkerboard of light.

On the cliffs, beyond the bay, the ravens have rebuilt their nest on the base of last year's. The sea swills or lashes far below, depending on the weather. It is a lonely spot, but time-honoured. The nest base that has lasted through years is once again tidied and built on, and is soon cosy and ready for eggs. Fresh twigs, some with lichen, form the walls and the inside is lined with horsehair. Because horses of many colours graze the cliff fields, the nest cup is roan and chestnut, black and grey. Set into a cleft, the whole is fifty feet above the waves, protected by an overhang from the south-west weather. Soon, we shall see eggs, green, blotched with brown, shiny and snug inside.

Ravens have nested on this site as long as the oldest villager can remember. They mate for life, and when a partner dies, a young bird takes its place. Thus there has been a continuum of ravens, an unbroken tenancy and genetic chain inhabiting these cliffs for perhaps millennia. How interesting it would be to find some ancient record of them, at this spot. They are storied birds in every mythology. Celtic legend credits them with prediction. The most feared battle standard of the Danes bore an image of the raven, and those who marched behind it must have been familiar with the bird, scavenging the dead.

The fine weather lasts; sunlight glitters on the bay, blue as the sky above. Cold February is on hold: the world takes off its overcoat. In sheltered corners, so warm is the sun that one can bathe in it. Walls gather the heat and flies buzz and bask, an early drone of summer. We know it may be short-lived, a passing isle in a sea of still wintry weather, but we are grateful for brief mercies, any respite being better than none. Walking the cliffs at lunch time – an hour stolen in honour of the sun – I spot a bright red hare in a green field where the grass is already growing. Through the binoculars, I can almost count the black hairs that tip its ears, standing straight up and turning like wind vanes. It looks so fresh and alive, such a symbol of frisky life with its whiskers tickling the air, its eyes wide and alert; because I stand stock still, it fails to see me. But, then, the dog! My faithful, hirsute hound heaves into my field of vision and the hare is up on its tiptoes and off, at a lope, the madcap springer bouncing after it. Not a hope, of course, has the dog – she wouldn't catch it in a year of Sundays. But I feel sorry for myself, losing the view, and for the hare, losing the peace and communion of the lovely day.

The first small celandines appear, shining like gold stars in the deep green verdure, on February 10th. Celandine was Wordsworth's welcome harbinger of spring. 'There's a flower that shall be mine,' he said. ''Tis the little Celandine.' With lines like that it is small wonder that the American critic Ezra Pound called him 'a silly old sheep with a genius'. Pound was, himself, silly, without being a genius; in Italy, during World War II, he backed Fascism and later, poor man, spent years in a mental asylum. Pound's *Cantos* have never entered the commonwealth of literature, but many of us know Wordsworth's 'There was a time when meadow, grove, and stream,/ The earth, and every common sight,/ To me did seem/ Apparelled in celestial light,/ The glory and the freshness of a dream.' He is still, I think, amongst the pantheon of great nature poets, especially in the 'Prelude' and 'Ode to the Intimation of Immortality'.

The celandine blooms on the verges of the road near Broad Strand, where it first appears every year. Spring fever abounds. Lambs gambol and play, white as snowdrops. Poor badgers, full of *taispeach* – the urge to procreate – cross roads recklessly and get mown down, three adults dead on a two-mile stretch near Bandon. Recently, I was shown an ancient sett so close to the sea shore that the waves, when high, must all but come flushing down the tunnels. On summer nights badgers may be seen rolling down the banks and nosing the weed in the rock pools. The sett may be as much as three hundred and fifty yards of tunnels, eight to twelve inches from roof to floor, displacing twenty-five tons of earth during the digging. Badgers cavorting on a beach must make a novel sight.

'Hirundo domestica!!!' cried Gilbert White, upon spotting the first swallow of the year 1768, at Selborne, on April 13th. Seizing his journal, he promptly wrote it down. The good vicar was forty-eight that year, celebrating the joys of spring and its arrival. One can almost hear him whoop. Perhaps it was because they were so late in coming that he feared the summer would be swallowless. But 'coming' is the wrong word; the great naturalist believed they hibernated under mud in local ponds and surfaced with the spring.

Irish swallows, most years, arrive in March but this year one was seen on Valentine's Day by a fisherman eight miles off Mizen. It flew around his boat a couple of times, then landed, rested, and flew off again towards land. A second was seen the following day, February 15th, on Cape Clear Island, by a bird watcher. Both may have caught the Saharan tail-wind that deposited a patina of red dust on cars along the West Cork coast. Just dust, no locusts, which are often carried huge distances after being lifted to great heights. I have seen locusts carried to the Canary Islands from the Sahara, but only as individuals and not in plagues.

We have rain – a February without it, in Ireland, would be very worrying – but it is rain, they say, as never before known. It falls, non-stop, for six days. Swans float where there were fields. Hedges are islands and trees are neck high. Water meadows are lakes, shining silver where, yesterday, they were green swards. Rain water runs off the ditchless land and forms torrents crossing the road at the field gates. Cataracts cascade down bye-roads and head-high water-falls leap from roadside walls. Many West Cork townlands are cut off from their neighbours. Long stretches of roadway are so deep in washed-down topsoil that diggers have to be brought in to clear the way.

Not 'holding water', or holding too much water, is a problem increasingly encountered on agricultural land. Many natural reservoirs, bogs and sloughs, are long since drained. Older farmers remark that the hedgerows, ditches and pocket-handkerchief fields of their child-hood are sadly missed in the deluges. The nitrates they have spread, too often and too copiously, are washed away and they worry how, if such weather continues, they will ever be able to farm. Prayers are said at Sunday mass for a few dry days, with winds and sunshine to sear the ground of surface water and allow them to enter their fields. Meanwhile, for wild birds and animals, and farm animals, this weather must be a time of tribulation. Are they ever dry? Where can a bird find shelter that is not damp? How can an animal hunt or forage in the constantly wet grasses? How do the cattle live, in mud up to their knees?

But after a night of floods and storms, there is a great, clean feeling to the morning, the air pearly grey, and then the sun burning through. The sea is flat out and the huge area of mud exposed is awesome. That all this, only hours before, could have been under six feet of water, square miles of it, which came in and then withdrew! How many litres to fill this estuary? The sea comes and goes, usually silently, creeping across the sand, welling in the basin that is the bay, and retreating without fuss when the cycle turns. But when the full moon draws it and the wind is behind it, then it is a massive, dangerous animal, rearing and bucking in its confines, smashing its way through all and every man-made barrier to stretch itself out over the land.

On February 18th, a frog left its spawn on a forest path, on one of the few half-dry square yards left in Ireland. Anywhere else it would almost certainly have been submerged. The incident reminds one of Jack, in *The Importance of Being Earnest*, who was left in a handbag at Victoria Station. To have lost both parents 'seems like carelessness', said Lady Bracknell; for a mother frog to have deposited so many youngsters so carelessly would seem profligate in the extreme. However, she may not have been so much careless, as short taken, literally bursting with spawn. Frogs lay a prodigious number of eggs and the aforesaid 150 lost embryos would have represented only about 6 per cent of the total 'brood'. Each egg is one hundred times bigger than a human embryo — frog embryos are not fed from the mother, and must start out large.

Happily, young Fintan found them as he made his way back from school — a bee-line route through woods and fields from where he gets off the bus — and carried the plum-sized lump of speckled isinglass in a wet leaf. It now resides safely in a bowl of water, on the dresser, out of strong sunlight. Soon there will be movement from the small black dots and they will begin to eat their way out of their nurturing jelly. Then we will find them fine, unpolluted algae or boil them lettuce leaves on which to dine. With luck, they will chomp their way through March and April, grow legs and arms and be ready for the road by May. Not the tarmac road, of course, but the woodland path where the boy found them. There is a pool up there where, a few years ago, we put swimming tadpoles, and perhaps the mother of the present spawn was one of these.

Each year, I find frog jelly in a *fulacht fiadh* in a prehistoric stone circle at Drombeg. *Fulachta fiadh* are ancient cooking places, pools that were lined with planks or stone slabs to make a trough. Our Bronze Age Firbolg ancestors would roll rocks, pre-heated in a nearby fire, into these pools. The water boiled remarkably quickly and the meat, possibly venison or boar wrapped in straw, was immersed for twenty minutes per pound weight. Their calculation of the pound weight or the twenty minutes must have been somewhat random, as they did not own scales or watches. However, many people are good judges of weight and it is my experience that when one is not in possession of a timepiece, one soon learns to gauge the passage of hours accurately, at least the hours of the day. Perhaps such ability is based on a perception of the light, the passage of the sun, and is an old, ingrained instinct. It is remarkable that, even in cloud or rain, one still has a sense of the time and it is surprising how often one finds the guess to be accurate when one encounters a clock.

The *fulacht fiadh* at Drombeg is, each year, a tadpole nursery; I have found them there, swimming robustly, as early as January 1st. Presumably it was not always an amphibian orphanage; only since its first function was abandoned. Venison garnished with boiled tadpoles would hardly have appealed even to a hoary Formorian, although our Continental cousins, the Franks, may well have had an appetite for infant frogs.

Storks, my brother tells me, began nesting near his home in Andalucia at the start of the month, high in thin trees and on the chimney-stacks of village houses. Flamingos, in gorgeous pink, strut through the shallows of Coto Doñana, and elegant avocets, with their turned-up bills, wade in the lagoons. I tell him I wouldn't give a lake full of pink flamingos for the flocks of golden plover on our estuary in West Cork.

Now, we have white egrets, just as in Spain. A dozen regularly decorate the trees over the River Argideen in the lovely gardens of Timoleague House and this year egrets are reported in many locations. On the 18th, someone phoned to say there were two on the Bandon River, in front of the church at Ballinadee. The little egret is a new bird on the list of Irish breeding species; bird watchers are twitching in delight. Just eight years ago, an egret in Ireland was extremely rare. Not long returned home after decades away, I was thrilled to see my first egret on Irish ground. Here was a bird I knew from Spain and India perched on an Irish tree, overlooking an Irish slob.

First, I saw some bird-watchers, then the bird. Crossing the causeway at Kilbrittain Creek, I spotted some gents hauling an enormous telescope out of a tiny car. They had a sense of surreptitious urgency, stooping as they moved and stepping as if they were walking on eggs. 'Twitchers …', I told my wife, as I slipped out of our car and set off on tiptoe towards them. 'Little Egret', they hissed, and kindly stepped back from the telescope to let me look. There it stood, beautiful, graceful, pristine, on the edge of a bog-dark pool.

Since then, little egrets have become a regular feature for bird watchers on the south coast and have bred on the River Blackwater in east Cork. The young birds seem to have dispersed widely and now over-winter in Ireland. Local people see them and marvel; their brilliant whiteness makes them outstanding in the shallow lagoons or in the tall trees above the water. In breeding finery, they carry a top knot of long feathers, lending a rakish air; once they were hunted for their plumes, much valued in the fashion industry. There is no bird so white except the swan, and no wading bird so elegant except our native grey heron.

The speed of their colonisation has been remarkable. Soon it is likely that other colonies – they are colony-nesters – will be established; the trees over the river at Timoleague House are a possible site. During the next decade they will, no doubt, also move to inland waters, becoming part of the Irish lake and riverside scene. They will compete only with the herons, or 'Johnny-the-Bogs' as country people call them, but there is no shortage of herons and, being taller, they in any case can fish the deeper shallows. These new-come birds are a singularly beautiful addition to our fauna, ornamental on the landscape or at the water's edge, their whiteness mirrored in the pools.

One February evening, a group of dedicated bird watchers and I ate a swan. Henry VIII ate swans but also beheaded ex-wives; it is to be hoped there was no connection. Swan-eating was once popular amongst royals, perhaps because of faith in sympathetic magic rather than cultivated taste buds; we found the flesh pleasant but – besides the novelty – nothing about which one might write home. Being 'royal' birds, perhaps kings ate them simply to assert their *droit de seigneur*; personally, I believe a Peking duck or a fat goose would be tastier, although our swan was young. Some folk, hearing that one has eaten a swan, respond as if one had consumed the family dog. However, past generations – my grandparents and parents – knowing the circumstances, would likely have applauded the recycling.

We had gone with some friends to a meadow on the Bandon River in the hope of seeing whoopers. Whooper swans are romantic birds, probably the swans of W.B. Yeats's 'The Wild Swans at Coole'. He described his swans as 'wild'; whoopers are wild indeed, arriving here from Iceland, the sky their thoroughfare and the stars their guide. Unfortunately, none was present in the meadow: instead, we found nine dead mute swans, casualties of overhead power lines. All were half eaten by animals, except one; it was freshly killed, its neck broken. 'I'll eat it!' I said. It seemed to me that eating it would be by way of an apology to the bird, a victim of our march of progress, and would save it from the rats and crows. We would complain to the Electricity Supply Board and demand the lines be marked (and, indeed, they immediately and effectively were) but meantime it was agreed that various members of the West Cork Branch of the Irish Wild Bird Conservancy would convene at my house some days later for a swan dinner.

The bulk of a swan is enormous; it almost filled the boot of my estate car. At home I hung it, head down, in our garage for three days, with wings outstretched; I was awestruck by the huge space it occupied. Wolstenholme, the secretary of the bird group, came with a sharp knife and skinned the carcass. To pluck a goose, they say, takes half day; to pluck our swan would have taken eight hours and we could have filled a duvet with the down. It so happened that I had a request from a young Cork artist for wild bird feathers; now, I could give her the impressive flight feathers of our largest native bird. They reached a wider public at, I believe, Cork's Crawford Gallery. After de-boning, the flesh was first boiled and then roasted; we ate in the evening, around a long table, beside a roaring fire. There was no fat, and not a lot of eating. The taste was gamey and more like meat than fowl. Michael O'Sullivan, the group chairman, said a bird watcher's grace for the bounty and afterwards we rose to toast the swan.

It is a warm February Saturday when our neighbour Micheál Hurley, proprietor of the Lifeboat Inn, pulls up on the dock, jumps out of his van, and bustles into a small portakabin on the pier. Micheál is in a hurry but not in a panic. Twenty seconds later he emerges with a flare gun and aims it at the sky. The kids, on bikes, are quick to notice. They whoop as the flare whooshes skyward, leaving a trail of smoke. It reaches its zenith and a loud bang echoes over the village. It is a Lifeboat 'Call-Out'. How long will it take the crew to put to sea? Minutes can make all the difference for a stricken vessel. The gun is hardly back in its box before the volunteers begin to arrive.

Seán O'Farrell, Ordnance Survey map-maker, is first, fast-walking onto the pier, disappearing into the hut – a temporary fixture – and emerging seconds later, pulling on his bright yellow oilskins. Vincent O'Donovan, accountant of Barryroe Co-op, is next, arriving by car, his sharp suit quickly replaced by sea-going gear. Now, cars sweep onto the pier every few seconds, builders, farmers, fishermen, unpaid volunteers abandoning trades and professions to set out on to the ocean. Soon, in a choreography honed by practice, they are all aboard the launching punt and skimming out to the big, bright, blue and orange lifeboat, moored in mid-channel. They climb aboard and take up stations. Six minutes after the flare exploded, they are powering out to sea.

The white frill behind the stern quickly churns into a cataract, the prow lifts and the RNLI *Fredrick Storey Cockburn* looks like it may take to the sky. At times it does, leaping the wave tops. I have been aboard; I have felt the thrill, seen the fishing boats bob wildly in its wake, watched the fishing guillemots scatter. Today the sea is flat calm — some pleasure boat with the engine stalled, the rumour has it — but call-outs come at all hours and in every weather. Ireland's first lifeboat was at Courtmacsherry, and village men have risked their lives for others since 1825. After rowing for four hours, they were the first lifeboat to reach the liner *Lusitania*, sunk by a U-boat off the Old Head of Kinsale in May 1915, with a loss of 1,200 lives. In 1979, in the Fastnet Race, a Courtmac crew spent twenty-one hours towing a yacht to safety through mountainous seas, saving her ten crew from drowning.

After Independence the British RNLI offered to maintain a lifeboat service around Ireland's coast and has done so ever since. This, along with some fine architecture, the parliamentary and legal system and, above all, the English language, were fortuitous legacies of an often rapacious colonial system. It was an Englishman, Mr Storey Cockburn, who paid most of the £1.1 million pounds to build the present boat, moored gleaming in mid-channel when the RNLI president, the Duke of Kent, visited Courtmacsherry on a May morning in 1998 and stood outside the Lifeboat Inn for an hour, chatting in the sun.

In such weather, it is easy to forget the power of the sea. Only a year before, the liner *QE2* had been hit by a ninety-seven-foot wave; these are the seas the village men set forth in. The 'lifeboat song', 'Carry us home, home, home from the sea, Angel of Mercy answer our plea …' is the village anthem, heard in the pubs whenever songs are sung. It is a rousing air, some may say sentimental but, fifty miles out in the Atlantic on a pitch-black night in a force twelve gale, its echoes perhaps strengthen the resolve of the steadfast crew. Courtmacsherry is a 'lifeboat village', and proud of it. With a population of less than 200, now as in the past, however dangerous the seas, however treacherous the weather, there are always men ready to answer the call.

There is a great stretch to the evenings as February proceeds and, one evening, our older son, Dara, crossing a stream near the house, finds some wood blewit mushrooms, normally unavailable after December. Hoping we may find enough for a side dish at supper, we rush off to search a path where I had found a small crop two months before. We find none – but, at six o'clock in the evening there is still enough daylight to search. Continuing through the walled orchards of a local ruin, we see, bright in the dusk, the remains of a few apples on the ground, these out of the thousands of windfalls that littered the grass in October. They show evidence of slugs and birds. Where have all the others gone? Such a crop, and hardly a scrap left – how economical is nature! Nothing wasted, creatures of some kind born to consume and recycle everything – swans or apples – a multitudinous, ever-present micro-fauna we never see.

These spring evenings are by far the loveliest this year. First, sunset over the millpond-still bay, with smoke curling straight up from the painted houses. Then this evening in the garden, just as the last sliver of red vanished and blue dark came down, a bonfire flared on the shore below and a minute later was an inferno, with sparks like sequins flying skywards against the trees. Young Fintan whooped and rushed off to join in the fun. Beyond him and the beach, the pier lights came on, throwing silver rivers across the water. It was mild out, and hard to turn away from that view. At last, as I walked across the dark lawn, lights came on in our windows, and inside I could see a big fire blazing. Yes, sometimes I miss the speed of cities and the thrills of travel, but I can think of nowhere better than here to make a home.

With the sunset, I had rushed in, like a tourist, to get my camera. Yet I know well, from sunsets on the Aegean, on the Pacific, on the Bay of Bengal that, however glorious the sky, my snaps will never even remotely do it justice. But the fever takes hold and Kodak and the film processors make another killing. How naïve we are! Sunset shots, more than any others, make little impression when later viewed. My father quite correctly said that photos, like whiskey, are of little interest until they are ten years old. Photos of people or places may, after a decent interval, elicit gasps of surprise or delight because people and landscapes change. But skies do not. Neither does the land beneath red skies. Buildings and features are usually black and lost against the background glow. Sunsets are eternal and, for most of us, it is a waste of money to attempt their celluloid immortalisation. Better take snaps of the kids or old folk. They won't last forever. Sunsets will.

It is a surprise to hear of butterflies – along with the swallows – on Valentine's Day, but one, at least, arrived in Courtmacsherry and flitted about the garden of a lady well known for her gardening and readiness, at all times, to stop for a chat. It was a painted lady, freshly painted, she said; it was surely an ideal butterfly for that romantic day.

The painted lady butterflies of spring come to us from afar, from south-west Europe and North Africa, a thousand miles or more. They are strong fliers but yet it seems a miracle that they should fly so far on such delicate wings. They are, as the name implies, brightly coloured. This one was fresh-hatched and 'new', the wings orange, with black triangles at the tip, mottled with white. Butterfly wings wear out or lose colour with time, and are at their brightest only briefly.

The species normally arrives in April, some years in huge numbers. One spring day in 1996, roadside shrubs in the village were almost weighed down by butterfly swarms. The migrants lay their eggs and a hatch in September or October provides a second generation to flit and flounce about our hedges. Winged life span – as opposed to caterpillar and chrysalis stages – is a matter of a few weeks, but some kinds hibernate, rather than die off, when winter comes. Painted ladys die; our familiar tortoiseshells hide behind a curtain or pelmet and survive to fly and breed again in spring. Stinging nettles are the favoured breeding grounds and LHPs (larval host plants) for the 'aristocrat' butterflies, which include the ladys, tortoiseshells, admirals and peacocks. The adults sun-bathe on the plants and lay eggs on the tender young leaves, while the caterpillars, when they hatch, spin webs of silk, impenetrable gossamer walls to deter avian predators.

Grazing animals stay away from nettles because they are tough, and sting. People also steer clear. Some forty insect species depend on nettles as a home and food source but neater farmyards, the replacements of meadows by blue-grass fields and the availability of cheaper herbicides have cut swathes in the nettle beds of yore. While not all the nettle bed-fellows are as pretty and innocuous as the aristocrat butterflies, it is my intention to cultivate a fertile nettle boudoir in the corner of my garden this spring.

T.S. Eliot said, 'In the mountains, there you feel free …' For us coastal dwellers, the inland mountains are another country and, last Sunday, walking the high ridges of the Galtees was as novel as a holiday in a foreign land. How convenient it is for us, on this island, that we have such a variety of environments within easy drive of home and can take an afternoon's holiday in another world. Pity the Arab, with featureless sand for days in all directions, the prairie dweller with his endless field, the Siberian with his taiga forest, the Eskimo with his endless snow. Even for Irish city dwellers, wilderness, in hills like the Galtees, is never more than an hour away. Treeless, with scalps of weathered rock and heather, and shoulders populated by sheep and pipits, they are there for us to enjoy at no cost. In most of Ireland, we can still wander such places at will, no gates barring us, no fences to negotiate, no landowners to appease. On top of the world, high on fresh air and endomorphs, we look down on misty landscapes stretching to far mountains or fading into pellucid plains. The trek into these heathered hills is a holiday for the soul.

The paths are not arduous. We are hardly spring chickens, my friends and I, not iron pumpers or gym athletes, but we managed it without any great strain. At first, a track ran alongside a Famine wall of outstanding workmanship, climbing for a mile into the empty hills. The topmost course of rocks, balanced on those below, were keyed so well together that, although the stones were unmortared and uncut, no human or animal pressure could topple it. Heavier and more stalwart than any block course we could build today, for one hundred and fifty years it had survived sheep and storm. Dividing only heather from heather, patterned with centuries of lichens, why it was built it was hard to know. Who would have wanted to wall off these uncommercial hills: to what purpose? We could only surmise that in Famine times someone had had a vision of this road leading from nowhere to nowhere. Perhaps the function was secondary. Its creation gave employment; it put the starving Irish to work. It avoided the dispensation of charity, the view taken by Lord Trevelyan and the British Treasury being that if the Irish were given alms, they'd never lift a finger again.

How tragic it all was, the potato famine of 1845 to 1848! In his *History of Timoleague and Barryroe*, Father James Coombes, our local parish priest, mentions a contemporary account of a Famine Relief Scheme where it is recorded that one Patrick Murray, sole supporter of a wife and six children, having subsisted on nothing but a few turnips for several days, died after one day's labour. This was not unusual. Even when there was work, the sixpence a day often went unpaid and men died of starvation on the roadside. As we walk this track into the hungry mountains, we cannot but think of those who built it. These were our great-grandfathers. In Ireland, if not yet everywhere, it is a more caring world today.

More caring, certainly, was the world we entered when, at sunset, after an evening picnic at the car, we drove down from the high 'three corners' of counties Cork, Limerick and Tipperary, to the streets of Mitchelstown in County Cork. There, in a pub known to one of our number, a fund-raising effort was in full swing, the house crowded, full of chatter and welcome. The cause was the provision of treatment for a baby girl born with a rare condition. Specialists in Boston, with a ninety per cent success rate in such cases, had undertaken to treat the child. Now money had to be raised, for travel, surgery and extended care. The Minister for Health had pledged that, when all local fund-raising efforts had been exhausted, he would make up the shortfall required.

It was the child's grand-uncle, a traditional musician, who came up with the novel idea of a music marathon, and this was in full progress when we arrived from the hills. Friends, fellow musicians and neighbours from his native Mayo had come to help him. There had been a non-stop twelve-hour session the day before. When we arrived, it was singing time. Crooners, chanters and chancers subscribed a fee for the privilege of singing a favourite song, or paid a fine for refusing to do so. The pub was in great voice, sustained by plates of local and exotic cheeses, compliments of a local merchant. We left at half past ten, a lady amongst us having selflessly abjured strong refreshment so as to take charge of the car. The friendliness, song and chat were heart-warming. Ireland is a continent of foreign countries, when one leaves home.

March

March is invigorating; it is the 'month of many weathers'.
In West Cork, this old adage may apply to any month, but
March is reliably diverse. Raw hail can change to tender
sunlight in minutes. After showers, the world sparkles and
raindrops bead the branches of the bare alders like crystals on
chandeliers. Once, in March, in Barryroe, we saw a cow up a
tree, so deep was the flood around her. Conversely, on warm
days, the air can be heady with the coconut smell of gorse,
baking in the sun. Wild garlic swathes the verges and
the laneways smell like Spanish kitchens. As usual, I try
to photograph the magnificence of the giant
rhododendron towering over the gate lodge at ruined
Kincragie House, covered in huge, scarlet flowers.
As usual, I fail.

In the higher reaches of the bay, below Timoleague Abbey, the water is infinitely still, broken now and then by the snout-wave of a mullet.

lready the evenings have a stretch in them and, given mild weather, have an almost autumnal feel. One evening last week, as I walked home across the meadow, the air was absolutely still. The tide was half out and, below me, the channel, red with the sun, wound between dark sandbanks. Farther up the estuary, drifts of mist hung in the valleys and hollows, grey against black. In the middle distance, the lights in the village came on, bright dots against the dark woods. Smoke rose straight from the chimneys. The sea in front was still as glass, clouds perfectly mirrored in the water, grey and motionless, hanging against the blue-and-pink background of the reflected sky. As I reached the first houses, a small horse walked ahead of me on the road, white, but very muddy, with a fringe, short ears, and endearing eyes. It seemed to be heading for the main street, but changed its mind, and went onto the beach where it stood still, looking out at the red sea. Farther along, in the gathering darkness, a young girl was riding a horse around and around on the sand. Peace reigned; it was a lovely March evening and all was right with our world.

Reaching home, I found Dara getting out of the car with a huge puffball that he had spotted in a field as he drove down from Cork. It was a foot in diameter, firm and good. Giant puffballs make excellent eating, delicious in slices, fried with bacon. From what he told me, it was growing on old land which, likely, had never known artificial fertiliser. It made a fine family breakfast next day. A horsewoman we know had also recently found one when out riding. Sadly, it was full, not with white meat, but with brown spore dust that ascended like a genie when it was squeezed. Puffballs can grow to a diameter of two and a half feet, enough to make breakfast for a village. If every tiny spore took root, we'd have a landscape of giant puff balls next year.

These days, abroad in the country, one meets nature waking up. If it's fauna, it is often still half asleep or so bent on procreation that it doesn't exercise the cautions of the winter, when the focus is on finding a meal while not becoming one. Humans seem to feel the urge, too. A country saying has it that 'Kissing's out of season when gorse is out of bloom'. In West Cork, there is no month when one cannot find a sprig of gorse flower but it blooms most vigorously in spring, when kissing is also thought to be rampant – the better weather encourages both, perhaps. On March 1st, walking down a sunlit lane, I saw, over a hedge of gorse in full flower, four roan horses grazing in a very green field, with veils of rain drifting across them. The sunlight on the gauze of rain was magical. Above the coastal fields, larks sang high in the heavens, fewer than in the past but, yet, to watch them made the heart soar. 'Split the lark, and find the music', the American poet, Emily Dickinson said. The sound of a bird singing its heart out on a March morning is more than just music; it's like the returning sun. In early morning Tokyo, we would hear bird song played from huge Tannoy speakers mounted on the buildings in the business districts. Bird song inspires optimism and euphoria. As the perceptive Ms Dickinson also said, 'Hope is the thing with feathers/ That perches in the soul'.

On the first weekend of the month, we drove west. Vast swathes of gorse draped the hills in gold. The tall variety, French gorse, was brought to Ireland by the Normans, while the Romans brought it to Britain many centuries before. The low-growing, western or dwarf gorse, which grows amongst heather and pricks the calves of those who walk the hills, is our own. Gorse is called 'furze' in West Cork, and 'whins' in Donegal. The Irish poet Oliver Goldsmith called it 'unprofitably gay' but nowadays there may well be profit in this rampant bush with its dark green, spiky foliage and bottle-brush, yellow flowers – it is, after all, one of the features of Ireland the visitors come here to enjoy. Perhaps we can farm its beauty as our forefathers farmed the prickly whins.

For centuries, on hill farms, gorse was a staple of animal subsistence. On the Cork-Kerry borders in the ruined yards of long-abandoned farms, I have often come across a rusted 'Pierce of Wexford' furze machine, although many have since been carried off to decorate rustic restaurants or country cotts. Hand-turned contraptions, like the ancient mangles that often stand beside them, they bruised the tough stems and thorns to make the gorse palatable for cattle. I had always believed only horses ate gorse; not so, I'm told. The gorse crop was purpose-grown as 'meadow furze', undersown to a cereal crop and cut and saved in autumn. Besides producing fodder, it provided bedding for animals and was woven into windbreak hurdles to protect them in the fields.

Dry furze was fired to build fast heat in bread ovens. It burns like wildfire, as anyone who has ever seen a hillside in flames will know; it is especially spectacular at night, over water. When burnt after the fledgling linnets and stonechats have flown, it does no harm to the landscape but fertilises the glorious gorse flowers of the next year. In the West of Ireland, the oar pegs of currachs are still made of furze branches; no other wood is so resilient to the bend and strain. Years ago, when we lived in the Borlin Valley, on the Kerry border, and could not afford the pub, we sometimes made gorse flower wine. It was a lovely drink in September, a beaker-full of the warm hillside in May or

June. Picking a bushel of flowers was no easy task, even for children's nimble fingers. Inevitably, finger tips were pin-cushioned with tiny spines. As soon as we got home we'd soak them in piping hot water. Instant relief and joy.

On the 6th of the month, as I walk along the cliffs at Coomalacha, the raven sits shtoom on the nest as I pass. The fact that it does not immediately take wing may mean there are eggs, and indeed, when it does take flight as two more walkers approach, I note that it returns a few minutes later, suggesting that there are, indeed, eggs to keep warm. A perennial germ is abroad that sets everything to budding and waking. In Courtmacsherry Woods the first bluebells have shown; the forest floor will be carpeted in purple before long. A few days ago a small tortoiseshell butterfly fluttered on my work-room windowsill, just emerged from hibernation. The weather was mild but a few warm days don't make a summer; I went to open the window but decided to let it find its own way out — if it would — into the uncertain spring. Perhaps it could go back to sleep, but I doubt it. Meanwhile, on mild days in sheltered lanes, drone flies buzz and flash on the ivy. As we have coffee in the sunlit garden, a ladybird walks by, and at night a few unidentified moths and a crane fly find their way in an open window, attracted to the light.

March 10th and after three days of spectacular gales, sleet and hailstones, it's suddenly again a beautiful morning, warm as summer in sheltered places, with the sun bright and lighting up the ivy on the tree trunks across our stream. 'Walk now, while the sun shines,' I tell myself but despite my resolve I dither, and by the time I leave the house there is the first spatter of rain. I head off anyway, the dog eager and springing at the prospect of a stroll. Soon I'm sheltering under a holly bush as horizontal hail flies past me, out of a lowering sky. Filling time, I decide to write a few notes and find the pages hail-splattered as I write.

Five minutes later, when I look up, a patch of blue is showing and within minutes the cloud has gone and the sun is shining again. The ivy glitters and the leaves of ramsons on the forest floor are rain-slicked and shiny; the woods smell faintly of onions, although the ramsons haven't yet bloomed. Early flowering wood anemones that closed under the passing clouds now reopen, as does the bright yellow celandine, like a child's drawing of the sun. A few stems of barren strawberries show small white flowers. There are great northern divers in the channel, their white breasts in contrast with the grey and sand-laden sea, stirred up by the storms.

On the estuary sands, widgeon, teal, mallard and shelduck have congregated in their hundreds. They seem less nervous than usual; they have other concerns on their minds. Nowhere is spring so evident as in the brilliant plumage of the drakes, arrayed in breeding finery; the ducks, although also spruced up, are much less eye-catching. Drake widgeon, their terracotta heads divided vertically by a golden stripe and roseate breasts puffed as wood pigeons', strut amongst their drab and delicate paramours. Every now and then one makes an experimental dash at the hareem. The females scatter, looking offended, as if trying to keep a sense of decorum in the face of such lewd behaviour. One cannot but smile; a waddling duck trying to look dignified is a comic sight. Teal females don't hold a candle to the decorative male, his chestnut head painted with a Chinese eye of metallic green and tail coverts as yellow as egg yolk. The female mallard, also, is dull alongside her elegant drake.

The dowdy colour of the females must be a survival tactic. It is the female who spends most time on the eggs, laid in a hollow of dried grass. With predators in the skies – grey crows, magpies, hawks – and predators on the ground – foxes, mink, stoats and rats – it makes sense that she should keep a low profile and look as much as possible like a clod. Quite different it is with shelduck which, locally, nest in abandoned rabbit burrows. Here the survival of the clutch owes nothing to the female's protective colouring; hence male and female are both gorgeous, with red legs and red beaks, snow-white breasts surmounted by a chestnut collar and dark green heads. They are big ducks, almost the size of small geese. Feeding far out on the mudflats, they are dazzling specks in the distance, mirroring the sun.

One evening, on a mission to find yet more hapless tadpoles a safe home, Fintan and I shelter under a magnificent blackthorn called, hereabouts, a *sceac*, a rough name for a tough tree. Its boughs, covered in a million white flowers, hung over a small creek near Kilbrittain. On the coast and on high land, one sees them growing out of rock, gnarled and wind-sculpted by the south-westerlies. Not so this specimen; it was healthy, well shaped and densely white, as lovely as any shrub in an exotic garden. In winter it will no doubt be black with sloes.

Later, as we dry out in a pub, a farmer tells me he's received a threatening letter – a Section 70 notice – from the County Council ordering him to trim his roadside hedges or face a thousand pound fine or six months in jail. What do civil servants know about trees anyway? he asks. His trees are big; if he trims along his road boundary, leaving all the branches on one side, what will happen in a storm? Should not the Council employ experts who do not, with Draconian disregard, issue these notices, putting the fear of penury or prison into farmers and sending them rushing for the hedge contractor or the saw?

Acres of flowering blackthorn and whitethorn still cover the countryside in white blossom in March and April and turn the middle distance into a haze. It is a mercy, not before time, that henceforth the cutting of hedgerows will be forbidden between March 1st and August 31st, allowing the birds to nest safely, and that Section 70 notices will be issued only to landowners whose hedges are a genuine danger to traffic. If not, Irish lanes would shortly have become as topiaried as a Hampton Court garden and we could kiss our wild and lovely *sceac*s good-bye. However, in what it is hoped will be the last March massacre, flail saws continue to flay the tender shoots of spring. It is hard to know which is loudest, the whine of the saw or the silent scream of the bush. Nature lovers close their ears and avert their eyes in horror. Meanwhile, truckers and motoring commuters congratulate the County Councils on making dangerous roads less dangerous, and saving lives. That human life should take priority over plant life is elementary. That over-cutting and indiscriminate cutting of hedges impoverishes our landscape is elementary, too. Roadside bushes, dressed in their flowers or leaves, are an integral element of pastoral beauty. With the monochromatic green of silage grass increasingly overtaking the landscape, never did we need wild trees more. Blackthorns in flower transform even the grey pavements of the Burren – indeed, in that stone landscape, the self-seeded *sceac* seems to thrive. Pink hawthorn breaks up the blue grass fields, and French gorse dresses bony hillsides. Fuchsia makes purple corridors of lanes in the south-west.

While roadside hedges cannot be allowed to make narrow roads narrower, to 'blind' corners or to endanger life, a universal complaint is the devastation wrought by tractor-mounted flail and disc saws. A hedge trimmed with a bow saw, or even a hand-held chain saw, may look shorn but respectable; a hedge mutilated by a mechanised cutter is an affront on a rural road. Branches are left half-cut, ripped and torn. The trees and bushes, nature itself, look violated. The force brought against them is wholesale, orderless, almost triumphalist. All is laid to waste. During World War II, the old 'bocage' hedges of France withstood advancing armies. They were actually too thick and strong for tanks, even with cutters, to plough through. By comparison, our Irish roadside bushes are slight as Wordsworth's 'hedge-rows, hardly hedge-rows, little lines of sportive wood run wild'. In fact, ours are rarely the edges of old woods, as some English hedges are. Our hedges are not endlessly resilient, and can be damaged irrevocably. I'm sure many Council employees enjoy nature as much as the rest of us, walk as much as we do, take photos, paint landscapes. They too will be celebrating the moratorium: let us hope it will last.

Meantime, however, some worthies continue to hack away at the vegetation with salacious zeal. Last Monday, at 9.30am, I saw a man take a chain saw to a slim and elegant little alder; it was as if he had said, 'First thing Monday morning, I must kill that tree!' The tree was doing no harm to him whatsoever. It was on public property, on a verge, where a new nature trail has got the 'go ahead'. The small grove of alders was to be one of the attractions. Why the man should choose to cut down a tree, seeded long before he arrived in the area, is a mystery. It harboured siskins in winter, acrobatic birds that hang upside down as they feed; perhaps he might have enjoyed them. But now the tree is gone. It was one of a small stand of five. Four remain. Let us hope he does not entertain grievances against the others.

Butlerstown village is a single street of multicoloured houses looking out across the wide, rich fields of Barryroe, Ballymacshoneen, Shanagh and Turkeyland, to the wide Atlantic. To the east is Courtmacsherry Bay, bounded by the distant cliffs of the Old Head. To the west, in the middle distance, are the coves of Dunworley, white surf breaking on dark rocks, with small sandy beaches in between. It has one pub, one shop/post-office and a population of eighty. Each year the Butlerstown Variety Group, country people, villagers, fishermen and farmers, mothers, fathers, sons and daughters, stages an evening out which, for fun and sheer theatre, 'Beats the West End'! So declared our London visitors who, like all in the packed-to-capacity audience, were enthralled from the opening curtain to the final bow.

I have sat through few two-hour shows in my life without finding a sag in the elasticity of the action. Not so at Butlerstown Variety Show last Sunday night. It had already packed the village Community Hall for five nights running, leaving standing-room only. Sunday was the last night; we came half an hour early in order to get in.

It is a marvellous thing for a village to entertain itself and the townlands all around it. In staging, costume, lighting, choreography, scripting, music and arrangement, and in the sheer quality of performance, the Butlerstown evening is outstanding, with a sophistication belying a small rural community on the Seven Heads. In the quantifying of 'entertainment value', if such is possible, surely the theatre of the people, at its best, can compete with the theatre of the professionals. I have rarely seen an auditorium so well entertained.

They were good; they were very good; they were 'polished'. They gave us an evening of glitter and sparkle, greeted by loud laughter, pin-drop silences, and loud applause. Act after act came and went, short, sweet, and with never a dull moment. Wide-eyed and open-mouthed, we gazed and grinned, shrieked with laughter, tapped to the music, swayed to the songs. To reach this paragon of parish productions, it had taken the cast and backstage auxiliaries, one hundred local people, a total of nine weeks, rehearsing four hours a night, four nights a week, come wind, rain or flood. Every one – from producer/director Annette Smith, and Michael O'Brien who wrote 'the book', to the scene-shifters, make-up artists, costumiers, principal actors and choruses – deserved our wholehearted praise.

As the show's last performance drew to a close, performers and spectators were one, the audience standing and clapping, and the company unabashedly smiling as we cheered them at the top of our lungs. It was a wonderful occasion, the soul of village, the Seven Heads and its people; so fine and heart-warming an evening of entertainment is not every day found.

The mid-March weather can be wonderful, but is not always so. St Patrick's Day arrived, warm and dry, Ireland as green as shamrock and speckled with wild flowers. The gala weather lasted into the weekend, blue skies with balls of cloud like candyfloss high above. The Great Creator, or stew of natural forces, does not always send such lovely spring days and the holiday gave everyone a chance to enjoy them. When the sun shines, country people say, 'It's a sin to be indoors.' They are fortunate; their daily business takes them out into the air. In weather like last week's, pity the city workers, catching as little of the glory as battery hens. I, myself, with a small walk book to finish writing, was another battery hen.

There is none of the brouhaha of an American Patrick's Day in West Cork or indeed anywhere in Ireland. It is a church holiday, but many people work. In the villages after morning mass, fresh-faced farmers stand around chatting, hands in their pockets, bushels of shamrock safety-pinned to their lapels. Children, in Sunday best, wear gilt paper harps and tricolour ribbons. The pubs have music at night and there is a buzz of celebration, but not even Dublin celebrates St Patrick's Day like it is celebrated in New York, where everyday life comes to a halt to honour an obscure trans-Atlantic saint who, although a Welshman, inspires an orgy of Irishness from coast to coast. Patrick's Day in New York is second only to Christmas or Thanksgiving; how on earth did this come to be? Why are the Irish allowed to paint the streets in tricolour and dye the Hudson green? Other nationalities enjoy no such indulgence. What is it with the Irish? Is it that the first Irish immigrants hugely influenced the city's culture or is it simply the Irish knack for throwing a party? Mardi Gras is confined to New Orleans; St Pat's is celebrated across North America.

Twenty miles west of us, the coastal villages of Rosscarbery and Glandore grow shamrock to export to America. I recall years ago a certain Irish entrepreneur had the bright idea of flying to New York with a big sack of it as personal luggage. He could see himself standing outside St Patrick's Cathedral on Fifth Avenue selling sweet-smelling shamrock at a dollar a smidgen, the freshest shamrock in New York. He raised the fare – I was a circumspect but loyal investor – and on March 16th set off for Shannon, scheduled to arrive at Kennedy Airport on the morning of the great day at 6am. All went well until engine trouble forced the plane to land at Gander, Newfoundland. There he waited, marooned, his hopes, like the shamrock, wilting in an airport lounge.

It was six in the evening rather than six in the morning by the time he lugged his jumbo-sized suitcase into the Big Apple. The Parade was long since past. His cargo, after thirty-six hours in an early version of a bin-liner, looked and smelled more like fresh Irish silage than shamrock; bin-liner over his shoulder, he made a forlorn sight trying to hawk his decaying asset around the Brooklyn bars. Next morning, when he turned up, penniless, at the Irish Embassy looking for a ticket back to Shannon, he was wearing the biggest buttonhole of defunct shamrock in America. 'Sic transit gloria Hiberniae'; he looked as worn-out as the shamrock itself.

While St Patrick's is celebrated in a month of rebirth and renewal, our national saint could hardly be called an ecologist. Young Fintan once drew a picture of a truck, with a lot of squiggles in the back, and a man with a halo and beard in the driving seat. 'St Patrick driving the snakes out of Ireland', he called it. When Patrick's name comes up in foreign parts, it is surprising how far his snake-expelling reputation has spread. Nobody believes it but people find it an amusing illustration of the Irish proclivity (as perceived elsewhere) for romantic mysticism and cavalier disregard of scientific fact. When it is quoted at me (particularly in Scandinavia) my response is to wax extremely earnest about disappearing Irish fauna and bemoan St Patrick's poor ecological record. I then move on, in deadly seriousness, to the vexing subject of the disappearing leprechaun.

It can surely be said that St Patrick rid the country of some of its wild life – never since has Irish society enjoyed the same pagan abandon – but he certainly did not rid it of snakes. Snakes never came to Ireland. This seems strange, considering we're only a short slither away from Britain, which has no less than four varieties, although their slow worm is really a lizard without legs. With the onset of the last Ice Age, when an ice cap slowly began to cover northern Europe, reptiles migrated south. Afterwards, as the climate warmed and the ice melted, they returned to re-colonise. Many species reached Britain, which remained connected to mainland Europe until 5000 BC. They were too late to cross to Ireland; three thousand years earlier, the low-lying land bridge to Britain had been drowned by rising seas from the melting ice.

Only one reptile, the viviparous lizard, had reached us; snakes, it seems, did not move as fast as lizards and remained east of the Irish Sea. No frogs reached us; our frogs were introduced. Our only toad, the natterjack, was probably a pre-Ice Age indigent that never left, surviving in the extreme south-west of Kerry, which the ice never reached. The natterjack is our sole representative of Lusitanian fauna, Lusitania being the ancient name for the Iberian Peninsula. We have Lusitanian plants, snails and scorpions, all of which are in West Cork, Kerry or Clare, and would have similarly survived.

The only other amphibian native to Ireland is the smooth newt. It is news to most people that frogs are an introduced species. There was no mention of them until 1696, when a Fellow of Trinity College

Dublin brought a jar full of spawn from England and poured it into the ditches in Phoenix Park. Soon there were frogs hopping all over Dublin. Why he should have done this is unknown. Our frogs are not the variety favoured for *hors d'oeuvre* in France; however, the common frogs' legs are eaten in the Low Countries in early spring when their larger edible frog hasn't yet woken up and put himself on the menu. There is a local story in Kerry that the first natterjacks came into Dingle Bay on a boat. If this is true, then the introduction must have been deliberate and the numbers imported great enough to succeed. But to what end? Toads' legs? Surely not comestible, even in Kerry.

A neighbour tells me that these mornings she has hares racing around her garden bird table. As we know, hares, in March, are mad, but they are usually seen running about in the cliff-top fields; she describes hers as uncommon or garden hares. Certainly we have seen our local hares box in March. Standing on their hind legs, they square off in Marquess of Queensberry fashion and pummel one another's ears. The bout is fast and furious; few boxers could get in as many jabs in as many seconds. I am not sure if a hare has ever been found feet up, after a knockout; whatever about a punch from the fore paw, I imagine the back legs can carry quite a clout. The woman's cat, finding hares in the garden, gives them a wide berth – perhaps she doesn't fancy a punch-up with one of these mad, March creatures which has survived in the wild for countless millennia. Like the Irish otter and the Irish stoat, the Irish hare is an endemic sub-species. It is a singularly beautiful and graceful creature. Last week I came upon one in full breeding colour. I had never before noticed so clearly the shining white fur that edges its ears, like ermine. It was as if a Tipp-Ex line had traced the outlines. It stood up and looked at me, so I got a wonderful view.

While hares box only in springtime, our stoat, wrongly called a 'weasel', is pugnacious and fearless at all times of the year. It will take on creatures many times its size and lift and drag them away after their dispatch. This is done economically and efficiently with a fatal bite in the nape of the neck. Stoats look very *glic* and charming, with their gleaming whiskers and beady little eyes. They are curious creatures and more than once I've seen a stoat stand on its hind legs, the better to observe me.

Some years ago I saw a string of stoats travelling along the roadside like Ten Blind Mice, each seemingly holding the other's tail, and travelling so smoothly and sinuously that I took them, at first, to be a stream of brown flood water snaking along the verge. Only when I got closer did I realise that the undulating snake was a series of small animals. They disappeared without breaking formation, like a stream diverted into the ditch. Such behaviour is probably the origin of 'a weasel's funeral' which most Irish country children will have heard about. While 'weasels' do not line up to bury their dead, it is known that they sometimes form hunting packs. The pack follows in single file behind a leader, only an inch or two separating the tiny hunters as they weave like a deadly anaconda through the grass. Remembering that they are fearless and will take on anything in their path, it is advisable to give them a wide berth if one would prefer not to have a flying column of weasels rushing up one's trousers.

An Irish stoat may give birth to as many as twelve young in spring-time, and the litter remains with the parents until early autumn, travelling in family groups. The parents seem very playful, chivvying the kits and rolling and tumbling and indulging in mock fights. However, this is probably important training in the nip-and-attack tactics of survival.

Years ago, one summer morning, we were driving along Dunmanus Bay in West Cork when we saw a mother stoat leading seven young-sters along a sunny bank. We stopped the car gently and sat quiet, waiting for them to come along. They did, in full view, and it was of course a wonderful sight because they were so neat and small and colourful with their red backs and white bellies and black-tipped tails. Just as they passed us, and as we were swearing, once again, that in future we'd always carry a camera, the mother suddenly sensed some-thing in the air. Hi presto! she and the tribe disappeared like a well-oiled roller-coaster over the summit of the bank. All but one of the tribe, that is. He missed his cue. Quickly he made an attempt to follow the rest but in his tiny panic fell, rolling onto the road. There he sat, mewling and squealing, a pathetic picture. Suddenly, above the crown of the ditch, we saw a sharp face, a pair of tiny ears. Mother! In two seconds, she'd hopped over the crown and down the bank and, looking up at the car as much as to say 'I dare you!', she grabbed junior by the scruff of the neck and unceremoniously hauled him to safety.

While stoats take game birds' eggs and chicks, their main diet is mice, rats and rabbits. Once they discover a colony of rats, they hunt them down until not one is left alive. Cats of course will equally well deal with rats, but I have sworn to bell my cat this nesting season.

On this late March afternoon, as I write, there's a stillness in the air and sound carries through the windows into my work-room, bringing the shrilling of a song thrush, the soft cooing of wood pigeons. Outside – I cannot resist leaving the screen and going out – not a leaf stirs and it is as mild as midsummer. In the garden, time seems suspended; even the water of the small stream seems not to move. I return and, as I finish up my work, the thrush continues. I can hear a robin too, now and then. Thank goodness for the birds.

In the woods the first few bluebells stand in deep purple shade. The brown carpet of last year's beech leaves is changed to bottle-green with new flower spikes bursting, tight-packed, from the soil; one wonders how the flowers themselves will find space to grow. Besides the bluebells and the white wood anemones, very delicate and, unfortunately, often slug-eaten, the first ramsons are showing, smelling of garlic. The unborn flower heads lie furled inside their spear-shaped parchment envelopes, like the chrysalises of burnet moths on grass stems, just about to pop. And pop they do, and bathe the woodland path in the sweet smell of garlic, no place for vampires. The flowers are white, tousled stars, with pointed petals. Arum lilies sprout, strange, dark plants, the stiff stamen rising from the white folds, giving them the name of Lords and Ladies. There are catkins on the alder; the catalogue of spring flowers grows by the day.

On a quiet lane I meet a man who shows me seven goldfish in his garden pond. He tells me he put in three fish some years ago and now, independent of human agency, they have become seven, with one obviously pregnant. Once, during heavy rains, the pond flooded and one was found by his sons walking home from school, in a roadside drain. What a surprise to look into a country ditch and see golden fish within it! Somehow, it reminded me of W.B. Yeats's 'The Song of Wandering Aengus', the mystic trout and the golden apples of the sun.

'Sumer is icumen in/ Lhude sing cuccu!' went the thirteenth-century words of the bard Anonymous. Perhaps if I could hear a cuckoo, summer might come in, sharpish, afterwards? I'd nail a cuckoo clock to a tree in the garden if I thought it would help. No country sound is more heartily welcomed than the ding-dong tootling of the male cuckoo. The female expresses herself in bubbling chuckles. Perhaps she cannot help laughing at the unfortunate pair who rear her young. Choosing a robust male by the sound of his 'Cuckoo!', she will mate and then begin to over-fly her territory on an hourly basis, searching for foster homes for her chicks. She will pick on small birds – reed warblers, meadow pipits, dunnocks; even robins or pied wagtails. When she lays an egg amongst theirs, although the egg will be larger, she will get the colour almost right.

Our family goldfish, the last of three, is twenty years old. She lives in a good-sized, rectangular tank. I have ended up looking after her; the small boy who bought her in Petticoat Lane all those years ago now has other fish to fry. One of her original companions died of 'piscine tuberculosis', an expert said. Then, when we were moving house, the tank was left in a garden shed overnight, the temperature plunged unexpectedly and, in the morning, her remaining companion floated belly-up. 'Blown swim bladder,' diagnosed the aquarist. 'No hope.' I shot her with an air pistol – an instant death. Departure by hypothermia, in a bowl of water in the freezer, was, I thought, cruel, nor was I going to knock her on the head with a 'priest', or flush her down the loo. I carried the tank into the sunlit garden and placed it on a flat tree trunk, then carefully rehearsed my movements so that there would be no panic, gasping or fear. One moment she was in the water, next moment she was held firmly on the tree trunk, next moment I blew out her brains. A neat hole in the forehead, and we buried her under a tree.

While she had been terminally affected by the temperature drop, her tank-mate — now twenty — did not go unscathed. She sometimes swam belly-up but after a year in very shallow water, she recovered. Even now, she sometimes does the back stroke, but otherwise leads a normal life. Science says a goldfish's memory span is but thirty seconds, so they live in a world forever new. Each time they reach the end of the tank, they have forgotten ever being there. Wonderlands open every time they turn.

It is not that the female cuckoo lays eggs of different colours at will but that having, herself, been born in, say, a reed warbler's nest, she is 'a reed warbler's cuckoo' and will lay eggs roughly matching those of reed warblers, whose nests she will seek out. 'Pipits' cuckoos' lay in pipits' nests and produce eggs of pipits' colours. However, host birds will often accept an unmatching egg. There are records of fifty different species being fooled in these islands and one hundred in Europe as a whole.

For the female cuckoo, timing is all important to ensure that her chicks are hatched on roughly the same schedule as those of the host's. She watches her intended victims constantly. Most small birds lay early in the morning. Seeing them lay seems to inspire the cuckoo to prepare an egg. That afternoon, when the parent birds are foraging, she slips into the nest. First she removes an egg and then lays her own; she can do this in as little as ten seconds. She carries the stolen egg away in her beak and drops it or eats it at some distance from the nest. Forty-eight hours later, she is ready to lay in another nest. In time, she has from ten to twenty-five eggs deposited about her territory.

Cuckoo's eggs often hatch a tad faster than those of the host. As soon as the naked chick is hatched, it begins to murder. Manoeuvring the eggs or chicks of its step-parents into a sensitive hollow in its back, it heaves them over the nest edge to oblivion. Chicks that cannot be ousted starve while the parents pander to the insistent usurper. After five weeks it is strong enough to make its own way. It leaves its tiny parents for a world empty of cuckoos; its parents have long since flown south. In September, with no guide but an inborn star chart, it navigates its way to winter quarters in lush forests beyond the Sahara sands.

It is a beautiful, golden evening, with my shadow long in front of me as I walk east from the Seven Heads at around six o'clock. The sea in the distance is very blue, unmoving, set against the shore as if carved from turquoise. The Old Head of Kinsale is sunlit, the lighthouse winking at the tip. A big ship stands out in the bay, riding at anchor – if it is a fishing boat, it is almost certainly a factory ship. At Coomalacha, the raven chicks are now hatched and raise their ugly heads, supported on scrawny necks, over the nest edge, with a maw wide enough to swallow one's hand. They are not a pretty bunch, but ugly ducklings turn into beautiful swans and these will be magnificent birds when they mature, living out here on the cliffs, part of the wildness, knowing every bush and cranny, every rock and pool where they can glean mussels or sea wrack. They will live here all their lives, pair for life, find a territory and stay.

How they have grown so big in ten days is a wonder. I try to count the pink gapes as they surface to breathe; they are four or five, snug in their twig and horse-hair nest on their inaccessible ledge above the sea, a round pool of blood-blue goose-flesh, shifting and heaving, dusted with blue down.

As I turn for home, a light north wind is in my face and a kestrel skims over a hedge and across a field, then gains height and hovers, russet brown in the yellow sun. Earlier, I had seen three turnstones on the shore, a small party, legs very red, taking turns to bathe in a rock-pool. Soon the flocks of warblers and flycatchers will wing in from the sea. No doubt the heavy twitchers – heavy with their binoculars, telescopes, bird books and warming flasks – will be there to greet them on the Old Head, at Cape Clear, Dunquin or Helvick, a welcoming committee of birders from far and wide. They will hoot and chirp with the joy of spotting the first whitethroats and their beloved rare American vagrants. Meanwhile they will say good-bye to the myriad birds of the slob – the dunlin, turnstones and godwits – off to the Arctic edges to raise their chicks.

April

April can be the best month of the year, sprinkled with
pet days. Perhaps it seems the loveliest month because
it ends winter; the swallows come, the woods are full
of flowers. T.S. Eliot, reflecting on age, said it was 'the
cruellest month ...' I often find it so, because it is a
working month with holiday weather. I stay indoors, at
my desk, in an act of faith that July and August will be
even better. However, April's glorious 'pet days' are often
better than any the summer that follows has to offer.

~

*'We were here…We knew about time
and we measured the sun's passage.'*

The weather is warm and bats flick over the hedges, where spirals of insects cloud the hawthorn tops. As the sun goes down, we find ourselves at a remote stone circle high in the Cork and Kerry mountains, watching gorse fires burn on the misty hills ten miles away. It is late in the season; the birds are beginning to nest. We have seen gorse burning every day over the dry weekend, in the Shehy Mountains and in Beara. The plumes of blue smoke looked pretty on the hillsides, with carpets of flame dramatic at night, especially over the black sea lochs. Burning adds potash to the soil and improves the vigour of the stock. But now, linnets, pheasants, perhaps even grouse will be nesting in the gorse, with eggs or chicks in the nests. These birds are becoming scarcer every year. Surely, upland farmers should allow them, their long-time companions of the hill country, some respite, given that they, like the farmers themselves, are on the brink of extinction.

In the Shehy Mountains we came upon Neolithic stone circles and standing stones miles from present habitation, untouched, on hill-tops with views over hundreds of miles of mountain and sea. The surprise was that there were so many and that such engineering had been done. Built monuments fall; where there is mortar it crumbles, but stones survive. However, while the stones that form the circles are all but unassailable, the science of their precise configuration is not. Now, in this secular age, with no pishogues or superstitions to pro-tect them and the awesome power of JCBs rentable by the hour, they can be moved and their science, their careful alignment to sun and stars, forever lost. Clearly, it is no accident that each placement is different; the sizes of the stones differ greatly, their orientation, the distances between them; all vary from site to site.

Sometimes families of stones are grouped together. We find an arrangement of pillar stones standing in pairs, with a circle of boulders and a radial cairn of loose rocks, thirty feet in diameter, all close to one another. It is as if the site was a laboratory, equipped with specific instruments to gather data or intercept natural forces. Scientific or spiritual, or both, they may yet have something to tell us which we haven't grasped. Raised over a period of three thousand years, it is not unreasonable to think that mankind then, with the same size brain as we have now, erected them for scientific use or to interact in some way with spiritual forces whose presence he had detected over many generations. They are still there, on the hilltops, magnificent in their resilience. They aspire to no subtle tones or shades of expression; there is only the rock, only the statement of the aligned rocks which tells us, simply, 'We were here. Our lives were ruled by more than brute survival. We worked in co-operation; we conceived of gods. We knew about time and we measured the sun's passage.' These stones, half-buried, are testimonials to those who went before. As long as we don't move them, they will survive, with whatever knowledge they have, though cities fall.

Later that Sunday evening, when we arrived home, a mains fuse tripped and, rather than fix it, we settled for candlelight. It reminded us of far-off, simple places where we once lived. In past ages, after dark, we humans saw only the close things, revealed by a small light source. These things were seen keenly, in areas of light and shadow, as the paintings of earlier centuries portray. Now, with electric bulbs, night is day and we see widely, everything in the view. Rarely are we presented with the minutiae of our lives in a frame of light, isolated from their background. Such things, seen by candlelight, are often intensely beautiful. In medieval times the colours of plants were held to indicate their medicinal properties – red plants for stanching wounds, and so on. In the same way, good whiskey is sympathetic magic and goes well with candlelight, bathing the brain in its golden glow.

Misty March is now gone and on April Fool's Day, at 8am, the air is sharp and clean as a curlew's whistle. Since our return to Ireland, we find April and May have become the best months of the year. Midsummer is unreliable but late spring and early summer have been consistently warm and sunny, often for a week at a time. Now, as the morning of the first day of the month proceeds, the world warms up. What a day to be out tramping the mountains, the Reeks, the Comeraghs, the Boggeraghs, or Slieve Bloom! By ten, those with thinning hair reach for a hat.

The dog, recumbent on the driveway, rises and moves under a tree. The belled cat sits on a wall, in deep shadow, perhaps awaiting the passage of some deaf shrews. A pair of goldfinches arrive on the lawn and pluck the dandelion 'clocks' for their small, downy seeds. Their red faces and yellow wings flash like enamel in the sunlight. Through the trees I see the bright crimson of rhododendron flowers, almost as high as the tall pines. The sea is blue below the garden, reflecting the dome of blue above it. As noon comes around I can resist the temptation of the sun no longer, and step out. A narrow strip of white sand edges the sea as the tide recedes. There are a dozen people on the beach. Already we have had this year's first intrepid swimmers, a hardy, athletic-looking woman and our own Fintan who, it seems, has neither sense nor sensitivity in his enthusiasm to usher in the sand-boy days of summer when he will come home at dusk, salt-rimed, with hair like it was combed by a bush and wet togs under his arm.

When the tide is far out, miles of rippled sands lie revealed. The squiggly casts of thousands of lugworms dot this landscape. They are almost pyramidal and, looking across the sand flats, it doesn't take great imagination to see them as primitive models for the ziggurats of Babylon or the pyramids at Giza. They remind me of the thousand Buddhist temples that cover many square miles of land around Pagan in Burma. I once saw them, on a golden morning, from a small plane, the mists of dawn hanging between them. They are one of the wonders of the world. Art imitates nature: who knows, maybe it was an anthill or a lugworm cast that inspired the first human pyramid builders in the world.

Spring fever is everywhere on the shoreline. Not only do excursions provide food for the soul – bracing air, oystercatchers piping in the wind – but also for the body, in the form of the many highly comestible shellfish exposed. Besides, there is the buzz of perennial regeneration and continuity, and the reassurance that the world-we-live-not-in is going about its business as robustly as it does with each new spring. After the tide recedes and leaves the sands bare, damp spaces under flat rocks are alive with procreating shannies, fascinating little fish that crawl about on their flippers and, because of a wet-suit skin, can miraculously survive out of water for hours at a time. During the breeding season, shannies of all sizes congregate on the sand, sheltering under flat stones and remaining stranded for the duration of a tide. Many are big-bellied with spawn. The problem with lifting rocks to find them is how to replace the rocks without crushing them flat. The answer is to scoop them to one side, replace the stone as was and then help them find their way back under it.

When we kept a marine aquarium, shannies and Montague blennies would sometimes climb out of the water and sit on top of the filter, basking in the Gro-tube light. Now and then they would flop back in, to cool off, like holiday-makers around a pool. I once met a Montague blenny crawling across our kitchen floor, ten feet from the tank. He'd climbed too high and, somehow, fallen out. When I returned him to the tank, he seemed immensely glad to be back. Although we live close to the shore, it would have been a long walk for a blenny to the sea.

Along the sand, tallin shells, wild oyster shells, smooth and rough cockles, clam and razorshells litter the tide line, empty but beautiful, especially when wet by the sea. I can think of nothing in nature that is unlovely when it is healthy. The tentacles of an octopus, the frills of sea slugs, the fans of fan worms, the skins of snakes, the agility and motion of garden eels, all are beautiful. Even a toad, or a lugworm, is a miracle of creation, and rats, although I would not want them as house guests, are as sleek and attractive as the squirrels or hamsters almost everybody loves.

Walking the Courtmacsherry shore below the woods, I am sorry to see yet another victim of coastal erosion in the shape of a huge beech that had slipped from thirty feet above and lies horizontal on the sand, seaweed drying in what were, last week, its topmost branches. The branches bear spring buds. On an alder sapling, similarly laid out nearby, buds have already opened. Despite the sea washing over them, despite the hopelessness of producing buds, flowers and seed, as long as earth still clings to the roots, they continue the cycle, spilling their seed on the sea. Some years ago, I saw a mature alder on the same beach, fallen from the same earth cliff – but this time standing upright – survive for an entire year until at last all the earth about its roots was taken away and it died. I thought, what a pity it couldn't have been lifted by a JCB and re-planted elsewhere. I had nowhere to put it at the time. The beech I now speak of is, however, forty foot from roots to tip, widely spreading and convoluted. How long it will live, how long before the root-ball is scoured of earth and it dies, depends on tides and the sea.

Homeward bound, I leave the beach at an old pier – a line of sunken rocks, covered in seaweed – where a small stream crosses the sand. Some image flickers in my mind's eye as I walk through its inch-deep water. When I was a boy, in such a stream entering the sea, we would always find eels under the stones, shoelace-thin elvers. Given that, in the long story of man on earth, we have only, so-to-speak, last week ceased to survive by hunting down our food, is it possible we carry a mind-picture of the bounty of such streams from long ago? I lift a stone to look. Not a shoelace elver, but a yellow eel, fifteen inches long, drifts down the current, away from me. Are the old skills still there? I wonder. Can I catch it with my hands? Yes – not immediately and not without strategy – but five minutes later I have landed it, squirming, on the sand. I put it back. I would have liked to have shown it to Fintan but it wouldn't have survived, out of water, while I carried it to the house. As it slid away into the stream, I was sorry for disturbing it. But the old hunter-gatherer will out.

Summer at Easter, and for almost two weeks now we have woken to sunlight streaming across the bedroom floor, sparkling on the sea outside. Not a drop of rain. It is as if we have moved to another climate. Oh bright new world, with sunny people in it! The sun is warm on our shoulders at 7pm as we sit at the edge of the garden, at the edge of the sea. The sea is still as a dish of set jelly, the boats bright as children's toys, each with its mirror image beneath. They point towards the bay head, the ocean. This means the tide is coming in. Four times a day they turn on their ropes, always facing into the run of the tide.

While the summers of my childhood were always sunny, the Good Fridays were always dark. At morning mass on Easter Sunday the sun would stream through the stained glass; bird song could be heard during the silence of the consecration. On Good Friday no birds sang. At four o'clock in the afternoon, as we shuffled past the Stations of the Cross, the aisles were already steeped in penumbra, the side altars dark, the skies grey outside. The day itself was dead, nothing to do but to sit at home and wait for the Resurrection and the Easter eggs. People didn't go walking abroad. The shops were closed, the streets empty, the way to the church the only pavement on which footsteps echoed. All day families came and went, to walk the Way of the Cross, to pray silently, to light candles, to go home to the fire. When they passed one another, they didn't stop. If they exchanged greetings, it was a half whisper. They walked with bowed heads. And the weather lowered or rained.

Not so last Good Friday, a good, an excellent Friday, possibly the best day this year. Celandine, the small early 'buttercup' of the verges and ditches, threw its petals open and shone like a thousand small suns against the green banks of its heart-shaped leaves. In the undergrowth, ferns unfurled in whorls like ammonites, the coiled fossil shells on sale in rock shops. I've read somewhere that fern tips are edible, but male ferns, at least, are very poisonous and shouldn't even be picked. Meanwhile, ramsons were appearing, the white, garlic-smelling flowers, and bluebells, in sheltered places. There were ladybirds, and red-tailed bumble bees, and hoverflies shining like they'd been dipped in lacquer. I saw a small tortoiseshell butterfly on a dandelion flower. Thrushes piped, robins thrilled; it was a great day to be out and alive, not like death at all.

While Courtmacsherry and our local world enchants us, what a country this is in general, our Ireland, jewel of Europe's western shore! The seclusion of undiscovered corners of this land never ceases to amaze me. We came upon another such spot over the Easter weekend. Scanning the Ordnance Survey maps for walkable, out-of-the-way bohreens, we found a lane leading down to a small pier on Bantry Bay. We had never noticed it before and, on that pet afternoon of Easter Saturday, no more idyllic spot could we have found. The westering sun streamed in from the mouth of the vast bay, turning the sea into a mirror so bright we had to narrow our eyes as we walked down the sloping road to the water. Although six o'clock in the afternoon, it was as warm as the Med. in June. And not a sound, not a soul, not a house, not a car, not a telegraph pole. But for the old pier, and a small rowing boat on the shingle, we might have been in the world before time began.

If we found such a place on a foreign holiday, we'd write home about it. Again, a mere hour or so from our everyday surroundings, we had found another country, as unfamiliar and magic a land as the high paths in the Galtees we walked in January, or the Mayo lakes we visited last autumn. The more I travel, the more I appreciate the beauty and uniqueness of home. As Fintan and I stood on the pier, we could see the sea floor thirty feet below us. In a wide channel between the beds of tall kelp, a spider crab wandered over the sand. So calm was the sea, the kelp barely stirred in the current. The depths were blue and clear as one would imagine on a Pacific or Caribbean island. But this was Ireland: Bantry Bay, the second largest natural deep-water harbour in Europe. What a place for a snorkel and flippers, to cruise between the kelp forests and find exotic fish. Only the knowledge that the water is at its coldest in April – never mind the fact that we had no swimsuits – stopped us from diving in. Fintan wanted to, regardless, but the shadows were spreading, and it would be an hour before we were home. We promised him we would remember this place for August and September, when the water would be sultry and the evenings long.

In summer, perhaps, people in holiday homes in Bantry would drive out to the pier and the tiny beach, and lounge about on the warm, sea-smoothed rocks until the red sun sinks into the red sea. It would do them nothing but good, I am sure, and instil the poetry of Ireland in their children. The rest of the year, there is nobody in this place, just the rowboat and a few lobster pots above the sand. For centuries the only people who came here would have been the families from the two farmhouses hidden beyond the headland. In the hills behind, there is little grazing and homesteads are few. Living in part from the sea, these families would have been familiar with this world of the huge bay, the wide sky, the unpopulated hills, the emptiness. They might even – seduced by the sirens of ambition or forced by cruel necessity – have exchanged its sublime charms for the pickings of Liverpool or New York. Would they have missed it? I think so. It is no wonder we have our plaintive airs of homesickness and exile, when we come from places of such awesome beauty and perfect peace as this.

The Easter weather was wonderful, but it couldn't go on. The farmers were praying for rain and even my eldest daughter, Lydia, and her English husband and family, on holiday from London, understood the need for it and had no complaints. When she and family escape London to holiday on the West Cork Riviera, they are generally greeted with downpours as soon as they get off the plane. This is an immutable law, and I think of placing bets with bookmakers. This year, however, it didn't rain when they got off the Ringaskiddy ferry; instead, the skies were black as Armageddon, and the green fields of Ireland lowered beneath an End-of-the-World pall. Now, there is so much mist over Courtmacsherry bay that one can't see the view. Lydia doesn't mind; a warm fire and family around her more than compensate. Also she knows there is a view, even if she can't see it. Not so, perhaps, our recent visitors from Japan, who must take our word. We tell them that, one morning, the light will be clear and golden and one will be able to see halfway to America. They nod, humouring us. A land steeped in myth and legend, indeed.

As happens always with our visitors, they tell us they love Ireland whatever the weather. Even if there's no sun, the colours are there, the dark and shining greens they talk about and, then, just two days later they can see the view. I remember, decades ago, an English stranger buying a stone ruin on an empty mountain on the Cork-Kerry borders. He bought it on a clear summer day, for its magnificent panorama. When he came back in the middle of January, the mist was down and he couldn't find it until Easter. The owner had gone to Boston, and the nearest neighbour, another old bachelor, wouldn't come out until the spring sun shone.

On one of these wringing post-Easter days, I walk the dreary slob and wonder why on earth our particular Celts chose to adopt this sopping isle as a place to set up home. A dense mist hangs over the sea, relieved only by deluges from the skies. You'd need waders to cross the yard and a dingy to ford the driveway. Tourists are being issued with life jackets at Rosslare. Why didn't the Celtic ancestors stay in Brittany or Galicia? While not exactly Mediterranean, at least they aren't underwater for eight months of the year. And where have all the birds gone? my companion asks me, as if I had personally shooshed them away. While only two months ago the sand flats and mud banks were bustling with bird tribes, they are now deserted. All that glorious mud, alive with free dinners, and hardly a feathered diner to be seen. Yes, there are a few adolescent oystercatchers and a few beautiful shelduck, which breed here, hoovering their crimson beaks over the shiny surface. I see whimbrels, a small group en route from West Africa to Iceland, where they will soon breed. But now as the human tourists come, the flocks have gone.

This timing is of course unfortunate. An estuary, in sunlight, with its filigree of creeks and channels, is an impressive sight; even more so when a look through the binoculars reveals thousands of golden plover or lapwing, or rafts of shiny teal. Visitors say their first reason for coming to Ireland is the people and the second is the scenery, of which this resplendent wildlife is part. But the wading birds do not oblige in the tourist season. They are with us from August to March; then they go. Others come, less visible, forest and farmland birds and the hirundines. But the huge winter flocks are gone.

Sanderlings, the little birds that run in and out of the surf along our storm beaches, head for the high Arctic to breed. So also do knot, large flocks from West Africa and further south joining the birds that winter in Ireland to make the longest of all migrations twice a year. The ten black-bellied Brent geese that swayed along Flaxfort Strand last November are likely to be nesting in Siberia, while their six light-bellied cousins that came later in the year will be doing the same in Spitzbergen or Greenland. The burgeoning larders of the Arctic summers is the attraction, although freedom from disturbance and predation also plays a part. I have heard of obdurate caribou cows making a trek to calving grounds so far north and so bitter cold that, eventually, even the predatory wolves give up and go home. Certainly, on the tundra, there will be predators, Arctic fox and wolf, stoat and grey crow and skua and gull, but at least, so far, there are few people to disturb them.

The main attraction, of course, is the food. The tundra, when the ice melts, becomes alive with insects. A French Canadian friend tells me that the principal impediment to the enjoyment of the summer sub-Arctic is the presence of millions of black fly which apparently would drive a saint mad. However, they provide wonderful food for the nestlings, so they grow fast and develop from hatchling to independence in half the time it would take a chick hatched here. For the parent birds, it is a question of investment. If they invest the energy to fly a few thousand miles north, they save on time which elsewhere would have to be invested in feeding young. Nestlings are growing machines and the faster you can feed them the faster they will fledge and free you of the chore. Protein is needed for growth and even seed eaters, such as our common sparrow, will catch insects for its nestlings. In the Arctic, apart from the proliferation of insects, the summer seas are pink with krill, so gulls and sea-birds can feed their chicks non-stop during the twenty-four-hour Arctic day. So plentiful is food that some of these chicks are ready to join their parents on a reverse migration a matter of weeks after hatching. It is worthwhile for such species to go north.

A theory holds that, during the Ice Ages, some birds moved the short distances to the ice edges to nest. There, summer heat on the shallow melt pools created an insect environment as fecund as the tundra is now. At the time, the ice extended south almost to the Mediterranean in the northern hemisphere – and vice-versa, below the Equator – and the birds did not have far to fly. Inevitably, as the ice drew back, reaching the edges meant longer and longer journeys. But the birds, hooked on behavioural patterns, continued to do it and so continue today.

As I make for home the sky lightens. Below Kilbrittain village, where the stream joins the tidal creek, I cross the old stone bridge. Small trout swim in the shallows. With all the washed-down worms, it must be a fat week for trout. The fires of their stipples would have been brilliant in the sunlight. I lean on the bridge and watch them. Now, ahead, I find the roadside hedges frilly with blackthorn blossom, fresh and frothy as if it had appeared overnight. A small band of long-tailed tits forage amongst it, and a cock bullfinch shoots past, his bright pink breast brilliant against the bushes.

The outgoing migrants have gone but on April 20th strong south-east winds are pasting pink petals of cherry blossom against our window panes and helping the incoming birds on their way. Swallows have been late in coming; now, everybody's seen one. It is extraordinary to think that birds weighing under a half an ounce fly two and a half thousand miles twice a year in a return journey from tropical Africa to Ireland. Such is the willow warbler, little bigger than a wren. Wear and tear on the feathers of this small, green bird is so great that, unusually, it moults and replaces them twice a year. Also, while in Ireland, it rears two clutches of chicks, probably to make the trip worthwhile. It is interesting to reflect on how wild our familiar garden birds can be. While we have year-round residents, some of the blackbirds hopping on our winter lawns may have come from Poland, and the starlings on the eaves may be Russian immigrants. Flying five miles high, in vast flocks, guided by the stars, there is little tame or domestic about them.

There is a long-tailed duck at Courtmacsherry and a brace of ruffs up along the Argideen river, near Timoleague. I haven't seen the latter myself but am told they are there by Peter Wolstenholme, the potter, who knows the Argideen well and has written a lovely tract on fishing the elusive sea trout of its waters. Ruffs are extraordinarily beautiful but, in Ireland, are rare birds of passage. At this time of the year males ruff up a great feathered collar and prance and strut like the proudest of proud dancers at the Argideen Haven *céilís* on a Saturday night.

The French and German motor homes, arriving on the ferries, are again beginning to move along the roads in westward migration and, at this time of year, are part of the wildlife of West Cork – wildlife, in that they often camp *sauvage*, meaning outside a camping ground, an activity that is not allowed in France. Here, happily, there is shore-line space a-plenty and it is a pleasure to see the children playing and enjoying themselves on a lonely beach. West Cork shares with Western Scotland the longest sunsets in these islands. We often noticed the difference when we arrived from London during the summer. It is a fine sight to see these families, after a long journey from the city, alone on the shore, sharing the sounds and solitude of a deepening West Cork evening. Of course, as the 'tourist providers' say, it is also nice to see them in the pubs or restaurants spending money. Fair shares!

I was at Shanley's bar in Clonakilty town the other evening and watching the rapt faces of the visitors – and being somewhat rapt myself – I could see why people choose Ireland for holidays. Maurice Shanley has his day job in Cork city but at night tickles the ivories to his heart's content, with members of his own family, in his own music pub. Such a life would, I imagine, be the envy of many a visitor. Perhaps this is why some stay, seeking an alternative to city bustle.

The first sandwich terns were seen on the West Cork coast last Sunday, and the weather immediately improved. Strong, graceful birds, our largest tern, they are called after the town of Sandwich in Kent, not because one can make sandwiches out of them, as my daughter Miriam, now mother of three, thought as a child. They sport quiffs at the back of their heads, with beaks entirely black. They breed here, on the coast and at lake colonies.

The return of blue skies has quickly transformed the country. Today, in the bright, sharp light, it's hard to credit our recent week of clouds and deluge. Irish country people don't ask for much and are quick to forgive. A few sunny days and the gloom is forgotten. Everywhere birds are singing and tractors revving. Farmers are belting about the fields like drivers at the *Mille Miglia*. Who can blame them? – seed the fields while the sun shines. The lizards are out, their glossy, new skins shining. They are green, yellow, brown, striped, jet black at times. They skitter over the warm walls of Lisheenaleen, across the bay. The sea sparkles below the cliff and, what with the heat and the lizards, we feel we aren't that far from the Mediterranean.

At an old *dún*, an earthwork fort overgrown with thicket, where gorse is fat as feather dusters on the stems, I found a gallery of badger setts, some very freshly dug – the ground must be a labyrinth underneath. The value of that fort is inestimable, a wild break amongst the fields of swaying grass, protected by magic or *pishogue*. Rabbits, wrens, linnets and badgers, ladybirds and a stag beetle, all made it their home. Maybe the old superstitions were nature's way of ensuring, at least in Ireland, that some islands of the old, natural world would remain. Their builders worshipped the sun and the oak and the ivy. If they left curses to protect that heritage, they did well.

April 25th is a pet day, the sky blue, the sun warm, the sea in front of the house flashing like diamonds. I leave the desk and whistle up the dog. She springs four foot into the air with excitement. Dogs on walks can be a disaster, disturbing everything in the countryside ahead. However, she doesn't chase sheep, or respond even when coltish horses come galloping at her; she acts as if they weren't there. Doggedly, she rushes on, nose-led, the landscape a melange of olfactory adventures. What she's looking for, I can't imagine. She looks like a springer spaniel but is she a truffle hound from Périgord?

It is a day when everything is outing. Every bird in the country seems to be piping in the hedge. Celandine, ramsons, dandelions and violets line the verges. Creamy breaks of white blackthorn hang over the river where the strimmers and flails couldn't reach it, 'the last honey by the water', perhaps, as in the Austin Clarke poem.

Sweater thrown over my shoulder, I take the bohreen down to the ocean. It's great to be on the beach again, a new summer beginning, sitting in a sun trap in the rocks with a riffle of breeze and the smell of the sea. Nothing to do but watch the odd ant hurrying about its business and the wolf spiders trying to ambush the flies as they bask on the slabs, knitting with their forelegs. The hot dog pants, sitting in my shadow. One could get an April suntan here, one could spend hours contemplating anything in sight and not get tired of it – the sea winking like semaphores, the surf rolling slowly on the sand, the thrift of sea thrift growing on bare rocks in thick cushions, the kelp rising above the sea surface, sinuous and shiny.

Beyond it, what I took for a pot marker turns out to be a seal. 'Hello, seal!' Could it be the mother of the small 'white coat' we found stranded on this beach last winter, and sent to Dublin in a fish box on a train? It can't be the father; the head is too small for an adult male. My American writer friend barks at seals, and Californian seals answer. Last week, when the weather was awful, we walked with him and his beautiful daughter over nearby cliffs in the driving rain. It was his first visit to Ireland; all six days, it rained. 'It's okay man!' he insisted. 'Mist and rain, like Northern California!' Yes, but where were blithe April days and blue Atlantic then?

Out here one wonders what we were doing in the city years, wonderful and cosmopolitan as they were, but not able to see the horizon for the buildings nor the stars for the streetlights, and always somewhat rushed. We did, at the weekends, get to the country; but often at the cost of a long and exhausting drive. We did steal hours to spend in activities more important than 'work'. Hours spent with children, lovers or friends are sustaining, hours at the movies or deep in a book – hours at the casino, if that is your fancy. But hours spent under the sky with no reminder of the century, let alone the day, nurture the deep soul. We are made of the elements of which the earth itself is made. We have been here before, have always been here, changing perhaps only on the surface, like the earth which is still the earth whether above or below the sea.

Perhaps the Irish business calendar should allow for three 'Blue Sky Days' per annum between December and March when, upon the advent of lovely weather, national holidays would be spontaneously declared and the staff of all the offices and shops of Ireland disgorged into the sun. For The Health of the Nation, everyone, short of hardened criminals, would be let out. A day under a blue sky, by highway or byway, lake, river or sea, would do the national psyche a power of good. Weather like this quite changes our self-image. No longer are we dreeping Celts, huddled in half-light, steam rising off us as we gather around the damp fire. On these sky blue days, I meet bronzed demigods and goddesses striding bare-headed from shade to sunlight. We are another race.

As April ends, the woods are in their greatest glory. For any walker or weekend stroller, they should not be missed. A billion bluebells make blocks of purple so dense beneath the trees that a dye might have been spilt over the forest floor, while other parts are entirely white with star-like, garlic-smelling ramsons. The ramsons in the woods and garlic on the road verges are completely different plants. Both are white, with green leaves, both smell of garlic, both are commonly called 'wild garlic', but there the similarity ends. The road-side garlic is like a white bluebell; the leaves are slim and spear-like, the flowers hang from the heads like small bells. The ramson has leaves widening from the base to an inch or more at the centre and narrowing again to end in a pointed tip. The white flowers do not hang but rather face the sky, from six to sixteen or more, star-like, standing on spindles. The petals are small spikes, splaying out from the yellow centre deep in the 'cup' of the flower.

Hardly a footprint-sized space of the woodland floor is now without a flower, and it seems criminal to walk off the path. Golden celandines are set in the moss around the boles of beeches. Pink herb-Robert, white stitchwort, creamy primroses and green arum lilies are all in flower, the last still somewhat embryonic, the club-shaped spadix just now arising from the sheath which, in rain, flops over it protectively. Bawdy medievals saw these flowers as sex symbols, by reason of the thick, upright stock rising from the green fold, shaped like a candle flame. Lords and Ladies, they were called. I wonder what Boccaccio's ribald peasants made of the stinkhorns that protrude surreal from the autumn leaf litter, white, thick, six inches tall with a bulbous tip, shiny and tight, like stretched skin?

Above the flowers and dappled shade, the trees are dyed in forty shades of green. Perhaps the prettiest of the opening leaves are the beech, pastel green and delicate, lacy against the light. The first leaves of sycamore are coppery and some of the oaks are almost red. The ferns are extraordinary. The lemon-green male ferns – those with brown scales on the stem and leaves rising directly from the root ball – are festooned with what seem like baubles hanging from the tip of the leaf, which is curled like a primeval snail, and from each of the 'fishbone' leaves branching off the central spine.

But even prettier amongst the ferns is, perhaps, the lady fern. It does not have the baubles and is a very dark, rather than pastel, green, but the fronds are marvellously light, with a pattern like intricate lace. The hart's tongue ferns stand erect, the unfurling leaves glossy and shining, as if they had been waxed and polished. The hart's tongues carry no fronds; the leaf is like a slim, green tongue, pale at first, then darkening. And there are many other ferns – light maidenhairs in damp places, polypodys on the tree branches; apart from the trodden path, nowhere on the forest floor is bare.

May

The village song thrush flutes each evening from a tall tree. The evenings have been very still, and his song carries over the painted houses, with their columns of smoke. Walking down the street, just as his song fades out of earshot, another thrush, high in the woods, is heard. His song is less fluid; maybe he's a younger, less experienced singer. But he has territory and, let us hope, will be raising a family of aria-fluting offspring before long.

~

Buddleia attracts butterflies like a patisserie attracts Viennese matrons.

As April gives way to May and the weather continues warm and sunny on the Irish Riviera, I wonder what our continental visitors must think — that stories of a sodden, rain-swept island to the west are slanderous lies, that their travel agent was ill-informed when he told them to pack sou'westers? Honest folk may tell them it is not always like this, but when the sun shines it is hard to imagine the rain. They will leave with a picture of a green paradise, an emerald shot through with sunlight. Roll on, the cloudless skies and halcyon days!

The cuckoo has been calling non-stop at Leap, pronounced 'Lep' by those who know. Peter Hill, farming at Droumilihy, tells me he saw two flying over his yard on May 2nd, with an irate small bird chasing them. That night, a cuckoo was calling close by the house at ten o'clock and in the morning it started up again before eight. Now he's hearing cuckoos everywhere. One cuckoo is inspiring but a convocation could drive one cuckoo, I suppose.

At the Hill farm there is also a cock pheasant which greatly relishes home-made buns. He daily appears in the yard to be fed and one day, when there were still downpours in this country, he was tempted indoors. After eating well, he stood in a window looking out at the rain, waiting for it to stop before again venturing forth. When a small child decided to chase him, he ran about the yard like a turbo-charged chicken but would not take wing. This is possibly his salvation; not taking flight, he presents no target for the guns. However, this tameness may eventually be his downfall. He has been in the locality for two years, roosting in a neighbour's tree throughout the winter. Currently he is lording it about the place, calling to his hareem of hens at various venues around the farm.

Last week, I heard an extraordinary story. On a sunny Sunday morning two amiable fellows were on the foreshore at Ballybrannigan Bay, near Cloyne, with sledges, bolster chisels, a compressor and a jack hammer, blithely chopping large sheets of stone cladding off the wave platforms that jut out into the sea. Happily, when the local Garda pointed out the error of their ways, they desisted without demur. They simply hadn't realised that the natural furniture of the foreshore has a more important destiny than the provision of crazy paving, and that the shoreline is for the enjoyment and protection of all the public. It is not up for grabs for those with the initiative to cut it into patio cladding or shovel it into trailers and take it home.

While land is owned, the sea is anyone's. It is strange that any individual, given the necessary skill and capital, can launch a boat and harvest thousands of pounds worth of fish that he hasn't farmed, cultivated or nurtured in any way. Fishing is a 'divine right' for those with the stamina and courage to do it; but fishermen sometimes pay a heavy price. Happily, we are increasingly aware that we must nurture the oceans or our greed will devastate them. Naïveté can be as misguided as greed and we are rightly appalled at the presumption of the lads with sledges on the foreshore. But what of the clubbable golfers, with JCBs and diggers, ever hungry for another eighteen holes? A golf links is a fine thing in natural parkland or on grassy plains, but what of fairways created in wetlands, fauna-rich scrubland and dunes? Like the wave platforms, such marginal places provide a habitat for thousands of creatures and act as well-springs, sinks and conservatories where nature can catch its breath.

Should we praise the Lord for the fine weather or should we pray for rain? Since the end of March, but for a week, the sun has risen, bright and constant, day after day. Have we ever known such weather? I have – on the Mediterranean, on the Aegean, on the shores of the Andaman Sea – but I would say that, last week in Ireland, one couldn't ask for better. It was the ideal climate, the climate of Paradise. How privileged we were. It was hot but not too hot. The vegetation was green and fresh, not burnt out and sere. It was dry but not dusty. If too hot, one could always find a breeze; if too breezy, one could always find a sun trap. Often it was possible to find perfection, with sun and breeze in perfect harmony. Only in such a spot can I bear sitting in the sun. I hate to bake, I loathe to fry. I like to take my sun on the move. Each day I justified a lunchtime hour of lawn mowing. Never did I go more willingly to work. Circuit of the lawn, one side in warm sunlight, the other in delicious shade. Build up a sweat and then cool off, the same effect as a sauna and an icy pool.

And talking of pools, last week I also swam. I'm no Spartan hero, no St Stephen's Day skinny dipper or the like. Unless the sea is summer-warm, leave me out of it. But late the other afternoon, walking across a wide beach with Fintan, we found a waist-deep pool which, while not exactly tepid, was certainly tenable. In he got and cried, 'Lovely!' I was distrustful; he'd been swimming out in the waves and said that was painless, too. I ventured a toe and then a foot and found that it was indeed lovely. We stayed in for fifteen minutes. A swim in Ireland in May; who would have thought of that?

Having heard, and indeed modestly contributed to, the Saturday night chorus in the pub and the chorus around the fire at home after-wards, it hardly knocked a feather out of me to catch the bird-song,

crack-of-dawn chorus at Inchy Bridge, near Timoleague. Rising at
4.30am, after barely two hours' sleep, I found myself surprisingly
clear-headed as, eyes and ears agog, I drove up the estuary in the
paling darkness at ten to five. A cup of strong, sugared tea rode on
the dashboard holder beside me. I had abjured the traditional stirrup
cup, feeling stimulated enough by simply being abroad in an empty
world, with not a car on the road and not a human stirring, although,
in the hedges, nature was no doubt stretching itself and yawning as it
woke to another day.

At 5am at Inchy Bridge there was one other human being, a mother
of three small children, who, she told me, were at home, tucked up in
bed. As the first birds chirped, bats still flitted over the water. We
stood leaning on the parapet, watching the darkness drain from the
morning, the only sound, the run of the river as we waited for the
chorus to begin. It was BirdWatch Ireland National Dawn Chorus Day
and I was there to dutifully swell the numbers of the West Cork bird
group which had been in such good voice the night before. In fact, had
I stayed at home, I could have opened the balcony door of my bedroom, high over the garden, and heard it all from my bed. But to share
the music with others was a little like preferring to watch a film in the
homogeneous stew of a cinema, rather than alone in front of a TV.

Dawn duly cracked with the fluid aria of a song thrush. No finer
or more versatile a singer have we; an arpeggio of liquid notes poured
forth, and the bats went home to roost. Day, in a subtle change of
tones, stole away the night. Sea trout softly broke the surface of the
Argideen below us; the midges also had arrived. Soon there were other
cars, the branch secretary, the owl man from Drinagh, a brace of
English twitchers, all wide-eyed and wide-eared early birds, scanning
the river banks for crepuscular life, expertly identifying chiffchaffs
from willow warblers by their song. A dipper, like a big, stub-tailed
robin, dark brown with a bright white breast, stood on the bank below,
ruffling its feathers, shaking itself awake. Dippers have the uncanny
knack of walking underwater – not swimming, but walking along the
pebbled beds of streams, hunting the caddis and crayfish that dwell

amongst the stones. It was a privileged sighting – dippers are usually glimpsed only briefly, between sub-aquatic perambulations. Now, as the light swelled, thrushes clarioned, blackbirds carolled, tits twittered, a magpie cackled, and a bird watcher belched. A mute swan swam upriver towards us, honking softly as mute swans do.

I went home for breakfast at six o'clock. By then the birds had quietened and gone about their daily rote. On the way home a young hare (clearly young, because it was so small) hopped with kangaroo gait ahead of me. I slowed and stopped, watching it through binoculars, its hindquarters in the air, its form quite different from that of a rabbit, its tall, thin ears tipped with black. On the tide-full estuary, the shelduck were roosting in the reeds, and a few curlew, very grey in the grey morning light. No contests, skirmishes or wars, they shared the reeded island, a peaceful kingdom. By habit, I reached to turn on the car radio. But I decided I didn't want to hear the news.

On these clear May nights, when one looks up at the millions of stars, it is hard to believe that there isn't life elsewhere and sentient creatures also looking up at the firmament in which we, for them, are just a twinkle. Now, after the glorious and memorable weather of early May, there is suddenly a touch of 'the scaraveen' in the air as the moon wanes. 'Scaraveen' – I spell it phonetically – seemingly comes from *garbhshíon na gCuach* or 'rough weather that comes with the cuckoo'. While many natives of West Cork, including my wife Marie, know the expression, it is news to me. This is not because I wasn't taught Irish at school – I was taught Munster, Connacht, Leinster and Ulster Irish, having attended school in all the provinces: and there the confusion lies. Straight from Blackrock College, Dublin, and genteel Gaelic, I found myself in a Donegal school, surrounded by Tory Island men who spoke, natively and volubly, a language that the stranger did not know. Compounding my stupefaction was my reverend teacher's bizarre habit of beating out – with hairy knuckles at the end of simian arms – the bars of Irish verse on my benighted skull, this the better to instil the rhythms of the guttural in my foreign and Dublin-adulterated brain. It is indeed no wonder that I do not know a 'scaraveen' from a 'sheegaoithe' to this day.

With the 'cuckoo weather', storms arrive: 'Rough winds do shake the darling buds of May', as the bard poignantly put it. It is indeed sad to see the darling new buds buffeted and sent streaming like pink confetti across the lawn; 'apple blossom snow', said Charles Causley in 'Cowboy Song'. On the seashore, the flora of the sea has also been torn adrift and carpets the beaches. On a strand near Garretstown, I estimated that twenty container loads of various seaweeds could readily be collected at low tide. Once, a harvest of kelp was considered worth days of hard labour with pitchforks; now, when it is no longer valued, it could be collected in an hour with a JCB.

John Millington Synge, in his Aran Island diaries of 1906, talks about the kelp burners of Inishmaan. The piece is worth quoting verbatim:

The work needed to form a ton of kelp is considerable. The seaweed is collected from the rocks after the storms of autumn and winter, dried on fine days, and then made up into a rick, where it is left till the beginning of June.

It is then burnt in low kilns on the shore, an affair that takes from twelve to twenty-four hours of continuous hard work, though I understand the people here do not manage well, and spoil a portion of what they produce by burning it more than is required.

The kiln holds about two tons of molten kelp, and when full is loosely covered with stones, and left to cool. In a few days the substance is as hard as limestone, and has to be broken with crowbars before it can be placed in curraghs for transport to Kilronan, where it is tested to determine the amount of iodine it contains, and paid for accordingly. In former years good kelp would bring seven pounds a ton, now four pounds are not always reached.

In Aran even manufacture is of interest. The low flame-edged kiln, sending out dense clouds of creamy smoke, with a band of red- and grey-clothed workers moving in the haze, and usually some petticoated boys and women who come down with drink, forms a scene with as much variety and colour as any picture from the East.

The men feel in a certain sense the distinction of their island, and show me their work with pride. One of them said to me yesterday: 'I'm thinking you never saw the like of this work before this day?'

'That is true,' I answered, 'I never did.'

'Bedad, then,' he said, 'isn't it a great wonder that you've seen France and Germany, and the Holy Father, and never seen a man making kelp till you come to Inishmaan.'

It is hard to fathom how the flora of the sea, so useful and so beautiful, came to be called sea 'weed'. Witness the rock pools, edged with pink coraline, olive wrack, iridescent carageen and brilliant green sea lettuce. What terrestrial rockery or formal garden can compare? Also, many of these so-called 'weeds' are healthy vegetables, edible and delicious. In Japan we often ate sushi wrapped in green 'nori'. In Glasgow I remember buying 'dulse' at a grocer's shop. In Wales they make 'lava bread' out of the purple laver which just now can be found in abundance, pasted like a shining cling-film on the seashore rocks. I tried laver recently. Raw, it was tasty but chewy. I tried boiling it, according to an old recipe, for five hours. It was supposed to turn into a jelly, very good when spread on fresh bread. It didn't jellify. However, it did turn out like tender spinach with a lovely salty tang of the sea. These plants, for which we have no name and no *meas*, are common on the coasts of Ireland. Surprisingly, we don't eat them, despite the fact that for centuries we've enjoyed carageen.

The free plastic bags once – but happily no longer – dispensed with such largesse by Irish supermarkets have come back to haunt us with the storms of last week. I feel sorry for a hedge with flitters of plastic stuck in it; it's doing its best to liven up the scenery with yellow furze, May blossom or wild currant and here comes a wind-blown old fertiliser sack and ruins the effect. I don't subscribe to the 'pathetic fallacy' that endows plants with intentions, but pathetic it certainly is – and no fallacy that this is a supreme insult to the hedge. On the Clonakilty road, there's a bag blowing like an ugly pennant on the crown of a bush, overlooking a lovely view. It's so high up that there's no way of getting to it and, if the bush lasts, our great-grandchildren will still be looking at it in fifty years time. It would be nice to think they could cherish it as a unique artefact but unfortunately there may be millions of other pre-millennium bags available. Few of them will quickly disappear.

There is an Irish story that, in the 1950s or 1960s, a country schoolboy found what he thought was the bottom hoop of an old zinc bucket as he walked home from school. An innovative lad, he rolled it along ahead of him, all the way home, for the fun. When his father saw it lying around the yard he said, 'We have enough rubbish around here!' and threw it into a hedge where it hung, unregarded, for a decade. Then, the story goes, a famous archaeologist found himself lost in that remote district and came to the house asking directions. Spotting the hoop in the bush, he took a closer look. It turned out to be a Bronze Age collar, a royal torc.

The details may not be perfectly correct but that is the essence of the tale, and the sub-text seems to be that anything that survives from previous centuries has intrinsic value anyway, whether a collar or a bucket hoop. Wood rots, metal corrodes, stone crumbles ('My name is Ozymandias, king of kings: look on my works, ye Mighty, and despair!'). Simply because the old is often unique, it is valued: should it have the intrinsic beauty of a thing made with pride and craft, this is an added worth. I fear that our plastic waste will be more of a plague than a pleasure for posterity. Should we take the view of Sir Boyle Roche, the highly original eighteenth-century Irish parliamentarian, who protested, 'Let us not ask what we have done for posterity but, rather, what has posterity done for us?'

Last weekend, we went to the Skellig Rocks, off Kerry, one of the most awesome sites of human habitation on earth. Here, in the sixth century, Irish monks raised stone beehive huts and oratories on the tight summit of a bare rock, nine miles from land and seven hundred feet above the sea. For six centuries their successors lived there, often cut off from the world by raging ocean. What were they doing on this rock, these brawny, death-defying madmen drunk on the soul and on God? What kind of men were they? Had they no homes, no wives, no comfort, no love, no warmth, elsewhere? Was it penitential? Had they committed dreadful crimes and felt the need to flee humanity to expiate them? Or was it that they were so intoxicated with the love of God that they saw His presence in every wave cap, in every storm-blown sea bird, in every cloud that passed, in every stone and storm? Was it that they wanted, somehow, to enter the elements of the world of God, to feel the blast of heaven far from the cloying concerns of human frailty?

The Skellig monastic settlement cannot be contemplated without a sort of intellectual awe. Its presence asks profound questions about the spirit. These were not crazed eastern Christian ascetics living on pillars in deserts, surrounded by wastes of sand. These men lived in community, wrote books, kept annals, preserved and protected the covenant of the early Irish church. They had a function, whether it stemmed from vocation or neurosis. One has only to look at the huts, still standing after a millennium and a half of wind and weather, to see that these men weren't simply contemplatives. They laboured; they got things done.

But other-worldly islands though they are, cut off from the mainland and the mundane, the Skelligs are not simply dramatic scenery. They are 'human', in the best sense, a testament to the transforming spirit, ladders hewn by human hands to reach for heaven. I huff and puff to the top, and reach the huts, the tiny gardens. It is one of the ironies of life that we don't get the eyes to look at such things until we are older, when we cannot enjoy them as athletically as we might. Teenagers perennially consider walking boring and sightseeing a yawn-a-minute, even when viewing the marvels of the earth. It could be that it's uncool to show interest in such matters, and I can understand this. For some reason, back in the early 1960s, when we made our trans-Europe-trans-Asia VW-van journeys, we considered it 'uncool' to carry maps. Where we got this idea, God knows: I realise now that we spent the night in a village only a mile from Ephesus and never saw it, that we drove a few miles inland from the Mediterranean coast of Turkey and never went to the sea. The mind boggles; we were so cool, we were uncool. There we were, pursuing an arcane alchemy which we thought would peel the blinkers from our eyes and change the way we saw, solemnly reading our *Journey to the East*, our *Doors of Perception* and *Gates to Heaven and Hell*, yet all the time we did not have the eyes to see the past, the history. Yes, when we stumbled on the Parthenon or Persepolis, we looked and marvelled, but we didn't seek out the past. Or maybe, in that nomad nation, there was no place for maps – only the wind in one's hair and the road unwinding, all roads untravelled because we were so young.

Cormorants are extraordinary birds. They can catch fish even when the sea is opaque with sand. I remember, when my son Dara was a small boy, I told him, tongue-in-cheek, a rhyme my father had told me. 'The lesser cormorant or shag/ Makes its nest in a paper bag …' 'Where do they get paper bags, Dad?' he asked me, earnestly. It was a good question. In that plastic age, the poor shag would have had a hard job finding an old-fashioned paper bag to nest in – and we'd hate to see her trying to raise a brood in a bin liner, we both agreed.

After the few days of storms, the wind drops, the sun shines and we flake out in sheltered corners, looking out over the deep, blue sea. After the showers, we marvel at the brightness 'drenching through the branches', as Austin Clarke put it, and the puddles shining on the pot-holed roads. Some parts of Ireland indeed are still in the realm of the older gods and goddesses. Out on the Dunworley headlands, when I cross the last field, climb over the last stone wall, and set out across the gorse and the bent grass for the sea, I walk across land unchanged since the legendary Fianna walked it. I could almost believe I will meet Oisín, the bard, with New Age hair and cloak and sandals, striding the clifftops over the sea. Behind me are the last vestiges of man's dominion; before me, none. Not a sail on the sea, nor a contrail in the sky, not a house, a fence post or a telegraph pole. I do not look back and, in the view ahead, nothing fixes time. For all I can see to contradict me, I might be the only person in the world, and it might be the dawn, or the evening, of the First Day.

My fellow creatures in this dimension are innocent of hours and minutes. A fox gets up and lopes away, unhurried. I see him canter through the heather a half mile off. Red admiral butterflies flutter from sun-warmed rock to sun-warmed rock and, on a small loch of water, I see a shining damsel fly, with shimmering wings and body like an enamelled brooch in the sun. Between the rocks and Bird Island, in a narrow channel, a huge grey seal hangs suspended. Is he asleep? I wonder; he is like an enormous fat man, lying back, bobbing gently on the surface.

These days, for the birds of Bird Island, the heat must come close to being a problem. The island is a large, roughly flat rock, with no shade. Upon its surface, seventy cormorants make their nests – not in paper bags, certainly. They sit, gleaming black in the sun, or standing above their nests, sometimes in pairs. Now and then a male arrives, and there is an intricate dance of arched necks as the female greets him. Home is the hunter, home from the sea. Black is not the best colour in this heat, and the hens, sitting on their sea-weed pyramids under the day-long sun, must surely swelter. However, if the eggs were left unprotected they would cook. While this year the sun splits the stones, last year I saw cormorants sitting on their eggs on this island in a raging gale, with sleet driving in off the sea and the Atlantic rearing and roaring around them as night came down. Now they preen in the sunset, black cut-outs against the mirror of the western ocean, and there is something wonderful, beyond our comprehension, in the very air.

Of all Ireland's cities, Cork is, I think, the most privileged in visitations by exotic wildlife – otters loping along Merchants Quay in daylight, a grey seal near the Maltings, and killer whales in the River

Lee below Patrick Street bridge. Now there are rare Alpine swifts roosting on the back wall of the Metropole Hotel. Alpine swifts have a twenty-one-inch wingspan, and skimming up and down busy McCurtain Street just above the traffic, they make a spectacular sight. Twitchers arrive from everywhere, hotfoot, to tick them. While 'twitching' and 'ticks' sound like spasms or infestations, 'twitchers' are not, in fact, victims of an ornithological St Vitus's dance but hobbyists who 'collect' sightings of birds, the rarer the better. They then proudly 'tick' them off on their 'Ireland list'.

Ah, for the aerobatics of swifts, that feed on the wing, sleep on the wing, mate on the wing and touch earth only when they make a nest. If clouds had crevices, swifts would nest in them, but nests must be anchored and, for forty days each summer, they relinquish their ethereal element and cleave to the terrestrial with sharp, clawed feet. On May 21st, as we sat in the yard of Dillon's Restaurant, the first Timoleague swifts of the year threw themselves about the evening sky like black, spinning swallows, as if exulting in Irish air. Back and forth they dashed, screaming in lover's pursuit, mating in airborne choreography. Insects are their sole diet. When the young fledge, they are fed on the wing but if the weather is too cold for insects, they resort to a sort of torpor, during which they can survive for up to fifteen days.

Swifts mate for life. They arrive in April or May, and leave in August. At dusk, those not incubating eggs fly higher and higher until they disappear from sight, and cat-nap amongst the clouds. They nest in church steeples or in the roofs of houses, but are very vulnerable to interference in their nesting sites. When we lived in a block of Victorian red-brick flats on Hampstead Heath in London, hundreds of swifts arrived each year and nested in the gables and chimneys. We looked forward to seeing them whizz over our first-floor balcony on summer evenings and, climbing to the flat roof, six floors up, to watch them hawk and skim. Then suddenly, one year, they came and went in a day. Dismayed, we discovered what had happened. Renovation of the roofs had sealed all niches. Now, the sky over Parliament Hill Mansions, once so full of life, was empty, no more acrobatics in the evening, no more squadrons in death-defying flight. The destruction of such nesting sites is now common, and the effects often go unnoticed until, suddenly, the birds are gone.

The synchronisity of migrant arrivals is wonderful. As warm tailwinds carry the flocks north from Spain, rising temperatures in Ireland ensure insect hatches to feed them. On the other hand, when temperatures are low and there are few insects here, head-winds from the north delay the birds' arrival. The swifts come late; by then, the swallows are in their barns, the sand martins in their burrows at Simon's Cove, and the house martins safe in their nests under the eaves of Timoleague Garda station. There they are undisturbed, their stucco homes unbreached, unlike those of some cousins who last year had the cheek to build under the eaves of new, expensive houses in Clonakilty town. There they were quickly routed, with a long-handled broom. How dare they stick primitive mud huts on the front of a dream home!

One year, in May, Fintan and I cycled to a ford on the River Argideen. Tresses of water crowfoot flowed in the eddies, like lace curtains drifting in the stream. There, in misty rain, above the water corridor, sand martins, house martins and swallows sped over and under the footbridge, carving swathes through the insect clouds. So many were there that, looking downstream through binoculars, it seemed as if the air was spun out of birds. Martins were boldest of all. They flashed, with beaks agape, high and low along the river. As we lifted our binoculars, they whizzed beneath our armpits. As we straddled the stepping stones, they flew between our knees.

Overnight they had appeared on the river. Less than two-thirds of an ounce, they had flown 6,000 miles from Africa, treading the sky over vast deserts, high mountains and stormy seas. They had flown over the great rivers Zambezi, Congo and Niger. Now they were enjoying their first Irish breakfast on our small river. Welcome to Ireland, we said – but keep off the new house fronts! 'The temple-haunting martlet', Banquo called them in *Macbeth*, 'Where they most breed and haunt, I have observ'd,/ The air is delicate.' The house-proud begrudgers are apparently too preoccupied with property values to heed this, while poor Banquo was too preoccupied with ornithology to watch Macbeth. It is sad indeed that the sealing up of nesting sites is threatening the future of swifts, swallows, martins, starlings, house sparrows and barn owls. They do little if any damage, and a human instinct for neatness should not deprive them of a short and temporary tenure. They are our guests and neighbours for only a brief spell. They herald the spring and uplift our hearts. They add immeasurably to the commonwealth of life. We are not here for that long ourselves.

I am entranced by the affection of wood pigeons. Their idea of heaven is a round white egg in a precarious nest you can see the light through. High on a branch, they lean on one another's shoulders and, side by side, breasts puffed out, heads under wings, they sleep in the early evening. Such 'love', if we can call it love, is evident in creatures. Nature has no plots or stratagems; it is innocent, it is direct. Now, in the evening, there is peace in nature, a cessation of hostilities. The peregrine and the sparrowhawk are at home. The pigeons rest, the thrush and robin sing. Another day survived, another evening reached. Summer and time to celebrate from the heart. The coos of wood pigeons fill the wood; they are the wood's natives. They, and the rustle of the leaves, are the voice of the wood.

Wood pigeons are lovely birds, fat, lovat grey, with pink breast and white collar. No wonder man made pets of pigeons, whose voices are so soothing to the soul. The soft, resonant coos are soporific; one could sleep to the sound of pigeons. Not the most intelligent of birds, they have been useful down the ages for enhancing dovecotes, carrying messages, sport racing, and for food. But they are distressingly ugly when they are fledglings in the nest, fat, untidy squabs. It is a miracle that they mature into such elegant birds.

A little over a century ago, the passenger pigeon was the most numerous bird species on earth. In the eastern US, they numbered over three billion, more than all other species of North American birds combined. The name 'passenger pigeon' was given by the French, who referred to the bird as *pigeon de passage*. Their migration, i.e. passage, was phenomenal. James Audubon, the great bird illustrator, noted that, while on a trip to St Louis in late 1790, during the entire three-day journey he observed a continuous flock of migrating pigeons overhead, with no beginning and no end. In less than 100 years the species was no more. The major reason for their extinction was sport-hunting by man. In one competition, a participant had to kill 30,000 birds just to be considered for a prize.

By 1896 there were only 250,000 passenger pigeons remaining, in one single flock. The newly invented telegraph lines allowed large groups of hunters to communicate with each other and on an April day they descended en masse. The carnage was devastating: 200,000 carcasses, 40,000 mutilated, thousands of chicks destroyed or left to predators. By nightfall, less than 5,000 birds survived. The last recorded wild passenger pigeon was shot by a 14-year-old boy in Ohio on March 24th, 1900. Its remains are still in the Ohio State Museum. One Joe Boyd, long-time resident of Chandler, Texas, recalled, 'I will always remember the last passenger pigeons I ever saw. It was a cold morning in winter, there were nine of them in a peach tree facing the rising sun, with their breast feathers fluffed out against the cold. The sun shining on their red breasts made them look like nine large golden apples in the tree. I will never forget the sight. I never saw another passenger pigeon after that.'

All through the glorious weeks of 10 to 25 May, I lamented the non-arrival of our American friends. They missed the beauty of Ireland, and the beauty contest at Leap. Leap is a centre of sulkie racing. Asked to help judge The Queen of the Centre Track, a fund-raising evening, I thought it would be a horse. Having little knowledge of horses, I demurred but then the caller told me it was a human beauty contest, and I had no excuse. The competitors were volunteers, local farmers' wives and daughters. The judges, men and women, voted anonymously, needless to say. The contestants, one and all, were ingenuous, engaging and talented, and I was intrigued by their comeliness and wit. Two tied for second place. The winner was outstanding; she could have won the famous 'Rose of Tralee'.

My sophisticated American friends would, I think, have enjoyed the innocent fun of rural Ireland, with no winking leprechauns but great natural beauty and charm. I was heart-sore they weren't there. Some weeks earlier, out of the blue, they had phoned from New York to say they were coming to Ireland for twelve days, and would we suggest an itinerary to include Dublin, Galway and five days with ourselves? Then, equally out of the blue yonder, we found a message on the answering machine saying they had looked up May temperatures in Ireland and were going to Greece instead. I tried to contact them, to assure them the weather was marvellous and, whatever the weather, they would have a wonderful time: but the Greek tickets were already bought.

As it turned out, the five May days they would have spent in West Cork were like days in heaven. Here was one of the most beautiful places in the world, at its most beautiful and, in the near total absence of tourists, the Irish had Ireland to themselves. Now was the time to 'do' the Ring of Kerry, with not a tourist bus *en route*, the small roads uncrowded and the black rocks and golden coves of Iveragh lapped by a turquoise sea. With the barometer at 23 to 27 degrees, our big local beaches, Garahfeen, Inchydoney, Owenahincha and Long Strand were littered with sunbathers from Cork. An hour in a sun-trap and you'd redden, an afternoon's walk and you'd come home bronzed. All Saturday afternoon we spent by the stream in the garden or down at the Courtmac coves, the sea smooth as oil, blinding as a mirror at midday, rich as stained glass at sunset.

On Sunday, walking west, we came on an unpeopled strand and basked on the rocks and skipped stones over the azure water, clear as the Mediterranean, the sun throwing patterns on the sand thirty feet down. At nine o'clock on the Sunday night we found ourselves strolling into a spectacular sunset in shirt-sleeves. Later we sat with friends on the sea wall opposite our village hotel and drank cool Murphy's stout, watching the boats turn to black silhouettes on the water as the sun sank up the estuary, dyeing it orange. How much I would have liked to show off our Ireland during those days of blithe weather. Our missing friends had visited us before but however warm the snugs in the pubs or bright the fires, it wasn't the same as sipping a Murphy's in a painted sunset.

This was the loveliest of Mays, each sight and sense and sound resplendent, flag irises bright in the bogs, the woods floored with bluebells and dappled light, the water lapping on a lake dotted with swans: all perfect, but our guests not here. I don't know if it was pride in Ireland or affection for these friends of thirty years that preoccupied me most. Both, I suppose. When one loves something, one wants to introduce it to those one loves. On a secondary level, one wants to show it off. I would agree with them that Greek islands are lovely, with guaranteed sunshine, but for people who love words and wit, I can't imagine that a Greek-speaking island, for all its time-worn history, quaint white villages, retsina and dolmades, could bear comparison with Ireland and its consummate conversationalists. And, in music also, could the strumming of bazoukis compare with the best fiddles in Ireland at the May music festival at McCarthy's in Baltimore? Could moustachioed men line-dancing in skirts compare with the batter-on-the-floor of an impromptu session we came across in a pub in Clonakilty?

I know the Greek islands a little; I lived on Corfu for six months, and on a then-unspoiled Rhodes for six more. I partied in Mykonos before they'd heard of a night-club. And I believe, without prejudice, that no Mediterranean island I know, in Spain, Italy or Greece can compare with Ireland when we get the weather. It was my friends' loss, local companions kept telling me. Ah, yes, but these were dear friends, and I would have wanted them to remember these perfect days in a country whose literature they love.

June

Annihilating all that's made
To a green thought in a green shade.

Andrew Marvell

~

*Fish-releasing day. Rock pools, clear as
crystal and beautiful as jewels …*

After a glorious May, June arrives with leaves flying in curtains across the yard, like summer suddenly become October. The scarlet petals of a rose lie strewn across the path. On the other side of our stream, nine huge beeches heave and thrash, their bottom branches lifting like the skirts of flamenco dancers. In the shadows, a billion leaves shimmer against the brightness of the field beyond, so that it dazzles the eyes to look. If the storm continues with such force, the pastel-bright grass and its hordes of juvenile rabbits will no longer be hidden by the May's green cloak, but as clearly seen as in November.

The leaves carpeting the yard are new, not old; as Shakespeare might have said, the weather is out of season, the times disjoint and winds do shake the June buds with a vengeance. Sunlight comes and goes – wonderful bursts of light when the clouds open and turn the grass bright green. Birds hurtle over the house, wings stiff, catapulted by tail winds. The aforesaid bunnies sit breakfasting in the field, ears flattened down. A magpie trying to alight is caught by a gust and goes arse-over-tip ten yards downwind. I've seen kestrels hover in such a gale, holding still against the awesome power of the blast. Apparently their name in Irish may relate to the idea of their having sex with the wind, perhaps suggested by the way they hang in one place, with tails lowered and wings beating up and down. How would poor Manley Hopkins reconcile this image? I prefer, myself, his name, the 'wind-hover', and his image of God in the bird.

Despite the storm, it is warm in corners when the sun is out; the sun has real June heat in it. The trees all around roar like the sea coming in, or waves breaking and drawing back on a shingle beach. Down on the bay the tide is full out and the estuary largely sheltered from this north-west wind. The channel between the sandbanks is so grey, it looks, itself, like sand, with moored boats high and dry on a huge beach. I meet a man who tells me he was out at 5am, securing his boats. I could well imagine sleepless boatmen fretting as winds buffeted their bedroom windows in the night. Sea angling brings some business to Courtmac, and from May to October doughty Dutchmen are seen heading down to the pier each morning to board Mark Gannon's boats and make for the wrecks, where the big fish lie. They return at 6pm with boxes full of ling, pollock and congers, often 'specimen' or 'record' fish. Then it's the pub for a pint and, after dinner, the pub for another pint, then home to sleep the sleep of the sea before another day's fishing. Many Dutchmen come again and again, and half a dozen marriages in the village have been Dutch-Irish unions. There are as many Courtmacsherry girls married into Holland as Hollander men married into and living in Courtmac.

When the weather is bad, the visiting anglers are greatly disappointed and wander the village looking for something to do. They are not great walkers or sea bathers and there is nothing, really, except the pubs. While these are grand for a few hours in the evening, after days they must become tedious, however welcoming. Neither is there any river fishing for most of this May, the rivers too swollen and murky to make any hope of a fish spotting the lure near impossible. Perhaps the Dutchman turns his mind from fish to romance and tries to catch himself a sweetheart instead.

On the subject of fish, a long-term mildly eccentric English resident of the village is currently stuffing gurnard. While recipes for stuffed gurnard may be found in Jane Grigson's cookbooks, Chez Jeremy's gurnard is better displayed on the wall than on the table. He is a marine biologist, not a chef, and is currently stuffing crabs, lobsters, gurnards and other denizens of the sea. He mounts them on boards, with a small plate giving the popular and Linnean names beneath. Hung on the wall, they look quite fetching, and would interestingly grace fish restaurants or seaside hotels. It is surely more original to stuff sea creatures than the usual taxidermist's salmon, pheasants or stoats.

Jeremy also has a brace of needle-nosed garfish in his formaldehyde tank. These are going to America whence he heard, via University College Cork, that someone required that particular species for study. Until five or six years ago, it was thought to be the ordinary, everyday garfish. In fact it is very similar but not the same. Like gurnard, garfish are somewhat bizarre indigents of our local seas. Gurnards grunt, while garfish glow. The French *gurnard* refers to the 'grunt' or 'growl', a noise they make by resonating an internal air-bladder. There are other fish, brown meagre, also known as drums, shoals of which, by the same method, can make such a racket as they pass several feet below the surface that they can be heard by a fishing boat above. Gurnard, both red and brown, have strange 'feet', three stiff fins behind the head for all the world like crabs' legs, with which they 'walk' along the bottom as they feed.

Meanwhile the glowing garfish is very slender, not much thicker than a mackerel, although it may be three feet long. It has long, tapering jaws, like a 'needle nose', and is sometimes caught amongst mackerel shoals in summer. One day some years ago, my son Dara and I went angling on a boat off Union Hall. We forgot to pack lunch and, though our companions would certainly have shared theirs, I opted to fry a few fish in the galley, a garfish and mackerel each, straight out of the sea. It was a glorious, sunny day and the galley was lit by the open door; if there was a light bulb, we didn't bother to turn it on, and the table was in deep shadow. Lifting the meat from the garfish, we revealed – like magic – bones that glowed with a bright, green light, eerie in the gloom. We were both intrigued. Dara, then eight years old, wondered, if we washed them and brought them back to London, could he make a luminous mobile to hang over his bed and watch at night, as it moved. A green, skeletal fish, turning in the darkness, would be wonderful. But alas we learned that the bones lose their luminosity before long.

Local hurling matches are a great diversion in West Cork on summer evenings. Our local sides, Barryroe and Timoleague, were meeting in a junior league game last Sunday at Kilbrittain and friends urged us to come along. It was a great game. One of the stars for Timoleague was a Japanese teenager, with a rich West Cork accent and hair dyed shocking-red. He and his family came to my wife's school to study English, some years ago. They fell in love with Ireland, stayed, bought a house, and son and daughter went to local schools, where they made friends and thrived.

Hurling, at any level, is a spectacle, one of the fastest, fiercest games one might hope to see. The pitch is nearly half as big again as a football ground, with tall goalposts at each end. The hard, lawn tennis-size ball, the *sliotar*, is sewn from leather, with raised seams. It is hit with the *camán*, a hip-high blade of close-grained ash, slimmer and flatter than a hockey stick, with a 'boss' three inches wide, often bound with metal hoops. The *sliotar* is almost constantly in the air, pucked or run from one end of the field to the other. The sheer power of the puck and the velocity of a well-hit *sliotar* is awesome. It burns through the air, beyond the speed of the eye.

The *camán*, unlike a hockey stick, may be swung at any height, and the legendary 'clash of the ash' occurs when two or more hurlers leap for the descending ball, their *camán*s clashing against the sky. It is a miracle — and a testament to the hurlers' skill — that no player is trepanned, or suffers the full force swing of the ash across the face. Nowadays some wear helmets, but it is a recent style and some players would rather trust the opposition not to decapitate them than wear an uncomfortable helmet for the seventy-minute-long sweaty game. Hurling, along with steeplechasing, is the most exciting sport in Ireland. Points scored usually run into double figures. Whacking the ball over the high posts from a hundred yards out is a favourite way to gain a point. This is not easy while running full tilt, bouncing the ball on the boss — it is against the rules to 'hand' the ball for long — and dodging the flaying sticks of the opposition. To score requires a cool head and deadly accuracy; glance up for a second, toss the ball in the air, aim, swing and let fly.

After the match we had a pint outside the pub in Kilbrittain. Last June we followed the Corpus Christi procession as it passed slowly through the village, the silences between hymns punctuated by the distant bleating of sheep. The procession moved down the main street — there is only one — between the freshly painted houses, the windows filled with flowers, holy pictures or Infants of Prague, to stop in front of the grotto and the canon's house, where that venerable churchman, as old as Time, gave out a decade of the rosary and the crowd stood against the background of the green hill on which cattle and sheep roamed.

Kilbrittain is a lovely spot, often missed by visitors. It has woods and woodland walks, and a picnic place with a wooden bridge and an old stone bridge, called Deasy's Bridge, below it. The grass is worn at the foot of the wall by Deasy's Bridge, testament to generations of water-gazers and meditative, poetic souls who peer into the flowing stream and, I suppose, dream. Half a mile farther, the river opens into the estuary and then, beyond, are the sand dunes and the fine, open beach of Garahfeen or Harbour View. To the left is Coolmaine Strand, a favourite of wind surfers. Coolmaine Castle, relatively modern, stands behind, the property of Roy Disney, nephew of the famous Walt — but do not expect to see Donald Duck or Mickey Mouse roaming the grounds. Behind Garahfeen are the dunes, full of yellow-banded snails and soaring larks singing their hearts out against the sky which, on a classic June day, should be heavenly blue.

It is a time-honoured tradition and a cruel irony that, as soon as the State school examinations start in early June, the weather, however bad it has been, assumes the air of the tropics. Giving a pair of over-heated, hitch-hiking, Junior Certificate candidates a lift home after a day of wracked brains and dashed hopes – so they cheerfully informed me – I suggested that, like exam students in ancient Greece, they wear rosemary in their hair to help them remember their texts. 'There's rosemary, that's for remembrance ...', said one, quoting Ophelia, tartly; but *Hamlet*, she said, was not on their course. Thinking of a neighbour's hare-brained son, I asked did she think boys would wear rosemary if it helped them remember. 'No way!' she said.

In fact, rosemary was a *memento mori* as well as an *aide-mémoire*; the Greeks also dropped fresh sprigs in graves to signify that the dead would be remembered. Memory, and the head, are rosemary's human province; it was also used as a headache cure and, patently, there is still some head magic left in the spiky green leaves and small blue flowers – today, it is an ingredient of shampoos. Perhaps then, if they knew this, boys might shampoo with rosemary on mornings of impor-tant tests. If nothing else, its smell would far outclass the pungent odours of teenage aftershaves, likely to pole-axe nearby competition in the examination hall. Herb rosemary doesn't grow wild in Ireland, only bog rosemary, pink or white, another plant. I well remember the bouquet of wild rosemary in the crackling Mediterranean heat on the hills of Ibiza when we lived there on pennies, before planes, hotels and discovery changed the island's soul.

But the soul of Ireland, the other evening, as I drove slowly home from a journey to the west, was as gentle and generous as that of any pre-tourist Mediterranean paradise. It was one of two heavenly evenings we had last week, a summer evening as it used to be. I made slow progress from Skibbereen, stopping the car every few miles to savour yet another roadside attraction: a blaze of gorse, a golden verge of buttercups, a dreamy landscape or a flock of yellowhammers on the wires. The lake at Rosscarbery was as calm as the Sea of Tranquillity. I couldn't resist pulling in to sit and watch a family of herons, fishing the shallows in the still evening. Herons move so gracefully. The stately adults, with yellow beak and black pigtail, step as delicately as if they are walking on wrens' eggs. The two young birds, more hunched, less white, stood nearby, stabbing at the water experimentally. A cormorant, black as a bin-liner, with a white slash under the throat and a disreputable crew-cut, ducked and dived between them; it almost swam between their legs. Surfacing, it looked surprised and indignant. Cormorants always do.

The West Cork bays are always there but that evening, under a warm sun, they were all one could hope for. Peace and harmony reigned. No wonder the Greeks were philosophers; olives falling off the trees, corn burgeoning on the stalk and every fruit of land and sea at hand, the sun itself and the clear, bright air. No wonder they had time to think. But why did they conceive the torture of exams? Scholars tell us it was to keep the mind sharp with maths and clear thinking. They were no bombed-out lotus-eaters, your ancient Greeks. Logic was a fast-track for the mind, a mental gymnasium. Warm-ups of arithmetic, knee-bends of algebra, trapezes of geometry. Stick a sprig of rosemary in your forelock and it's as easy as Pythagoras! So the Greeks would say.

Just before home, as I round the last corner, I see Dara and Fintan in the sea. I stop. 'It's like Gomera!' they bawl, referring to the balmy waters of the Canaries. I'm persuaded. Soon, I'm squatting in the bay, the sea up to my chin. It isn't cold and it's even warmer over the mussel beds – all those little mussels, busily pumping water through them, must be raising the heat. I look around, head revolving like a conning tower. The sea is still as a mirror. From our tall trees, pigeons coo. A dozen oystercatchers wing down the bay into the sunset. Not a car passes. A buzz-saw, or strimmer, snores like a sleeper in the distance. The boys sit on a surfboard, absolutely still. Behind them, multi-coloured Courtmacsherry is hazy in the last light, a painted street upon a painted ocean. I sit, chin deep, in the hush of it. It was Wordsworth who said poetry is emotion recollected in tranquillity, if my rosemary shampoo serves me right. But tranquillity itself is, surely, inexpressible. Words, even written words, are noise, and even the best painting or best music interrupts the stillness.

As I philosophically schlep up the dark green lawn to the house, the night dew is cold on my naked feet. When Ireland smiles, no mistress is more seductive, and there is grilled wild salmon and brown bread for tea. I finished exams long ago and can rest, for worse or better. Good luck to the gallant triers. May angels sit on their shoulders and whisper the answers in their ears.

Our cat keeps bringing in shrews. Apparently, they are not very nice to eat but, while she disdains them herself, she seems to think they are good enough for us. She leaves them on the doormat as offerings. Shrews are, of course, the Pinnochio-nosed, tiny 'mice' that spend their frenetic lives burrowing and foraging in our back gardens. They are almost always there, but rarely seen unless the cat gets them, or we sit very quiet and listen. Then, their snufflings and squeakings can be heard. They are, like hedgehogs, insectivores, and have no relationship with mice, rats or stoats. They are very bad-tempered and belligerent, certainly to other shrews. They must eat their body weight each day, so they have no time for niceties. Of shrews, we have just one variety in Ireland, the pygmy shrew, which could comfortably curl up in a runcible spoon. In Britain there are six kinds. They are all distinguished by their long hairy noses and their dynamo activity. They are so small they must forage constantly. Life's too short to stand and stare. There is no such thing as an unstressed shrew.

Our cat, on the other hand, leads a life of leisure. She sleeps when she fancies, wakes when she pleases. Upon waking, she yawns, stretches and preens. Then, off to the garden, to terrorise the wild life and show who's boss. We have her belled so that she can't do too much damage. She is a singularly fortunate cat, an inner-city alley kitten who, during her nine years of leisured life, has enjoyed pleasant Hampstead flats and extensive Irish gardens. She lives the life of a queen.

Today is fish-releasing day. The thumb-length denizens of our temporary marine aquarium will be returned to their rock pools. This, no doubt, will be a great relief for them. During five days of confinement and observation they have behaved impeccably; no ethnic prejudice or cannibalism, no exclusion zones – except perhaps crabs excluding other crabs from their lairs. They have rubbed along well as a community, living in closer quarters than they would normally be used to. They have provided education, entertainment and excitement for a horde of small persons, my grandchildren. Not that, as a diverse selection of wild, intertidal life, they had any such intention; they simply adapted to their new surroundings and made do in somewhat smaller space than usual, the usual being any one of a thousand rock pools on their familiar coast.

They may have had to tighten their figurative belts somewhat, in that we may not have given them all they wanted to eat. But on the other hand, neither did we kill them with kindness as uneaten food degraded in the bottom of the tank, de-oxygenating the water. This is the fate of many goldfish won at agricultural fairs. Our shore creatures may have missed the come-and-go of the tides, but we had a strong electric filter at work day and night to agitate and oxygenate the water, so there was some simulation of natural conditions. We provided a 'reef', a piece of rock, overgrown with coraline and sea oak, in which to hide. Other, smaller rocks were footholds and anchorages for beadlet anemones, and holdfasts for limpets and acorn barnacles. The aquarium was out of doors, open to the sky, to sun light and star light, and to the rain which fell once or twice, gently, over the long bank-holiday weekend.

A sea hare was one of the more exotic inhabitants. A very small grandson, who took to poring over field guides to the seashore, identified it. It is a sea slug, deep purple in colour, with frills on its back. This specimen measured all of one and a half inches. Happily it did not discharge the sticky, blue ink the sea hare uses to deter predators. Had it done so, the bucket in which we carried it home would have become untenable for other life and we would have had to launch an emergency rescue operation. Why a sea slug is called a sea hare, I can't imagine. It doesn't move fast (on the contrary, it browses) and I have never seen a purple hare. The studious small boy — embryonic marine biologist, perhaps — wanted to take most of my seashore library home to the UK and carried heavy volumes about with him when he wasn't actually down at the sea.

Another small grandson who, during a few minutes of a seashore TV film in which he and I had once appeared, had reached into a pool and instantly captured a pipefish to show to the camera, trawled pool after pool for specimens, without his usual success. Outstanding amongst our family foragers were two small girls, formidable hunters, who found starfish and brittle stars, and many crabs which they fearlessly seized and put in buckets. We had so many crabs, nine out of ten had to be released. In the rock pools, shannies and Montague blennies were everywhere, along with bearded rocklings, sea sticklebacks, two spot gobies and goldshinnys.

It is most useful to stuff a clear plastic freezer bag in one's pocket when going rock pooling with children. Filled with sea water, it provides a portable and temporary aquarium in which the 'specimen' can be viewed from all sides before release. This is much better than the traditional bucket. The sheer open-mouthed wonderment of small children looking at a fish in a bag is a joy to see, and they understand that they must let one specimen go to make room for another. Catch-and-release becomes established practice. Meanwhile, finding marvellous things under rocks, they learn to replace the rocks gently, just so. We found scorpion fish, none larger than a thumbnail and, despite their name, not harmful at all. There were periwinkles and dog whelks and netted whelks and top shells. Our crabs were shore crabs and porcelain crabs, and some of the shrimps carried eggs in their abdomens, as did some crabs.

For the younger children, I searched in vain for baby lumpsuckers, like small, chlorophyll-green cubes with big eyes and whirring fins. Perhaps we will be lucky next year, but I cannot leave it too long. Interest in wild life abates (possibly only temporarily) after puberty, when other agendas, like hanging-out and flirting with the opposite sex, intervene. So I can afford to waste no summers if I want to enjoy rock pooling with small persons who are still wide-eyed with wonder at the marvels of the shore.

Hardly had they gone when the proprietor of a local pub arranged that I be delivered a pink octopus that he had, inadvertently, caught on a rod and line while fishing for bass. It is an enchanting creature with large, sympathetic eyes, black with a large yellow iris; I only wish my grandchildren could have seen it. It is well known that octopuses can quickly change colour to match new surroundings. It was mottled pink when I put it in the sea tank but quickly changed to red when it climbed into the terracotta flowerpot I'd provided.

Later, when I went to commune with it, it was gone. Eventually I found it sitting on the dog's blanket, ten feet away; being molluscs, minus a shell, octopuses can live for quite a time out of water. The dog blanket was Black Watch tartan; so now, also, was the octopus. Given its resemblance to a highland wind instrument of which Oscar Wilde said, 'Any gentleman could play one, but doesn't …', I could see a great future in octopus bagpipes for the Scottish market.

A member of the 'lesser' rather than the 'common' octopus species, it was a foot across. More amazing-looking than even the most imaginative cartoon creatures, it ate prawns, which it stalked theatrically, catapulting itself like a jet-propelled handkerchief to envelop them. Local youngsters loved watching it but, at last, too busy to daily trawl the rock pools for live prawns, I let it go.

The other evening, Fintan told me that he and his pals had found a nest in the woods, perched directly above their camp which, in consideration, they had decided to evacuate. He begged me to come and look. Sure enough, on a laurel branch only four feet above the ground, a blackbird had nested. Beneath the nest, in the thicket, tin cans and log furniture composed the remains of the children's camp. There were two eggs in the nest. We watched it for three days, and even went there at dusk when the hen would be sure to be sitting. No blackbird appeared, and no new eggs were laid.

All around the coasts of Ireland, the fulmars, kittiwakes, guillemots, razorbills and puffins are nesting in their hundred thousands, to
mention but a few species. Often, one can get close enough – without
tempting gravity – to see them through binoculars, standing shoulder
to shoulder on cliff edges and ledges in vast, cacophonous colonies,
raucous, ebullient, quarrelsome, even possibly issuing cries of delight.
Because sea-birds do not sing, as we know it, and yet land-birds sing
all the time, we can only assume that the fault lies in our ears, that
they are not attuned to the dulcet notes of shags. Sea-bird colonies
can be seen at the Mizen and at the Old Head of Kinsale where, from
the cliffs beside the car park, one may look down on a city of birds,
nesting on the sea stacks and rock faces. It is thrilling stuff, watching
them glide and hover and ride the thermals to alight on the inch or
two of ledge that they call home.

A guillemot's egg is pear-shaped, with the fat end heavy and the
pointed end short. Thus, if disturbed by gales or careless neighbours,
it spins, rather than rolls, and does not fall off the ledge. There is of
course no nest, but each egg is a slightly different colour so that
parents can recognise theirs; also they lay only one. Each guillemot
chick has a different cry, so that the parent can pick out its mewling
note from the mad orchestra of the cliff face. Baby guillemots will
leap 3,000 feet off a nesting ledge to bounce or fall into the sea. They
have small bags of fat attached to their undersides, avian shock-
absorbers. Most survive the death-defying leap and the fat bags prove
useful in sustaining them while their parents hunt for fish to feed
them for their first six weeks at sea. The parents in this case – and
the same applies to razorbills – moult at this time and so can't go
anywhere, anyway. After six weeks they have new feathers and their
chicks are fully fledged and can make their own way. Another example
of nature's synchronisation.

Yesterday at the Old Head I saw a thieving raven fly in off the sea
and land on the kittiwake cliffs, near one of the colony's outlying
nests. Bold as brass, it hopped onto the ledge and shouldered the
kittiwake aside. The kittiwake did no more than hiss feebly – it looked

like a hiss through the binoculars but it might have been a shriek. The robber simply picked up an egg in its beak, flew out over the sea and landed a quarter of a mile away. Seagulls' eggs are tasty and the yolk is very red. I remember, as a boy, on the Mayo lakes, we would collect a dozen black-headed gulls' eggs for Mrs May, my pal's mother, and she'd bake them into a sponge cake that was as light as a feather and bright pink.

The other evening, after work, we drove up to Cork to see the killer whales, in the harbour but they weren't there. They *had* been there only two hours before, breeching and blowing a mere three hundred yards offshore at Passage West, in a narrow channel alongside the Cork road. Panicked mullet and salmon skipped out of the water in all directions. What a nightmare for a trans-Atlantic salmon, arriving back at the nascent cradle of its own lovely Lee only to find three massive killer whales steaming up and down the waterway, saw-tooth mouths agape. And the unfortunate city mullet can't have imagined an invasion of leviathans in their muddiest dreams.

I had heard of the whales via a message on my answering machine expressing anxiety at the foolhardiness of punters who rowed out to take a close look at the 'pack', as they were described by Dr Simon Berrow of the Whale and Dolphin Group, who certainly would know a 'pack' from a 'pod'. Orcas in the Lee; three huge black-and-white killer whales, with teeth as big as your hand, surging up and down the channels of the city, reaching Morrison's Island alongside the South Mall, where august financial institutions and grand hotels lean from the river banks. Whales in the city! Sharks, I believe, abound – but never before whales.

Last week a tragic drama was played out when a pair of bottle-nose dolphins expired on the sand banks opposite Courtmacsherry. The male, eleven feet long, and with a tail almost three feet across, was clearly visible from our house; we could see him raising his head weakly from the sand every minute or so. The tide did not refloat him, only turned him to face out to sea. What to do? Obviously, he was on death's threshold. Blood was seeping from his mouth on to the wet sand. Probably his ribs were broken because dolphins' ribs are not made to take weight, the creature being waterborne from the moment it is conceived until the moment it washes up on a shore.

When dolphins want to die, there is often little we can do. Our kindness can perhaps be cruelty, frightening and distressing the creature in its last hours. Dolphins have died alone on mudbanks and lonely shores for many millions of years. Perhaps all creatures have their own way of reconciling the arrival of death; perhaps we have too. To feel that we can in some way assist in the passage of this creature with a brain almost as large as our own, is a vanity; to interfere may be an intrusion. The creature 'clicked' every minute or so, the 'click' sounds which are known to be a sophisticated 'language'. Maybe it was calling to its mate, dying farther down the estuary. It would perhaps be fanciful to think it was 'clicking' to some force beyond our ken – but we know not of what 'fancies' such a brain is capable.

Its mate was younger and half the size – in toothed whales, females are smaller than males. While the big animal had likely reached the end of its natural span (up to fifty years) the smaller creature showed no signs of ill health, no wounds or damage. Why did it also beach itself? Love amongst dolphins? Let us not be anthropomorphic, but they are sentient creatures and they do seem to 'think'. Brain weight in humans is 1.9 per cent of total weight; in some dolphins, 1.5 per cent of total. When first spotted, the pair were heading in tandem for the sandbanks. Some fishermen steered them towards the sea, but they were soon back again. As the tide receded the larger animal grounded. The other stayed a few hundred yards out, then disappeared only to be seen, at 10pm, 'climbing' the seaward end of the sand bank, as if trying to reach its mate. Rescuers attempted to dig beneath it and pull it off the bank with a boat. The effort was quite useless. However, the tide would turn in half an hour and the hope was that it would refloat and go back to sea.

In the morning it was found, again high and dry, where the male had been. The male, now washed farther up the estuary, lay slowly dying, in view of the village street. Calling a vet., with a humane-killer gun, was considered but killing a dolphin isn't easy. Kilos of blubber cover the brain and much suffering can ensue in trying to locate and reach it. Besides, dolphins have cognisance and may even be self-aware. As with aged humans, death is part of life and surely no one (except the dying) has the right to shorten the experiencing of death or to usher it in prematurely.

The following evening a local lobsterman, when pulling his pots close inshore, found many dolphins around his boat. He had never seen them so close in, and thought that there was about to be a mass stranding. Happily, they went out to sea and haven't been seen since. The ancestors of whales and dolphins were primitive ungulates, grazing the swamps on four legs, 60 million years ago. As they spent more time in the water, their nostrils migrated in a backward shift and developed valves to seal them when they dived. The tails of these creatures moved up and down like present-day dolphins, not side to side like fish, and over time their legs shortened and their bodies grew streamlined. Dolphins, proper, appeared about fifteen million years ago. They have a far older claim to earth and sea than we have. Some scientists believe that when cetaceans, distressed by disease, polluted water, or injury, strand themselves, they are trying to return to the security of dry land whence they came.

The June downpours came, as they often do, and last week as we travelled west from Cork, the rain lashed the windscreen so hard the wipers couldn't cope and we might as well have been driving through a waterfall. Earlier, as we had driven up to the city, rain water rushing down a hilly road was so deep that the jeep was bumper-deep in the surge and, at a flooded lag, we had to divert, although our wheel base was a foot higher than that of most vehicles.

The rain had been, since morning, heavy and incessant, unrelieved but for occasional even heavier showers which lasted ten or fifteen minutes and reminded us of Tokyo during the monsoon. We would hear them battering on the roof of the jeep; later, we could even hear them on the roof of the house. The jeep was Japanese, so the wipers would have been designed for monsoon rain. But Ireland, this mid-June, out-rained the monsoons. We had never seen anything like it, and the only verdict could be that climate change, whether cyclical or man-made, was indeed apace.

The farmers are devastated. The grass is ruined. It is hard enough for the small farmer to survive, without this. As we know, for him and his family, their holding isn't an industry but a way of life, work quite different from that of an office or a production line. For the dairy-man, it begins when the animals wake and ends only when they sleep, with milking seven days a week, every day of the year. For the tillage farmer, it begins when the sun starts to warm the ground and doesn't end even as frost first dusts the land; there is urgent winter ploughing to be done. Small farms have been with us for millennia: the ringforts that occur all over the West Cork landscape were small farms. Over centuries, the character of the independent farmer has added much that is positive to our national character. He, his wife and family have contributed invaluable elements to the culture, not least an ethic of hard work, decency and hospitality. One finds little indolence, thievery or aggression in rural places; these are city things.

It is sad that, since agri-biz times, small farmers are no longer able to subsist on their own land but often must find supplementary work in a world that has little time for values other than the commercial. There is, we all know, more to life than material comfort, although a modicum of the latter is not to be scorned. As always, balance is the problem, but when the farmers, reeling from weather that was none of their doing, ask for public help, let us not be too concerned about the euros and the cents but rather consider the value of the culture they embody and make a sincere attempt to keep it, and them, alive on the land.

In weather such as we experienced that June night, how do animals fare? Out on the roads, we saw, in the fog and the driving rain, two red eyes caught in the headlights and a large fox ran across the road. Foxes have no option but to hunt, whatever the weather; neither have their prey species any option but to come out to graze. However hostile the elements, they must go out into them and succeed in spite of them, or die. In pelting rain, in darkness, through sodden fields and storm-lashed hedgerows, they must forage and find. They have no stores except their own fat, and they carry little of that, especially at a time of year when they have given birth and have been run ragged providing for the young. A wet June is disappointing and tough for holidaymakers, but they have the hotel or holiday home to go to, the television to watch. It is much, much harder on wild life; and one cannot but have sympathy for nature. The creatures that should be playing with their young on sunlit evenings are instead out foraging in the dark and the rain.

It has been a June of many weathers, but by the end of the month the ground is once more dry. The land has survived the deluges, beauty abounds and I ask myself again, why are the forms of nature so lovely? One can see why brightly coloured flowers might attract a bee, or a brightly coloured male attract a female, but what about the beauty of conkers, hidden in their shell, or the concentric rings, hidden in the heart of the tree, or ivy on a tree trunk? The ivy leaves didn't have to be shaped like that, like a thousand hearts, black-green and sombre, or shining like shellac in the sun. A leaf like a prize fighter's ear would have fed the vine as well.

Along the sea, blue butterflies flit past on the breeze and sea pinks are blooming in bunches on bare rocks, with trefoil pouring like golden spills down the cliffs' shoulders. So many blooms, so marvellous a landscape! It could presumably have been all, and only, green. If nature or the Great Creator had had less imagination, we might live in monochrome. Instead, there is more diversity of shades on a roadside ditch than on any painter's pallet, and more diversity of shape and form than any artistic imagination could devise. We are surrounded by miracles. In this country, all one has to do is look at an old stone wall and one will find a mini rock garden, with self-seeded ferns, and forget-me-nots, navelwort and mosses, wall rue and a dozen other plants colonising every crack and cranny, making a rampant organism and a roadside attraction out of a stack of bare stones.

The beauty of so much in nature would seem to presuppose an observer who will take pleasure in it. It is as if a Great Maker said,

'Next, I'll create this plant [or rock or creature] and, while I'm at it, I'll make it beautiful to set eyes on …' For what eyes? To the non-human eye, form and coloration seem to have to do only with survival. Certain forms and colours mean danger, or food. Breeding adults 'read' the subtleties that distinguish 'quality' from 'lesser quality' but it may be argued that the only purpose is to better ensure the perpetuation of their kind. It seems doubtful that non-human life can 'enjoy', rather than simply 'discern', the multi-colours, multi-sounds, multi-smells of this Garden of Delight, as we can. Does a fine-looking pheasant admire a fine-looking goldfinch? It is hard to believe that plants – the most gorgeous of creations – enjoy beauty at all. We humans seem to be the only objective sensors to the beauty of natural or man-made things. If nature was not made beautiful for us, then its great beauty must be a happy accident. But it is hard, on a country walk in Ireland in June, not to think otherwise. The glory of the wild flowers, the loveliness of the birds, seas and skies would seem to presuppose an observer. And, it follows, an ultimate artistic director, making works for the fortunate observer to enjoy.

July

Exultation is the going
Of an inland soul to sea

Emily Dickinson

~

*Thoroughbred racing may be the sport of kings but
sulky racing is the sport of agricultural princes.*

In Ireland, July has always been the month for family holidays. Suddenly, Courtmacsherry is full of smiling strangers greeting one another, once-a-year friends since childhood. The weather is a lotto but, being Irish, they are inured. A sense of humour is a great stand-by and, short of a downpour, they sit bravely on the sands in small and large families, wrapped in towels, with goosepimples and pink legs. In such weather, only the very young or chronically numb dare the sea. But sometimes we have heat waves too.

Foreigners, we are surprised to learn, find contrary summer weather refreshing, a relief from broiling Italy or Spain. They cycle doggedly on, rain cloaks billowing in the wind, threatening to carry them into the sea. No problem, they say; they come with no expectation of sun, and no desire for it. They love the soft rain, the warm pubs. They shelter under roadside hawthorns, relishing green thoughts in a green shade.

The sprats are boiling in the bays of West Cork and the halcyon evenings seem set to go on forever. We Irish are a pink people, turning brown. Office men, just back from town at half past six, pile the kids into the car and rush to the beach for a pre-prandial dip. Throwing off the city jacket, they rip off the tie and make a *sugán* of the shirt in their urgency to get into the water. These nights, they don't have to hurry. The sand is hot and the air is balmy, and at eight o'clock there are still twenty people on the beach. Beyond them, mackerel break the surface like fairy winds riffling the bay. Gulls hover and squeal over sprat shoals in the shallows. A couple feathering for mackerel from the pier say they haven't seen the like for years, their every cast a glittering winner. At nine, the sun on the sea still dazzles and the village street is the promenade of locals and visitors out to see another glorious sunset. The women are bare-armed and shining, the men wear modest shorts. It stays bright late; one could read the paper on the lawn at eleven and the garden walls still radiate like fire bricks long after the sun has set. Nevertheless, a turf fire or two is burning, perhaps for old time's sake.

Courtmacsherry has long been the favourite resort for Bandon and Cork families. Some have enjoyed centuries of summers here, the bungalows and Georgian terraced houses passing down through the generations. I regularly meet visiting strangers who know more about the village than I will ever know. Each summer they reunite and perhaps the elderly like to gather around a fire. Over the years, come wash-out Junes or sodden Augusts, these families have faithfully arrived – and stayed.

In summers like this we Irish become a Mediterranean people. A month more of this weather and we would move out of doors, eat in the garden, drink in the street, sit in the shade and snooze in the afternoon. The womenfolk, most especially, transform. She who appeared doughty and deliberate now, in a summer dress, moves with an angel's grace; she who was pasty is freckled and glowing. Happily, most of the men do not wear shorts, but those that do cut a decent figure, provided they do not wear woolly socks with their sandals. The farmers look well in the sun. Compromising little, they wear the usual shirt and long trousers, but with their sleeves rolled up, displaying muscular, sun-tanned arms. While not under-going such a transformation as their wives or daughters, they are, nevertheless, new men.

Mornings begin with spider webs of silver on the lawn. By noon they are long since gone and the landscape staggers in the heat. As we walk the shore, the beach ahead curls and shimmers. Children, far out near the surf, are like Giacometti figures, black spindles cut with a blowtorch out of a sheet of iron. The sea isn't yet warm below the rocks, where it is deep, but the incoming tide, crawling across a beach heated by hours of sun, is almost tepid. Swimming with Fintan and his friends, I make the mistake of diving off the rocks into a deep pool. It is so cold, it almost scalds me. A few minutes later, however, the pain gone, I duck and swim through jungles of sunlit kelp. The rocks that wall the cove are flat slabs of slate inclined at seventy degrees, catching the sun, with ledges to stand on. Wet from the sea, we rest back against their warm, smooth surface. Below us, the sea glitters and laps. The climate, like the place, is heaven.

For Marie's summer students from France, Spain, Japan, Italy, Austria, here to improve their English, a fishing trip is a highlight of their Irish visit. They've seen school photographs of students in other years, eyes shining with excitement, holding aloft lines of glittering mackerel like big-game fishermen displaying their marlin, sailfish or sharks. This evening, it's their turn. We are scheduled to set off from the pier at 6.30pm. It is almost 7pm before we get going but there's no great hurry – West Cork is on summer time.

Now, the thrill of the sea, of the big, fast boat throbbing beneath us as we sweep out of the bay, of the fat, white wake, of the land receding, the village growing smaller, the wind pulling at our hair – an Irish summer and the mackerel season, and we are off to catch serious fish. It is a golden evening, perfect for our voyage. The angling boat owner, sea-beaten and red-faced as the sun in splendour, predicted the weather would be grand. Right he was; it could not be more beautiful, a blue sea under a blue sky, the sun dancing on the water like a million lights – and soon, there will be a host of mackerel, dancing on the feathers. Our captain this evening is a part-time tutor at Marie's language school and, by good chance, also a doctor of marine biology, angling boat skipper and fish finder and fish stuffer of expertise.

The engines thrum, the prow rises, the French girls shriek. Of our passenger list, most have never fished before and some have never been to sea. Will there be sea sickness, *mal de mer, mareo, funa-yoi*? Hardly; the sea is flat as a mirror, barely a stir on the surface except for the small black guillemots that rise and whirr away on their short wings to land a hundred yards off and continue their fishing. As we pass the bay mouth, we see terns diving, a sign of sprat shoals, a good sign. To the east, the Old Head of Kinsale, with its lighthouse and the grey cliffs, catches the sun. Headlands to the west are shadowed, their dark green fields, banked by stone walls, pouring like green rivers down to the shore. Cameras are soon clicking but there is no photographing the reality, no way the camera can catch the wind, the salt breath of the sea, the throbbing of the boat, the 360 degree ocean. But the on-board shots, the eyes bright with delight, will later tell of an evening off Ireland, the emerald isle behind them rising from a turquoise sea. *Phoque!* shouts a French boy, *Foca!* the cry goes in Spanish, and I realise they have spotted a seal. *Azarashi!* I tell a Japanese girl. While they learn English, I learn polyglot words relative to these voyages, adding one or two a year.

Soon, there are gannets, big, white, cruciform, with black wing tips, rocketing into the sea a hundred metres beyond our prow and the fish-finder screen shows strata upon strata of fish below us. We have hit a shoal. Coal fish, they turn out to be – black pollock, not favoured for the table, but easy to catch. A few dozen are taken, and dropped back. We leave the coal fish and set off in search of the mackerel. Who needs a TV fish-finder, when the big, soaring gannets show the way? An Italian doctor, here with her two daughters, tells me that she is amazed at the amount of fish we are catching. She holidays in Sardinia and, although the Mediterranean thereabouts is clean and clear, there are very few fish. Wait until we hit the mackerel, I tell her; then you will see serious fishing. I am sad to hear that the Mediterranean is so over-fished that its lovely waters are almost barren inshore. I remember Ibiza in the early 1960s, the octopus boats at night less than a kilometre off the terraced town, their carbide lamps flaring on the pitch black of the sea, and I recall the huge amount of fish in the fish halls every morning. But that was forty years ago, when nature's bounty burgeoned in almost every corner of the earth.

The mackerel! Seven rods off the side, with feathers on each, and the fish coming aboard by the new and old time. Shrieks and screams of excitement, photo opportunities, cries of alarm – 'It ees too 'eavy! I 'ave caught a shark!' All the fun of a classic mackerel evening but, once again, and as always, my sympathy is with the fish. So many fish, so many and so beautiful, so perfectly formed, so sharp and bright and strong. It seems criminal to be murdering them, a dozen every few minutes. How can the stocks last? So, I calculate numbers – which of the students' host families like fish, which don't. I arrive at a figure: nine households to be fed, at six mackerel per household, and the odd pollock for variety. I relay these mathematics to the fisherpersons and, when the catch box is half-full, we start throwing them back, a quick release and over the side, and they flash down into the depths whence they came. I could never be a commercial fishermen. I am grateful to the professionals, and one of the attractions of living by the sea is that I can enjoy the bounty they daily bring fresh ashore. But I am becoming a softy. When I think of the Mediterranean and of other depleted waters, I think, more than ever, that we must take only what we need and not a sardine more.

While mackerel fishing is a summer sport on all the coasts of Ireland, here we also enjoy a distinctive West Cork pursuit. Every year on a July Sunday, sulky racing is held on the broad sweep of beach at Inchydoney, at low tide. Added to the heady air of horsey excitement is the gamble that the sea will prematurely reclaim the track. A few hours available and many races to be run. Sulkies are lively little horses that race in harness, pulling a light cart and a driver. Thoroughbred racing may be the sport of kings but sulky racing is the sport of agricultural princes. Most owners are farmers, and not rich. It doesn't cost a ransom to own a harness racer.

Last Sunday, all over the beach, and in the dunes, bronzed holiday-makers joined horse-mad farmers with flat caps and weathered faces, probably as white-skinned from the neck down as the day they were born. It was incongruous indeed to see sun-bathing men in bikini swimwear queuing at the on-course bookmakers. It was a new racing experience to listen to the list of runners reeled out, while lying flat on one's back on the sand. A mild flutter, followed by a quick dip, was the order of the afternoon, then back to watch the excitement of horses and drivers raise spray from the near pools or race far off in a dark string against the sun-bright Atlantic. Racing *au natural* and *al fresco*. Tide and the starter's whistle wait for no man.

Amongst the horse boxes and trailers, I met James Jennings of Cononagh. 'James has the bug,' his wife, Lily, told me. 'He'd talk horses in his sleep!' James, a leading light in the West Cork harness racing fraternity, breeds, trains and drives. 'It doesn't cost a lot.' he told me. 'If you have bit of ground, the rations don't work out so pricey – and if you're any way lucky, you'll win a bit of prize money and cover costs.' Even as we talked, he was busy grooming and tackling his mare for the 'Surf Breaker', the sixth race in the programme, with the tide now so far in there was every chance the wheels of the carts would indeed splash through the surf. *Fleet I Am* was his horse, and fleet she was. Drawn Number One, and first off from the start, she held that position all the way, beating a tough challenge from a larger rival that raced neck and neck beside her for the last hundred yards to the post.

After the dainty trotters, the unfettered flat races – horses ridden by jockeys rather than pulling sulky carts. These made a sight to be remembered, the spray and sand rising from their hooves as they galloped flat out on the open circuit, the cries of the punters, the galloping commentary on the Tannoy, the whoops and cheers. For visitors from the cities of Britain or continental Europe, it was certainly a sight worthy of the Ireland they had come to see. Here was racing in the vernacular, Everyman's racing, country men with their steeds racing across a sun-blessed Irish strand.

There can be marvellous runs of blue sky days in July, with warm sun but not the white-out or desiccation of Mediterranean shores. The green fields are gentle on the eye and nowhere I have ever been is lovelier. On such a day last week, entranced with it all, I drove around a corner of a back road on the West Cork coast and came upon a view so beautiful I gasped. Below me, coastal fields, golden with gorse, basked under a blue sky and, beyond, huge green islands with tall cliffs and small white strands rose out of an azure sea. It was a view to equal any I have seen on four continents and, once around the dangerous bend, I planned to pull over and enjoy it to the full. But if nature's sheer magnificence had overwhelmed me, what I was about to meet was like a blow that took my breath away.

There, between the road and the view, amongst gorse and heather, a new, huge house was going up, two storeys with dormers and large garage. The site, a natural viewing place where there should have been a lay-by and a *mirador*, as they call it in Spain, was now occupied by this vainglorious edifice. On the hairpin road above it there was no place to park. From the road below it, the scene was of farms and houses, a rich landscape but without the overwhelming majesty I had seen. That majesty, previously available to the poorest traveller on the public road, was now blocked out and in the future would be enjoyed only by the house occupants. For these privileged few, a public amenity, an uplifting spectacle, a hundred square miles of world-class landscape and seascape had been spoiled.

Every week we hear of beautiful places in Ireland being lost to the public. The county planners do their best, but the cheek and arrogance of some aspirant home-owners know no bounds. I could point to a headland, the natural arm of a very popular beach with a long tradition of summer homes, where someone has attempted to build a huge house on a green field near the tip. This structure, isolated from any other by half a mile, dominates the view and, had the house reached completion in all its multi-roofed glory, it would have been an aberration on the face of Ireland. Happily, it was stopped. But three years later the block-built edifice, in places two storeys high, remains, roofless, with empty windows, grey and monolithic, a blot on the view. Presumably the county planners will insist on its removal. Not before time.

These days, to expropriate an entire landscape by putting one's home in a position that destroys it for others must be recognised for what it is: greed. In the past there was much land unbuilt upon and few to see it, the average citizen travelling no more than five or six miles from his or her door. Then, the first consideration for house-building on the coast or in the country was shelter. Thus houses were often fitted into hollows or behind hills. They were not salient and generally had no negative impact on the overview. Now, with money for insulation and double-glazing, with the means and machines for re-landscaping and earth-moving, houses can be sited where they could not have been in the past. As a result, the landscape of Ireland is being destroyed by isolated new buildings. And some of those that would call themselves aesthetes or lovers of the landscape are most to blame.

They move to the country and seek a remote site with panoramic views. The planners don't easily grant permission, but the culture dictates that it is the right of the individual to build in the pristine landscape; at least, that was the culture until now. It is high time it changed. Huge swathes of scenery are being undermined for the sake of a few dwellings. The fact is that, while a house with a view is wonderful to show off to relations or visitors, the occupants soon become accustomed to the backdrop and, in time, hardly notice. In everyday domestic life, we look in, rather than out. However, if, beyond our town or village, we can almost entirely escape from houses into a pristine vista, wonderful! We can take a stroll and enjoy it. We can drive out on Sunday. But if we continue siting solitary houses as we have been doing, there will be no natural vistas left.

An annual feature of July is birds with short tails, not because the cat has got them but because they are newly fledged and, particularly in the crow family, tails are slow to grow. We see tail-less young magpies along the roadside, awkwardly trying to get enough lift to avoid oncoming cars. Similarly, jackdaws, on the wires, like commas with the tails cut off. Young birds often appear gormless. Perhaps this is the destiny of teenagers, feathered or fleshed, as may be. Also on the roads we see many tiny corpses, baby rabbits, a tiny stoat, baby birds. Recently we have twice come across families of young foxes all over the road at night, asking to be run down. Every year we meet fox cubs like this but, while we see dead adults, happily we never see pretty young foxes dead on the road.

When July is warm and dry, showers are welcomed by nature with new growth, insect hatches and the sudden appearance of birds one never knew were there. When blessèd rain from heaven fell upon the place beneath, young blackbirds and hedge sparrows could be seen busily wrestling on the lawn with worms that, unwisely, surface for the rain. Most welcome of all in the garden is a young song thrush. We are happy to see that the cock who so proudly sang from a cherry tree in March has succeeded in finding a mate and has borne issue. Those lucky enough to have song thrushes nesting in the garden can count upon summer evenings full of bubbling, exuberant song. But song thrushes are nowadays in decreasing supply. While blackbirds – another type of thrush, in fact – supplement their creepy-crawly intake with fruit and berries, song thrushes are almost entirely carnivorous. Pesticided slugs and poisoned grubs lead to death or infertility, so our summer evenings are not always orchestrated as of yore.

At the start of the month the road verges are golden with tall buttercups, and flag irises still wave their yellow banners from bogs and ditches by the West Cork roads. They stand tall amongst the deep green verdure of the damp places where they grow. Towering over them are the last foxgloves, thirty and more fingers and no thumbs. I warn small children I know not to poke fingers into foxgloves – there may be a bumble bee inside! Meanwhile, navelwort, that round-leaved plant of stone walls, seems sometimes to be almost competing with foxgloves, which it resembles in small scale. Some years, it flowers to unprecedented heights, a metre from root to tip, covered in creamy, bell-like flowers. That it is named for the navel and stands a metre high seems to me appropriate. Our one-time agricultural neighbours in the Canary Islands would make a metre measure by breaking off a stick at navel height, it being reckoned that the average Canarian man's umbilicus is approximately a hundred centimetres above the ground.

Throughout July the procession of wild flowers goes on and on; it is a great month for a hedge scholar. As one flower bows out, another flounces in, painting the hedgerows in fresh colours. The wayside ditches are an education for botanically curious ignoramuses like myself and, when next spring comes, an entirely new perception will inform our perambulations. No longer will a ditch be simply a ditch but a charabanc of delight, a catalogue of the season, a repository of rarity and surprise. Life is full of delights. As our school Tennyson put it, '… every hour is saved/ From that eternal silence, something more,/ A bringer of new things; …'

When I was young, I thought wild-flower-spotting a sissy pursuit, the preserve of spotty persons in bifocals and Oxford bags, with funny hats and flower presses. I happily admitted an interest in fish, flesh and fowl but thought flowers, wild or otherwise, beneath the notice of a robust boy. Later, as an adult, when I again came to live in the country, I was greatly impressed by the flowering of certain species in certain months, to find that I could tell the month of the year by the wild flowers and that their cycle evidenced the fecundity of summer, the sleep of winter, the first stirrings of spring. I had by then gained confidence in my convictions. If anybody thought me a pansy for pausing to admire a dog rose, they could say so and I would defend the charge. The floral landscape is of constant interest, changing every time we walk, with fresh roadside attractions as the months go by. Historical artefacts don't change but nature is never the same two days running. Birds migrate, return, feed or roost, animals hibernate or mobilise, trees shed or grow, plants die or flower. The vegetable kingdom is especially diverse and un-boring. Even in deep winter, when there is no colour anywhere, blue, red, orange and green mushrooms grow beneath the trees.

Peter, the rabbit-wrestling cat, is suddenly gone west, after twelve years with us. West, I suppose, because that is where the sun sets, and Peter's sun has set; it was a painless demise, as far as we know, dead in bed, no trauma. In spite of the name, she was a female. Her transgressions were few; she was politic, cautious and meticulous, like J. Alfred Prufrock in the poem. Domestically a paragon, she caught mice and never ate the goldfish, although she would drink delicately from their tank while, beneath the surface, the poor fish turned a paler shade of gold. She was the terror of the garden; early on, I belled her, thus to save fledglings and sun-basking lizards from an untimely end.

Cats have been caught eviscerating everything from barn owls to ornamental emus but Peter's number one prey was pygmy shrews. Not to eat – for shrews are reputed to be foul-tasting – but simply to stop shrews from taking over the world. One felt sorry for the tiny, elephant-nosed little creatures, but more concerned for the viviparous lizards because these are rare and localised and we feared she would wipe out an entire colony on the side of Courtmacsherry Bay. At viviparous lizard-catching, our Peter was a dab paw. She became so skilled that they even kept their tails on. At first this was not the case and there were so many tail-less lizards about that I feared she would initiate a sub-species. She didn't kill them, just frightened their tails off. It is well known that a lizard's first and last line of defence is to shuck off its tail. There it sits, wriggling like a live thing, while the lizard body-corporate makes itself scarce. Less intelligent predators will be diverted but not Peter. No, she would ever-so-delicately seize the truncated reptile and carry it into the house, there to deposit it somewhere safe, such as under the bed where it might crawl into my wife's slipper. Yes, Peter had some exquisite moments to answer for. But, reptilian company excluded, she was a very well-liked cat.

She was born in a Kentish Town housing estate but moved at an early and impressionable age to Hampstead where, beside the Heath, she settled amongst literary and artistic cats as one to the manner born. A tortoiseshell of delicate build, she liaised with a sleek Siamese and duly delivered what was to be her one-and-only litter before paying a discreet visit to the vet. Soon afterwards, she moved to salubrious Ireland where she again fell on her feet (as cats will) with a very pleasant home and overgrown garden by the sea. There she led a maidenly life until weak kidneys smote her down at the grand old age of eighty-four, on the human scale. Not a bad life; nobody, to my knowledge, ever kicked her, inadvertently sat on her, or stood on her tail. We shall all miss her. She was always there when one came in late at night, mewing a greeting and offering company, if feline company one sought.

For children up to a certain age, many everyday things are new, and being with children inspires, or restores, the art of seeing the world as they do. I have been lucky in having the chance to take each of my children, as they grew, on a summer holiday, sometimes together but more often alone, usually when between the ages of six and twelve years old, this apart from the family holiday. In West Cork, we have explored many wonderful places – islands like Sherkin and Cape Clear, in Roaringwater Bay, and the Blaskets, off the wild coast of Kerry.

One mid-July day, my then ten-year-old son, Fintan, and I crossed to Clear Island on the evening ferry from Baltimore and set up the tent in a fallow field overlooking South Harbour. We could hear the sea lapping far below us and watch the water arriving in slow ripples from America. We knew it was coming direct from America because, when we went down for a swim, we spotted a drifting plastic drum which I suggested would make a good seat by the camp fire. However, when we examined it, its submerged side turned out to be covered in gooseneck barnacles in their white shells, their delicate fans extending and retracting, trawling the ocean for plankton. It was a colony that could not have grown so large and vigorous had it not been in the sea a long time. The drum was labelled 'Oil Company of Kentucky'. It was drifting towards shore and the barnacles towards certain desiccation. We steered it back out to sea; such is the magic of Clear Island.

Perhaps, if one lives there, it is much like anywhere else, the marriages, births and funerals. Next day we saw a funeral, the hearse a blue Volvo estate car, with the coffin laid in the back. It was followed by nine cars, most of them old and rusted, processioning up a steep narrow road to a pink church on a hill below lowering clouds. The grief was theirs, the small community of mourners on that dark day, poignant and no business of ours. We passed the open door of the church, our heads bowed, wishing we were invisible and not, by our very foreignness, intruding. While we were enjoying summer holidays, someone's mother, father, daughter, son, brother or sister was being mourned. But those that saw us didn't look resentful. The Irish bereaved are humble and don't expect the world to stop, nor blame it for not stopping, even if their personal world has utterly changed.

That night, over our camp site, a half moon sailed across black spaces between ragged clouds. At 3 am, the first rain came. The boy and I stirred in our sleeping bags as the fly sheet cracked and flapped like aluminium foil shaken behind a stage. My toes grew wet with driven rain, a not entirely unremembered sensation – indeed, almost an annual one, as the children have grown. 'Dad, I'm freezin'!' hissed the boy. 'Here's a sweater,' I offered, captain in the flapping dark, our hands meeting in the storm-torn night, both of us enjoying every minute.

In the morning the sea was clear, the world new-washed and bright from the storm. The waters in the harbour were crystal to twenty feet down and we dived in, never mind the blast of a sudden shower and the rain drops peppering the surface. A good time for campers to swim, with a free shower from the sky afterwards. And then off to fish for our supper, from the rocks below the camp.

The silver spinner flies and plops and a silver swirl follows as Fintan reels it in. It is a long, thin, silver garfish, its three-inch beak breaking the surface. Tonight there will be green, luminous bones on the supper plates. 'We could hang the backbone in the tent, Dad. We could read by the light of the garfish!'

Next day, in milky sunlight, we climb to the highest point on the island, where we find an old-fashioned furry caterpillar, and gleaming white mushrooms in a field. The land, like the sea, is different at Clear

Island. *Oileán Cléire* – it is Irish-speaking – has been left, largely, as the Great Creator made it, too poor to deserve 'improvement'. I don't know the statistic but perhaps no more than 20 per cent of the island is under grass or crops, the rest a wild medley of purple heather, gorse, bracken, montbretia, fuchsia, vetch, cornflowers and the rest. The rocks are bristly with lichens, green or grey, or like seagulls' eggs have dropped from the sky and splattered them in orange. We had elected to make our annual camping trip in the second week of July and our decision was well rewarded. The island was lovely, whatever the weather. On the boat back, three-quarters of the passengers stood on the open deck in driving rain and flying spray, rather than miss a minute of it. Two seals and a deluge greeted us as we pulled into the quay at Baltimore. Although we looked forward to home and telling the family of our marvellous adventures, we were sorry to be back on the mainland, in the everyday world again.

During the following week, as the temperature dropped and the downpours descended, our friend, the ardent walker and singing veterinarian Jim Buckley – welcome, for his fine voice, in any pub where we have ever repaired for a post-walk drink – phoned to insist we went walking. 'Once you get out in it, it's all right,' he vowed. 'And, for the love of God, if you can't go for a walk of a July evening, when can you go?!' We went, the rain cleared, and his mantra proved right. Once we got going, we warmed up and it turned out to be a grand walk. As we arrived back at the cars again at eleven, it still wasn't really dark.

When my living-abroad children visited us in early June, my eldest daughter, Lydia, marvelled at the length of the evenings compared with London, and fondly recalled the long evenings of the Borlin Valley, west of Bantry, where we spent two precious years when she was a child. It is true that the evenings of the west remain light unusually long; I recall experimenting with reading a newspaper (*The Irish Examiner*, with its lambent prose) out of doors at 10.50pm in mid-June and finding I could do so. Marie, a geography graduate, says we get four minutes more daylight for each degree of longitude west of Greenwich. Looking at the map, I see that we are slightly less than nine degrees west of the meridian, so our evenings should be about thirty minutes longer than at Lydia's home. Not so, she says; where she lives, in Hertfordshire, it's always dark before ten. The explanation our geographer offers is that in Courtmacsherry, on the western seaboard, we have a wide and bare horizon; there is no topographical feature or source of atmospheric pollution between us and the setting sun. So roll on, then, the long evenings; given the weather to go with them, we will be casting for mackerel from the rocks or diving into the crimson sea until eleven o'clock!

The following evening, without encouragement from the wandering minstrel, Marie and I took to the outdoors again. This time we got drenched. I found that my increasingly minimalist hairstyle obviated the need of a cap, and this was a bonus: in long-haired days I disliked getting my head wet because my scalp prickled; now I found that warm July rain hopping off my stubbled skull and running down my forehead was a not unpleasant experience. The rain began almost as soon as we stepped out at about 10pm, a grey curtain drifting down from Barreragh, a mist slowly becoming rain. By the time we had walked a mile, our jackets were sodden.

The route home took us down a disused road with hedges overhanging on both sides and thigh-high grass in an unbroken corridor between them; it is a most pleasant lane on dry days, with wild flowers in profusion. Meadowsweet, foxgloves and bramble blossom were indeed everywhere and the scent of honeysuckle – in spite, or because of, the drenching – hung in clouds. 'Swish!' went the tall, wet grass as we passed, and 'Slap!' went the sodden hedges. 'First in a wood, last in a bog …', my father used to say, but it was hard to know which was best, so we took turns, the follower walking six feet behind the leader. Gradually, our trousers, summer-beige, turned black with drenching and, by the time we reached the bay at Abbeymahon, we might as well have walked into it, for all the wetter we could get.

However, turning south on the seaside path, the prospect brightened. Familiar Courtmac, as we tramped sodden towards it, was a place enchanted, the street lights hazy, the pier lights swimming on the soundless bay. Water met mist, and mist, water; the village might have been a ship, the ghost of the drowned *Lusitania* lying twelve miles distant, off the Old Head of Kinsale. It was great to be out in the half-darkness, out in the night and the weather, Marie, myself and the half-drowned dog, with the occasional car passing. In Ireland, it is unlikely that the cold or the heat will ever kill us, or that we will drown in a flood or a tidal wave. We have this to be grateful for; and there is great novelty in the deluges of midsummer.

One July, late in the month, the temperature dropped and a cool breeze blew in our bedroom window. Downstairs, the dog was in labour. At any minute we expected to hear the squeal of pups. Although she was a pure-bred springer spaniel – and the kindest, most sociable dog one could hope to find – her pups would, as usual, be black-and-white nondescripts. They were always the same. Undistinguished they might be, but they were invariably pretty, and a photo in the local supermarkets always secured good homes.

When the second litter came, I asked a small grandson, visiting at the time, to pose with a pup exactly as he had done in the first 'publicity' photo. We consulted the old photo to compare. However, when he cradled the pup, we all saw that it was an exact clone of the first. Since then, we have pinned up copies of the first pictures and saved on expenses. Whoever the father, the pups look the same. In personality, they take after their mother. They are not gun dogs or show dogs, simply amenable family pets.

Sally, as she was called when we got her, might well have had a pedigree but she turned up at a neighbour's house as a stray. She was in a bad state. We saw her and said we'd take her, but then the original owner arrived. He explained that she was 'gun shy'. All his efforts to train her had failed and we were welcome to her. She came to us as a cowed, frightened dog, shell-shocked, we supposed. She would not respond to any command. If you wanted her to leave a room, you had to carry her; if you wanted her to come in the car, you had to heft her in. It was six months before she began to gain confidence. At last she no longer cringed at every command and came out of the corners in which she hid. She was only a year old, young and beautiful, liver and white in colour and as enthusiastic and fearless over land and water as only springers can be.

Now, she is part of the family. Her pups, for all that they are hybrid, are civilised hounds, good with children; they retrieve thrown sticks and prettify the hearth rug. We are not dog-breeding people, nor organised enough to find her an aristocratic beau. She is still terrified of loud bangs. When one of the children got a cap gun, she left the yard, tail between her legs, and did not reappear until the caps were used up. She is everything a family dog could be – and, rightly, she does not like guns.

My German friend Mr Alphonse Straub, who, after twenty years married into this part of rural Ireland, speaks the vernacular like a native, says, 'See you next Monday, please God!' I reflect on the meaning, 'If it pleases God …' God must be mightily pleased with this little part of the world, I think to myself, as I drive home over the highlands between Bandon and the sea. And aren't we lucky to have blown in, Alphonse the Romanian German, and I!

Yellowhammers sit on the roadside telegraph wires, with their yellow bibs, imbibing the sunset. Friendly children, out walking the dog, wave to me as I pass. Fallen fuchsia reddens the road between the hedges. Every corner I turn presents a prospect of fertile fields, patch-worked with crops. The silver estuaries are dotted with birds. In nine miles of driving, I don't meet another car. Mr Straub's recipe for life is, 'Don't lie, don't steal, and, if at all possible, avoid drawing welfare. …' Like many local people, he has survived by sheer energy and a job-lot of practical skills. I first met him when he cut up my trees for me.

In our first winter we had three giant macracarpa pines knocked by phenomenal gales. They lay, like the ruins of a primeval forest, across the lawn. Mr Straub agreed to deal with them and the next day, when I looked out my work-room window, I saw six or seven men, with tractors and chain saws, ready to begin. Spot the German, I thought, and talk to him. As it turned out, the most 'Paddy-looking' of all, the one with the turned-down Wellingtons and the build of a Firbolg, turned out to be Herr Alphonse Straub. The trees were duly cut into neat, nine-inch deep, swiss-roll slices, perfect for chopping. The whole job was accomplished in record time and at a very acceptable price. Next time I met Alphonse, I asked how he was getting on with the wood cutting. He'd 'put it on the long finger', he said, 'for there was little money in it'; he was dealing in cattle now.

August

August is the month for festivals and regattas in the villages
of West Cork. 'Commit-tees' — emphasis on the last syllable
— of local residents are formed, meetings are held. Those
houses that haven't already been painted are painted — any
colour the owner admires — and baskets of flowers are
perched on windowsills or strung from lamp-posts. Tidying
is carried on, as if for a Tidy Towns competition, chip vans
are franchised, musicians are engaged and pubs apply for
extensions. The priests are consulted about blessings and the
Garda Síochána about traffic and, in the case of Timoleague,
the local Garda station is dolled up so colourfully, it is a
place one would almost love to be detained in.

Still and sheltered, Dunmanus Bay.

When the sun shines the Irish are, again, a pagan people. Mass is attended after sunset on Saturday, so that not an hour of Sunday sun-worship will be lost. For the few who do attend on Sunday morning, the priest foregoes the sermon, and lets them out early so that they may make the most of the Lord's bounty of good weather. Being a down-to-earth country priest, he knows that the sun streaming through the stained-glass windows and pouring through the door is distracting them anyway – '… the sun is brighter/ Than God's own shadow in the cup now!' as Austin Clarke said. In such weather, the entire population abandons the television in droves. The world is transformed, the children come out in freckles, and the nation turns golden brown.

It was the American Murphys, whose ancestors likely came from Cork, that began the vogue for suntans. Born rich, they left the rarefied society of the Hampshires and Cape Cod, and migrated to the South of France and stayed there. Friends from America's east coast elite came to visit and found them sun-tanned as peasants, but looking wonderful for it. So they too, instead of hiding under sun hats, fedoras and veils, came out into the sun. Suddenly, sun-burnt skin no longer signified labour in the fields, but leisure on the beaches. Not poverty, but affluence. And the cult of the suntan was born. Scott Fitzgerald's characters in *Tender is the Night* likely all had sun-tans. He and his wife, the lovely Zelda Sayre, were friends of the Murphys and, with them, resorted – perhaps cavorted – on the Mediterranean; it was the extravagant, hedonistic thing to do. While it all ended in tears, sun-seekers and dedicated party-animals of the new millennium might reflect that the in-crowd were doing the same thing in the 1920s, often with a lot more style.

Sun is always better when there is water, and the West Cork week began with the best Courtmacsherry regatta weather for years. Regatta Day is a big occasion. In his eponymous lyric, our local bard and librettist of the Butlerstown Variety Group, Michael O'Brien, nostalgically recalls what it meant to him and friends when they were young. 'In June, July, the time would fly, 'til August came the way,/ To bring the high point of our lives, Courtmac Regatta Day …'

As always, volunteers set up a stage on the pier, while gawpers gawped and hurlers-in-the-ditch offered unasked-for advice. By mid-day, crowds began to gather and the village was lined with cars. The band played and the white boats glimmered. Fr Hurley, in white vestments, blessed the occasion, scattering holy water far and wide. The Church of Ireland rector, the Reverend Johns, delivered a brief homily after which the Chairman of the Courtmacsherry Development Commit-tee (hard '*tee*'), Mr John Young, and local politicians, made speeches.

Then the real business of the afternoon began, sail-boat racing, yawl racing, skiff racing, swimming races and pillow fights on a greasy pole over The Dock. While the lifeboat crew, in unseasonable oilskins, gave a demonstration of sea-rescue skills, beyond them white terns flicked over the bay, plunge-diving into the glittering sea. The sky

from which the 'rescue helicopter' descended was cloudless and innocent; it was hard to believe it could ever have been brooding and dark.
Classic August weather continued, following upon the idyllic regatta
Sunday of 1998. Evening after evening was so perfect that at seven
o'clock we could put a saucepan of boiled new spuds into the car, a
bowl of salad, fresh-cooked crabs straight from the pier and a bottle
of chilled wine, and dine above the beach at Dunworley. After the sunset and the red sea, we drove home in the light of a harvest moon, huge
and golden over the fields. If I had to choose a location in which to spend
eternity, it would be the coast of Ireland on such perfect summer days.

The tricks of hot weather. … In the early afternoon, a heat mist
hangs over the bay and a couple walking on a sandbank half a mile off
appear to be drifting in the middle air. Grey mist and grey sand merge
into a single element. An opaque curtain veils the other side of the
estuary with a few hill-top fields suspended above it beneath a Delft
blue sky. Mirage is something not often seen in Ireland; I rush in for
my camera. The photographic result will probably resemble a blob,
with two fly specks. Magic isn't easy to capture, but I try.

While the morning was lovely, I think I have never seen anything
so beautiful in weather as the sun filtering through rain that same
evening, looking out the open French windows onto the lawn of the
Courtmacsherry Hotel. The bay was glittering, silver rather than
gold, as the sun set beyond it to the west. It so happened there were
palm trees in the view, the Cordyline palms we have here. Green and
Medusa-headed on the dewy lawn, they added to the exotic air. But
more than anything, it was the rain. It fell straight down, each drop
following on the other like a bead curtain but falling slowly, as it is
indeed possible for light rain to fall. I have somewhere seen clear,
slightly viscous liquid run down a long, silk thread, drop following
drop, slowly descending, filtering the light as it went. That was how
the view appeared, the rain itself a curtain, the palms, lawn and bay
hazed behind it, all glittering as if shot through with silver dust.

While our weather, summer or winter, is a bagatelle, it is rarely
tedious; variations are infinite, never repeating. A foreign student told

me that on a day's outing to Kerry, she and her friends knew they would have to pass over the same route – Bantry-Glengarriff-Kenmare – twice. However, on the return journey, they kept wondering if they were on the same road. Even after consulting their map, they weren't sure. Clearly, something uncanny befell them in the Cork-and-Kerry mountains. They talked about it with great intensity afterwards, what they called the 'tricks of the Irish light'. It is true; the sleight of light can transform a view from gloom to glory in seconds, as clouds scud over or disperse. What was a deep green, misty corridor on the outward journey was, upon the return, vast with views over Bantry Bay and distant mountains. A grey, barren landscape had become a palette of colours.

I can imagine their surprise when, coming down the Tunnel Road, they saw the huge bay below, stretched out in the sun, and the road-side bedrocks splashed with brilliant lichens, none of this seen on the outward round. 'The magic of Ireland' is a phrase become clichéd but it is not to do with leprechauns; it truly describes the marriage of landscape and light. We have not one Ireland but an infinite number. We live in a country of illusions; we never see the same prospect twice. A guest told us that the view from her window was theatrical, like the rise and fall of a stage curtain. Perhaps, she speculated, the Irish verve for theatre and drama was engendered by the changes of the light.

Late Sunday afternoon, as we set off to walk west across the sands, our visitors felt cold. Indeed the setting, just then, might have well suited a bleak, northern tragedy, a forum for Ibsen or Bergman. The huge, flat beach, with the tide far out, seemed more suitable for bird watchers or surf fishermen than for holidaymakers. But then the clouds opened. Suddenly, all was golden, including ourselves, and we might have been walking into Paradise down gilded sands. To our left, the sea, transformed, flashed blue as sapphires and the grey surf was as brilliant as white lace. Above the vast proscenium of beach and sea, spotlights had suddenly switched on. It was pure theatre, and Prospero's island couldn't have been more magical. Facing out to the ultramarine ocean, one might have filmed *South Pacific*.

Visitors certainly get value for money in Ireland. In a few hours they can savour all the seasons and the 'forty shades of green'. Sometimes, however, an act of faith is required. Once, in July, I proudly took some overseas students to see Kerry. We drove to the mountain top of Priest's Leap, near Bantry, where the marches of Kerry are laid out in glory below. Alas, like the Kingdom of God, the Kingdom of Kerry was invisible. In vain I pointed into the dense rain, describing it. But I think they didn't believe Kerry was there.

I heard reports of seven large basking sharks drifting on the surface near Rosscarbery. A family I know paddled amongst them, in a small boat. They were seventeen feet long, their dimensions easy to gauge by the boat's length, and as harmless as rafts of flotsam. Although toothless plankton-feeders, they were amongst shoals of sprats, and the mackerel milled on all sides. With their huge gapes, wide as open dustbins as they drifted, how did they avoid swallowing mackerel and sprats? Basking sharks are an abiding memory of my own childhood summers. We don't see so many now. My friends say they were graceful and beautiful. I wish I had been there.

Later in the week we had mackerel skies over the bay. The clouds lay like a giant fish overhead, daubs of white mist, like scales, laid on the midnight blue. One can't but wonder about ancient belief in sympathetic magic; that particular night the inshore sea was teeming with mackerel. Fish in the sea, and their image evident in the sky? Maybe the name refers not only to the sky's appearance but to the fact that such cloud formations presage mackerel close to shore.

We had mackerel sashimi at sea a few evenings later, and I would highly recommend it to anyone with a bit of culinary nerve and a taste for the exotic. As the mackerel came dancing over the side of the boat, they were humanely dispatched, then gutted and handed over to our two on-board Japanese chefs – actually, language students – who skinned them and cut them into thin slivers. These were briefly bathed in a marinade of soya sauce and wasabi, a type of Japanese horseradish paste available in the English Market in Cork. Delicious, they were wolfed down by captain and fisher-folk alike. What more tongue-tingling a treat than a raw-fish feast at sea.

Afterwards we took the student group to Clonakilty, which must have the best and most varied music in any small town in Ireland, with as many as ten pubs offering everything from traditional to country 'n' western, rock 'n' roll, jazz and techno, at weekends. As we filed into De Barra's to hear Noel Redding (Jimmy Hendrix's one-time sideman) in an atmospheric back room, the sight of a hirsute Irish Traveller belting down affluent Clonakilty's main street on a flat cart pulled by a hairy piebald pony elicited surprised 'Ooohs' and 'Aaah-Sos'. Our visitors wanted to know about these 'different' Irish and their culture and why, if we had native nomads, we did not flaunt them proudly rather than hide them as if in shame.

As we waited for the gig to start, I told them the little I knew about the Travellers' claim to be the descendants of the ancient High Kings of Ireland, about the greater likelihood that they were families displaced during the Great Famine or dispossessed clans that took to the road when Cromwell, in 1649, told them to go to hell or to Connacht. I told them about their lavish marriages and funerals, their mourning rites and special way of dealing with death – burning the deceased's caravan to ashes and burying his horse's reins and bridle with him. I told them I thought the time might come when our native nomads would be ikonised, like the Native Americans, rather than marginalised, as they are now, and when there would be a Travellers' TD speaking Shelta in Dáil Éireann and appearing beside our Taoiseach to welcome foreign delegations.

If we ever do have a Travellers' TD, it will mean that he or she reads and writes and has thus taken aboard our cultural luggage. The fact that Travellers have not rushed into literacy has preserved them, for better or worse, as they are. They are, not without reason, suspicious of the settled Irish. We have all heard of the quaint parent who tells his child, 'Reading books will only lead you astray!'

In mid-month, my brother visited from Seville, the 'frying pan of Spain', where temperatures reach 44 degrees centigrade in summer and to step out of the shadow is to be hit a pile-driver blow by the sun. The population adopts a crepuscular lifestyle. Daytime is spent

indoors, with air conditioning; only at night do those who can otherwise avoid it venture out. For a Sevilliano in summer, Paradise is a
cloistered corner of the Alcazar Gardens, within earshot of running
water. While Courtmacsherry could not offer the Alcazar, it could
offer the cool Atlantic, and for brother Gerry, just arrived from Cork
Airport, it was 'out of the fire and into the Frying Pan', the English
name for the small, deep cove at Coomalacha.

We had its clear waters to ourselves for half the morning. We lay
back against the heated slabs of rock, ahead of us the ocean winking
with a million mirrors, without a symbol of time or mankind. Later,
teenagers arrived to swim and dive in the blue lagoon below, boys and
girls flirting, appraising, competing, relaxing. Our hours were short
and, for that, all the more precious. Once, like them, we had no
thought of summer ending, and endless summers yet to come.

At six o'clock we sit drinking Murphy's stout outside the Pier House
Bar, waiting for the boats to come in. The angling boats always have a
catch, and the foreign anglers, with no cooking facilities in their guest
house rooms, are generous. Persons loiter about the pier, plastic bags
sticking out of their pockets. We are in search of lemon sole or John
Dory and are waiting for one of the three small local trawlers to arrive.
It is extraordinary that the Irish, surrounded by fish-rich inshore waters,
are circumspect about many species and have little or no interest in shellfish or *fruits de mer* – it is even possible that some of our forebears died
during the Famine because they could not conceive of eating limpets.

Some years ago, our son Dara, then seventeen, wondered how he
and his pals could raise cash for a three-day stay at a famous music *Féile*
in Cork. Private enterprise, suggested his mother and I. Mackerel, so
plentiful the angling boats couldn't give them away, were arriving on
the pier every evening; why didn't they take them a few miles inland?
Surely there would be market galore for fresh-caught mackerel, the
succulent chickens of the sea?

The boys duly sought out a boatman, who generously said he
would give them half a box 'on spec'. If they were sold, they could buy
him a few pints; if not, they would serve as rubby-dubby for shark

anglers or bait for lobster-potters the following day. It was the perfect no-foal-no-fee arrangement. Next evening the boys collected and gutted one hundred and twenty mackerel, and drove to Bandon town before teatime. 'Fresh mackerel, ready for the pan, four for a pound, straight from the sea!' Surely it was a bargain. Eight mackerel will feed a family of four. But did the inland Irish rush to the car and queue to buy them? No: one family bought twenty fish; nobody else showed an iota of interest and the remaining hundred mackerel became shark bait, next day. The lads tried again, two days later, with the morning catch, this time calling at rural homes, bringing fresh fish to the farmers. Again the same result. The Spanish, Italians, Greeks, Scandinavians, even the largely landlocked Germans all value fish, and sea creatures that the Irish 'wouldn't be seen dead, eating!' are savoured by some of the most discriminating palates on earth.

Was it the fish-on-Fridays fasting laws that caused the pious Irish to treat all that swim with disdain? Was the reason historical, that the poorer land was on the coast and only coastal dwellers ('Fish eaters!') would have to stoop so low as to have a fine cod on their plates? Did the inland farmers look down on them, the poor shore dwellers who could not afford steaks of fat Golden Vale cattle? For whatever reason, fishing, on this island surrounded by the riches of the continental shelf, has never been properly exploited. In the early days of the Common Market we swapped our fishing rights for entrance to Europe, sought farm subsidies and surrendered our protein-filled waters to the Continentals, who well appreciate their worth.

'A remarkable bird is the pelican/ Its beak can hold more than its belly can ...' was another of my childhood lessons in avian lore, compliments of my father. What with his capacious pelicans and bag-nesting shags, it is not surprising that I developed an early curiosity about nature. The fact that I didn't know a shag from a cormorant was academic. Armed with my father's arcane data, my eyes wide as saucers and sharp as eagles', I went forth into the world to view the wonders thereof, confident that at any minute I would see pelicans with beaks like flour sacks, cormorant clutches in sweet bags, a stork flying by with a baby, and a phoenix rising from the living-room fire. I was also interested in reptiles and expected crocodiles to contain alarm clocks and wooden legs.

For fear readers would think me an exceptionally naïve child, let me say that, unlike some Irish country children of the time, I did not believe in fairies, and clearly saw that leprechauns, gnomes and elves were the brain-children of altitudinally disadvantaged Celts or Picts who wanted to look down on people smaller than themselves. 'We daren't go a hunting for fear of little men ...' the school poem told us. Rubbish! I thought. I'd only be glad to meet a leprechaun, if they existed. I'd tame him and take him to school in my pocket.

'Look, Dad!' said Fintan to me, one August evening. He held it out, along with a few sea-polished shells, in his scooped hands. It was only two inches long by one and a half wide, the shape of a small turtle shell. He had spotted it, half buried in the dry sand, when he took me to 'the Diving Board', a small cove off the path to Wood Point, where I had never swum before. It was nine o'clock at night, and I was privileged to have his exclusive company – he had left the gang to take me to this special place. We swam for nearly an hour and came home through the woods, after dark. How a tiny sea turtle's shell could be washed, wave-worn and rounded, into a cove on Courtmacsherry Bay was beyond us. Giant leatherbacks, large as single-bed mattresses, do drift by on the Gulf Stream, far offshore, in a circuit from the Gulf of Mexico, but no way could a baby Caribbean turtle come this far.

If it wasn't the shell of a tiny turtle, then it was surely the shell of a land tortoise. It was the perfect shape, not shell but bone, with the hump and the arch where the head stretched out, and the scoop for the tail, and the signs of small, rectangular plates on the carapace. But tortoises are Mediterranean creatures. How would a baby tortoise end up here? As we walked home that night, and all next morning as we dived off the rocks where the sea was clear as the deep ocean and we could see the bottom five metres down, we speculated. Might it in fact be the shell of a tortoise? It did have a high hump. But tortoises roam the lands of the Aegean. Was it perhaps bought at an Irish pet shop and, after an untimely death, given a Viking burial? Was it the pet of some lonely Greek sailor, passing in an oil tanker on the horizon who, when he found his small compatriot dead, cast him into the sea?

We have great summers in Ireland; and we have half-baked, soggy ones too. Nineteen ninety-seven brought parka weather in June and an Eskimo on an Irish holiday might have longed for the summer tundra. In July 2002 the farmers couldn't get into their fields, for mud, but the end of July 2004 brought in an August, September and October of unbroken sunny days, and a winter mild and often sunny, auguring, perhaps, a climate change for the better in the south-west of Ireland. Wild primroses bloomed at Abbeymahon on Christmas Eve, the first 'spring' flowers, while some fuchsia blossoms still hung on the bushes, the last of summer's.

Diary notes tell me that on Sunday August 15th, 1999, waylaid by showers on the dunes of Inchydoney, we had a picnic under a golf umbrella, the diurnal downpour like a curtain between us and the sea. Later, 'Drips from the umbrella spokes plopped into our wine glasses but failed to dilute the summer cheer. Although a grey cloud hung like a dirty duvet over the dunes, we were optimistic; it had started suddenly, so it might, likewise, stop. Meanwhile the dunes, while no longer golden, were not without interest. Half-drowned cinnabar moths clung to ragwort in a semi-coma, so wet the shiny black triangles had leached out of their wings leaving them see-thru' as gossamer, with their scarlet margins as pink as watered wine. The cinnabar caterpillars, in black-and-amber Kilkenny stripes, continued, despite the soaking, to munch industriously on the poisonous yellow flowers, digesting the toxicity and in the process making themselves inedible to birds. Would that the big black dune slugs, fat and long as an index finger, could eat ragwort; they would make short work of this noxious weed which, if it strays into hay, can kill the horses that eat it.

'After the rain stopped, slugs by the pound poured across the dune paths, eliciting theatrical shrieks from my eldest granddaughter, Elishea, much to the delight of her Uncle Fintan, her junior by three months. Fin's older brother, Dara, and friends, had sensibly gone to seek an Indian summer in Simla, and venues sim'lar, the previous week. I have never been to Simla, or Shimla, once the favourite summer resort of the Raj, a hill station to which the British memsahibs, their children and servants retreated during the summer heat, leaving their menfolk, the soldiers and the "box-wallahs", to swelter on the plains. Simla, and the towns around it, are graced with fine period houses and beautiful bungalows, and the area is replete with walks and treks. Despite the charms of the Inchydoney dunes, the cinnabars and fritillaries, in weather like this I would quite like to be with Dara. While I adore the great black slugs sliding viscously over the wet Irish grass, I am sure they have splendid slugs in the Himalayas, and a myriad of undreamt wonders to admire. …'

The Irish remember famous summers and sunshine, as skiers remember famous winters and snow. It seems every child has his summer, as every dog has his day. Fintan was very fortunate; we moved back to Ireland when he was only two. He was eight – the perfect age – when the summer of 1995 arrived. In his memory, it may eclipse all others. 'Ah, yes,' he will tell his grandchildren, 'we don't get summers like that any more!' From April, it was blue skies dawn to dusk, and never a spit of rain. School holidays stretched ahead, like a long bohreen staggering in the heat. He and the village kids left home at breakfast, with togs and bikes, and but for running buffets of lettuce and tomato sandwiches taken at one house or the other, stayed out until ten o'clock at night. At the end of August the sun still streamed through the bedroom curtains each morning, as if the golden days would never end.

They swam off the strand and in the coves. Swelled by the summer families, they were gangs of children, eight-year-olds, ten-year-olds, twelve-year-olds, each in its own tribe. They dived into the shoals of mackerel beneath the pier. They fished and surfed and made camps in the woods and caves. They smelled of salt, their hair went streaked blond and they were as brown as hazel nuts. The village, seashore and meadows were their domain, and they were lords over a secret world beyond adult eyes. They found rocks that glistened like diamonds; they found 'human bones' under the wreck of an old car. They found a fish's backbone that could be played like a concertina. Fintan found his tiny 'sea turtle's' shell in the sand. We adults watched, bemused; we thought of our own childhood and thanked God for children, their innocence and joy.

All societies love their children; even in the direst poverty they nurture them as best they can. It is sad to reflect that as a species we suck dry the bountiful planet we inherited and pass it on, depleted, to those we love. The richer the society, the more it ransacks the earth's surface, squanders its fuels, pollutes and rapes its seas, overheats its skies, burns holes in its protective ozone. Those who bring the bad news are derided as softie Green-Peacers with flowers, and probably lice, in their hair. This perception makes our children's future increasingly precarious. Credence is given to men-in-suits who scoff at scientists in anoraks out on the ice edge. 'Alarmists' they are called by the deluded, self-serving salesmen of oil and power who, while they love their children, lobby governments to exploit ever more fossil fuel. Men and women of conscience are dismissed with a contempt reserved for flat-earthers and loons, their message drowned out by the orchestrated corporate snigger. Meanwhile the ice is dripping, the time-bomb ticking. When I look at children, I hope, first, that they will survive in security; second, that nature's wondrous diversity will still be there to enjoy, as it was for me.

While fossil fuel use turns the benign sky into a lethal greenhouse, there are non-threatening technologies to hand. There are practical, realisable options to the subordination of benevolent nature to the short-term interests of multinational corporations promulgating a philosophy not of conservation but of greed. But we buy into them and if our first loyalty is really to our children, rather than ourselves, then it is our values that must be looked at. However affluent we may have become, we have the same stake as the poorest of the earth in those most valuable of all assets: the air we breathe, the water we drink, the seasons that ripen the crops, the earth that feeds us. No amount of share holdings will save us, or our so-deeply-loved children, if our money cows eat up the earth. The corporations and governments are us; and by controlling our greed, we may bring their extravagance under control. Surely, at the turn of the millennium, on this threatened planet, it is in the moral values of the empowered that the salvation of our future lies.

'It's dreadful stuff!' pronounced a mildly eccentric West Cork dowager, referring to ragwort. Even genteel ladies hold a grudge against it. Perhaps it goes back to the age of horses. Like my genteel habit of always walking on the roadway side of a female companion — 'Gentlemen should be on the outside to protect ladies against runaway horses,' my mother used to tell me as a child.

Ragwort, the tall weed with bright yellow flowers that swathes our verges in August, is universally despised. Most grazing animals avoid the live plant but, where it invades fields and is inadvertently cut and dried with hay, its active ingredients quickly destroy the livers of animals unfortunate enough to eat it. Its seeds, in common with those of many of the daisy family, travel by 'parachute' and disseminate far and wide.

Oxford ragwort, a rare native of the mountains of South Europe, has an extraordinary story. It first 'escaped' from the Botanic Gardens at Oxford and was noted on the walls of the town in 1794. In the railways boom, with its parachutes conveniently swept along in the slipstream of the locomotives, it took wing and soon travelled and colonised all over Britain. Bombing during the Second World War gave it a new lease of life by creating great swathes of the waste ground upon which it thrives. Its first landfall in Ireland was around Cork city in the early nineteenth century. It is still spreading its range, even appearing as a garden weed.

While common ragwort begins flowering about July 25th, Oxford ragwort's phenomenal success can be attributed to its amazingly long flowering season, April to December, during which one plant may produce 10,000 seeds. Only one control seems effective: the caterpillars of the aforementioned cinnabar moth that strip it, figuratively, to the bone. However, while so numerous in places that they eat every morsel

and wander about looking for more food, they are entirely absent elsewhere. Perhaps be-gloved school children might be employed to harvest
the surplus and carry them about in match boxes for distribution
where required. The warning patches on the moth's wings are the deep
red of mercuric sulphide, otherwise called vermilion or cinnabar. The
striking colours of both moth and caterpillar warn predators that they
are inedible. Ragwort is rich in alkaloid poisons which, stored in the
caterpillars' bodies, are passed on through the chrysalids and imagos
to the moths. The cinnabar is amongst the most poisonous moths in
these islands, inedible for amphibians, reptiles, birds and mammals.

The nights of this tropical August are filled with winged creatures
of all varieties that fly in from the jungle-like gardens of our house,
doomed to perish by seeking the bright lights, a somewhat tired para-
ble for ourselves. There are beautifully patterned moths and dull,
camouflaged moths, moths of infinite finesse, style and aerodynamics,
creatures that live in a glimmering we know not, amazing evolutions
from eggs to chrysalids to a splendour-in-the-night of which we catch
only glimpses, and know even less. To match them, in the day, all the
wild flowers of August bloom in gay profusion. Orange montbretia –
another import, a garden escapee – flares along the verges, with
creamy, nodding meadowsweet, spears of purple loosestrife, swathes
of scarlet fuchsia, hands of sweet-smelling honeysuckle. The paint-
box of nature is a kaleidoscope. This is no ragwort world.

When I think of meadowsweet, I remember Adlestrop, the tiny
village in Oxfordshire where a famous poem was written by a man
whose steam train stopped there briefly, one June afternoon in 1902.
He said: 'What I saw/ Was Adlestrop – only the name/ And willows,
willow-herb, and grass/ And meadowsweet, and haycocks dry …'
Meadowsweet and willow-herb in June, and haycocks dry? Was it
poetic licence or was the weather different then? Now, it is always
August before these flowers bloom. But the poet, Edward Thomas,
surely deserved the licence, portraying as he did the warm, summer
fields stretching to the horizon, which I and my companion saw a
century later. He continues: 'And for that minute a blackbird sang/

Close by, and round him, mistier,/ Farther and farther, all the birds/ Of Oxfordshire and Gloucestershire.'

But while I cavil about the blooming dates of wildflowers – a reflection, surely, of my West Cork ease – the new, widely publicised sex stimulant manufactured at the Pfizer plant on Cork Harbour may be great news for endangered wildlife. Asian ancients whose amorous aspirations caused rhino to be slaughtered for their horns, and tigers for their testicles, are now queuing up at chemists' shops.

Jellyfish, although possibly equally electrifying, are not an aphrodisiac. They can be eaten, so a Japanese friend tells me, after pickling, and are chewy, like squid. In Japan I tasted many exotics, and in Hong Kong I ate everything that moved which wasn't a bicycle, but I have yet to try jellyfish. I don't think I will. Were we a jellyfish-dining people, we would now be able to harvest a half-year's supply on some beaches in West Cork. It is a temporary and, happily, harmless 'plague', happening some years but not others, and soon gone. Some folk say jellyfish augur an Indian summer. The theory is that they drift in when the water is warm. The Japanese say August 18th is the beginning of the jellyfish season, and they are wary of sea swimming after that date.

Jellyfish in Irish waters are either 'pumpers' that propel themselves, or 'drifters' that leave progress to the vagaries of the currents and winds. The moon jellyfish, now on south-west shores, is bluish white and named for the four mauve 'half moons' on top of the transparent 'bell'. Fine stinging tentacles and four frilly mouth tentacles hang beneath. Tiny fish are immobilised and slowly ingested. The sting is too weak to be painful, even to children. Some fish fry – horse mackerel, haddock and others – have immunity and live amongst the tentacles, where they are safe from predators. The compass jelly, the same size, also pumps itself along in swarms and is a familiar casualty on beaches. Yellowish, it has dark brown lines radiating from the centre of the bell like a compass. It does not sting humans and, apart from feeding on small fish, leads a blameless life. Another pumper is the dangerous lion's mane jellyfish, so called because it is golden and hangs hundreds of thin stingers beneath it, like the hairs of a lion's ruff. If one finds a floating marmalade blob of, say, three feet across in the water near one, it is best to retire to the beach.

Amongst the jellyfish 'drifters' are the salee rovers, also known as by-the-wind-sailors. These are sometimes washed up in legions after south-west gales. What is found on the sand afterwards is both intriguing and pretty, hundreds of three-inch see-thru' plastic discs, patterned with concentric rings, each as regular as if it was stamped out by a machine. Salee rovers have a soft body suspended beneath the 'plastic' disc upon which is mounted a blue, triangular sail, an inflated bladder, thin as cling film. For the sail, they are named after the Algerian corsairs that roamed European coasts in the seventeenth century, plundering ships and taking slaves, as at Baltimore, Co. Cork, in 1631. Usually only the disc is left after they are tumbled in surf and scoured by sand. They are harmless to humans, the colony of which they are composed finding nutrients in plankton.

The infamous Portuguese man-of-war, like the rovers, move at the vagaries of the wind and are not true jellyfish, which are self-propelled. The English named them after seventeenth-century enemy gunships, possibly because they were unfriendly and carried a sail. The man-of-war is a colony of creatures, living in symbiosis, one killing the prey, one digesting it, one providing the gas-filled bladder with its shiny sail, like a cockscomb, on top. With it, the colony sails the wide oceans. The man-of-war was the most feared peril-of-the-deep for Greek sponge divers. The tentacles, almost invisible and up to twenty feet long, can cause severe injury, even paralysis. Dead or alive, whole or in parts, the man-of-war can still sting dangerously. Some years ago, a friend, wearing a diving mask, searched a rock pool on the Sheep's Head for a lost knife. Suddenly he was struck as if by a cattle prod. A yard-long piece of man-of-war tentacle was responsible. The scar on his forehead took weeks to heal.

The Sheep's Head, or Muntervary, is one of the loveliest and least known of the five peninsulas that reach out from the south-west coast as if fingering the sea. On the north side is vast Bantry Bay, the second largest deep water harbour in these islands and, on the south, still and sheltered, Dunmanus Bay. Our friend and his partner had moved there from Kilbrittain with their children, deserting a Queen Anne villa and formal gardens for a cottage in a quiet cove near Ahakista with the sea washing in on the rocks below. One summer evening after a day at Ahakista we hied ourselves to Castletownshend there to hear Anúna, a group that plays the haunting music of the ancient Celts. The venue was perfect for plain chant and sanctimony, St Barahane's Church of Ireland, looking out on Castlehaven Bay.

Castletownshend – called 'CT' by its inner circle – is a shrine of Anglo-Irishry. Cradle of a self-appointed West Cork 'gentry', it was for centuries sustained by a genteel rapacity at home and service in the Empire overseas, serial intermarriage and the English traditions of huntin', shootin', fishin', and 'is-there-honey-still-for-tea?'. A unique and pretty village, the Home Counties – rather than the Atlantic Ocean – might well begin at the end of its single street, plunging headlong to the sea. The CT 'families' were the inspiration of a seminal tome on their class, *Some Experiences of an Irish RM* (1899), which told amusing tales of English administrators struggling to bring civilisation to such recalcitrant rogues as Flurry Knox, a local squireeen adept at running rings around them.

St Barahane's is a lovely church, shining and polished, with an ambience of solid sanctity and patriotism. Patriotism to Britain, of course; wall plaques attest to the gallantry of Castletownshend officers (they are all officers) in the Empire's wars. The authors of the *Irish RM*, Edith Œnone Somerville and her cousin and collaborator, Violet Florence Martin (Martin Ross), are remembered in a plaque erected by American admirers. Their simple graves lie behind the church, two Irish yews over them, the sea below. All around rest the remains of the ancestors, headstones graven with the revered patronymics, names hyphenated and double hyphenated, narratives of English consanguinity etched in Irish stone.

From the seventeenth century, CT was a unique Anglo enclave, with the wild Irish all around. But the usurping 'gentry' were unlike the Anglos elsewhere. Only the founding family, the Townshends, were planters, occupying confiscated Irish land; the rest arrived later and largely by chance, Calvinists fleeing Scotland, Huguenots fleeing France. Having 'bought in', this self-appointed, self-regarding ascendancy prospered; they built glorious houses with large gardens and left a unique architectural and literary heritage behind. One of them, one-eyed Tom 'The Merchant' Somerville, ran a transatlantic passenger line to Newfoundland from Castlehaven Pier. Unfit for the service of crown or church, he stayed at home and made a fortune while his fellows fought in European wars or administered the far reaches of the Empire. Their women, often formidable, ran the large houses with the help of Irish gardeners and maids, meanwhile maintaining – to paraphrase Rupert Brooke – 'a corner of a foreign field that was forever England'.

To their credit, the CT 'families' developed a unique interface with the Irish. They contributed to Irish law and letters, to Irish Home Rule and to their own peaceful integration into the Republic. When, during the War of Independence, Anglo Irish 'great' houses were being torched in every county, the West Cork IRA – a foremost unit in the fight for freedom – burnt no Castletownshend house. It is a measure of West Cork people of both persuasions that here was achieved something unimaginable in Ulster: the reconciliation of an imported culture and its eventual integration into a new Ireland. Thus, in a remote corner of West Cork, the summer house-parties, croquet and dingy-sailing culture survived into the 1960s, with bumptious old colonels and captains, still walking the village, and the brilliant Edith, author, painter, horse-woman and horse-dealer, still playing the organ in St Barahane's, overlooking Castlehaven Bay.

Also overlooking the bay, and a panorama of sky and islands, stands an ancient Irish ringfort, Knockdrum. On a hillside opposite, three tall, pillar stones point dramatically at the sky; they were once five. Ironically, while Knockdrum Fort owes its rather lavish 'restoration' to a archaeological Somerville, it was a Madam Townshend who long-ago took away one or more of these prehistoric relics for garden ornaments. Robert Salter Townshend, her descendant, tells me he would happily restore it if he could find it, but it hasn't been seen for years.

September

Autumn again, mists and mellow fruitfulness,
glimmering mornings and red evenings, growing
shorter as the days pass. The 'season' is all but over,
the summer families going back to the city, the children
going back to school. The September story-telling
festival 'knocks' a last weekend out of it, with the best
yarn-spinners in Ireland in the village and sport in the
pubs. The irony is that, as the holiday crowd leaves,
the best weather of summer sometimes arrives. We have
it to ourselves, but wish the absent friends could
be here to see it.

~

Lapwing: they stand, shoulders hunched,
top-knots jigging in the breeze ...

utterflies are in profusion. Speckled woods chase one another in the sunlight beneath the garden trees. Small tortoiseshells bask and feed on the buddleia, red admirals gorge on fallen apples, the caterpillars of cabbage whites have made a banquet of our nasturtiums. The leaves are ragged and full of holes, but the flowers are still bright and a favourite venue of carder and bumble bees.

Brighter than the brightest flowers these mornings are the West Cork villages, where the natives are fearless with paint. In the morning sun, house fronts of gold, pink, purple and pastel green jump out at late tourists, more colourful than any Caribbean conurbation and garlanded with Tidy Town flower baskets brimful with exotic blooms. Amidst the blooms, flower bees and honey bees forage and fumble, drunk with summer's lees. Indoors, wasps are a nuisance, the queens seeking hibernation quarters, the workers dizzy and dangerous, falling into the folds of clothes, half dead on curtains, but still with a potent sting.

Robins sing competitively from high spots in the garden. The other day a foolish young robin, with fiery breast, took fright and flew straight into a window as Dara sped past on a bicycle. It died in his palm, neck broken, beyond help. End of robin. Speed kills.

It is a lovely autumn to be abroad and the sensible among us – of which I am not always one – walk in the mornings, the best part of the day. Grass then lies slicked and silver with the dew, and the spider webs glisten like gossamer. This morning the sea was as still as glass, in places flashing like mirrors, in places dark, although these too were in strong sunlight. The cobalt water reflected all upon or near it, the blue sky with wisps of white cloud, the bright boats, the green banks, the dark abbey, the bridge arches; also, the white swans and the seagulls sitting on the sea wall, warming up with the day.

The tide being full in, hundreds of curlew and godwit were still at roost on the cord-grass islands, heads under wings, sleeping late; the mudflats, their breakfast counters, were still under water, so they might as well. Lapwing rose and flew lazily over them, alighted and roosted or took off again. The winter flocks are building up; more birds arrive each day. In the soft brown carpet of roosting birds, the oystercatchers are vivid, with black and white plumage and bright red beaks. Black-tailed godwits came early this year, the males still with russet breasts, their breeding plumage. Dunlin arrived a few weeks later; they seemed to be early too. The egrets have returned; they have once again bred successfully on the Blackwater and a flock of forty-five were seen in east Cork after the young were fledged. Mullet, two-foot-long fish in nine inches of water, make slow ripples in the shallows, unhurried, unworried by our presence on the bank. Close-focus binoculars provide a wonderful view of their sinuous progress. One stays dry but is in the world of the fish.

In sheltered lanes the warm sun cooks the blackberries on the briars. Wild flowers are in decline but fuchsia is rampant. Lady's bed-straw grows on verges and banks – a tall, yellow flower, named for the

Virgin Mary who is said to have lain on a bed of it when she gave birth to Christ. Thus it earned golden flowers while less favoured bed-straws have to make do with white. In times past it was popular for stuffing mattresses and, I would have thought, was more aromatic than horsehair if not as long-lasting. It was also used to curdle milk. Now, it is found less widely than before – but it brightened up clearings in the dark-canopied woods where we walked last weekend.

Myrtle is in flower, the trees with lovely rust-red bark and tight white blossom, and tai trees – a.k.a. cabbage palms, cordylines and so on – are throwing up their strange white buds. Pigeons perch high on the beeches in the evening sun, round pink breasts shining metallically in the light, white collars very bright, chests heaving with effort as they coo resonantly, incessantly, like demented didgeridoos. Smoke begins to curl from chimneys, of evenings. We gather in early for winter, but can still walk abroad on these glorious days.

September is the mushrooming season; while the white field mushrooms and button cups of summer can still be found, now we seek the exotics of the woods. On mainland Europe, mushrooms known in the British and Irish Isles as 'toadstools' have household names. The *Boletus edulis*, for which we have only the Linnean term, is known to every French child as a *Cep* and to every German as *Steinpilz*. From Cherbourg to Siberia ceps are as well known as onions. Here, the mention of eating strange fungi is usually greeted with a 'Yuk!'

'Boletes' have a strong flavour and dry superbly; few people know that they are the mushroom used in most tinned and package mush-room soups. Quite different from the Irish idea of a mushroom, most of my neighbours describe them as toadstools; they ignore them or some – from ancient superstition – stomp on them or give them a kick. In 1984 I used to get a sterling pound a pound for boletes from London's top deli, Justin de Blanc, in Elizabeth Street, Knightsbridge. This might give boletus-kickers some food for thought.

The boletus tribe are fat in cap and stem. The brown, velvety cap of the *b. edulis*, the best kind, will be two inches thick when it is four inches round. The stem is bulbous at the base, more than an inch in diameter, and the boletus does not have gills underneath but 'sponge'. In edulis, the sponge is creamy white; in other boletes it may be lemon yellow, orange or red. In the stem, and above the sponge, is the firm, clean, fat mushroom-meat for which the variety is famed.

The only dangerous boletus is a red-sponged variety, *b. satanus*, but I haven't seen more than a dozen in my mushroom-picking life. It isn't necessarily deadly, if one is taken quickly to the stomach pumps. With the deadly *amanitas* – the *Pantherina*, *Destroying Angel* and *Death Cap* – once one has eaten even a small amount there isn't a great deal anyone can do. The victim feels bad, then good, then terminally bad. The liver rots, the brain deliquesces. It is a nasty business, fungus poisoning. All aspirant fungi foragers should check the edibility of their specimens in at least two, if not three, books.

Forest mushrooms often grow in symbiosis with trees. *B. edulis* grows in coniferous and mixed woodland, chanterelle grows under oaks, saffron milk caps under spruce. On my first fungus forays, I spent as much time looking up, to identify trees, as I did looking down, to find mushrooms. After many a cricked neck I realised the leaves at my feet would tell me the trees above. The forest floor is full of interest. I see ferns in West Cork woods standing as high as ferns in the Amazon jungle and blink my eyes and ask myself where I am.

Buddleia attracts butterflies like a patisserie attracts Viennese matrons and two years ago I set a buddleia bush in my garden, a small stick with a root given to me by the ageless Ms Peggy, whom one will see gardening her plot or energetically carrying buckets of water to it from the village pump. She told me to simply dig a hole, fill it with water, and half-bury the stick. Now, two summers later, twenty or thirty multi-coloured butterflies rise or sit three and four together on the purple flower-heads that are like slimmer versions of lilac flowers. The velvety patterns on tortoiseshells' wings always remind me of Persian carpets – perhaps they were the inspiration for some patterns, given that nature is often the inspiration for art. While no carpet could reflect the brilliant hues of butterfly wings fresh from the chrysalis, natural dyes and the weaver's art can achieve a brilliance that still leaps from old carpets long after hundreds of generations of butterflies have flowered, and faded, and turned to dust.

In September 2001 when the terrible events of the 11th unfolded on TV, I thought of our New York friends, living in Greenwich Street, only seven hundred yards from the scene, and of my eldest son, Niall, on a business trip in America, flying from city to city, with a meeting each day. A phone call to his wife assured me that he was safe. He had, indeed, been in New York on the 10th, and had often attended meetings at the World Trade Centre, but not this time. He had flown to Washington that night and was at his hotel, a mile away from the Pentagon, when it was hit. For four days, he wasn't able to fly home. When we heard he would be back on the Saturday, we flew from Cork to Heathrow to see him and other children and grandchildren. We walked in the Hertfordshire woods, holding the hands of the small ones; how different it could have been!

The Chiltern woods were, as always, verdant and lovely, shot through with patches of light. We were doing what we had done so many weekends when these, now adults, were children. We found much to wonder at and enjoy, unusual toadstools, oak apples and a small toad. Marie and I had brought mushrooms from Ireland, agarics, like huge field mushrooms, but difficult to identify. As usual, I had pored over books. Deciding they were edible and probably good, I tried them myself first – at this stage, I am the most expendable. When I showed no ill effects, we all ate them. They were excellent – *Agaricus augustus*, commonly know as 'The Prince' and given their Linnean name because they were the favourite fungi of Caesar Augustus, who apparently liked his mushrooms too.

Back at home, red clumps of fuchsia brighten the field hedges and turn the roadsides into scarlet corridors under the cloudless sky. Blackberries, fat and full, catch the sunlight and shine as if lacquered. This year autumn is cruelly beautiful, and it goes on and on. For myself, you can keep your blackberry pies, tarts, and fools; just give me a warm, fat blackberry off a sunny hedge, bubbles of warm juice, with the bouquet of brambles. A friend of mine used to quaff berries without even looking to see if they contained foreign bodies. If there are foreign bodies, he reasoned, they are what they eat, which is simply more blackberry. 'Ah, for protein on the hoof!' he used to say. 'Meat with the veg!' As I gorged, throwing the occasional berry to the dog (she will eat only the ripe ones), I recalled our son Dara, when we first arrived back in Ireland, coming home with a half pound of squidgy blackberries in his lunch box; he'd picked them on the hedge opposite the little Gurranahassig Primary School. No doubt half the country children in Ireland were supplementing their lunches with a diet of blackberries and small insects. I once ate a flash-fried daddy-long-legs that flew into a pan when I was cooking a camping breakfast, and it did me no harm.

Rutting dogs again litter the lawn as our superior bitch, Sally, again comes into season. Dirty Harry, a prime mover amongst the unusual mélange, has been doctored and happily is no longer swinging with us. I don't know how he spends his emasculated days, but he hasn't shown his face around here since he lost his testosterone. However, the rest of the gang has shown up, widdling on the gate posts, scratching up the lawns, snarling at one another at unearthly hours, scuffling under the feet of our visitors. We may have to take out special insurance against falling over dogs.

Meanwhile in the hope of repelling the bad, the ugly and the outright appalling, we allowed our bitch a live-in lover, a pure-bred Springer like herself. I fear, however, that he has been cuckolded. In an unguarded moment, she disappeared into the wilderness we call a garden and was shortly seen *in flagrante delicto* with a rangy, black and white animal which, I believe, has the legs on one side shorter than on the other. It is an entirely dysfunctional dog in that it spends its days crouching behind gate posts and dashing out to nip the back wheels of passing traffic: this is its *raison d'être*, its vocation, its very life and soul. Little else did it do, I fondly thought, but now discover that it has talents as a bushwhacker, and pheromones that make it irresistible to cultured bitches. While the rest of the crew were parading like a troupe of canine Chipperfields, it was having its way in the bushes.

Our friend Hanley, however, opined that it might be firing blanks and advised that we board Sally at his kennels until her season was over. Since her departure, her retinue of shaggy, waggy and short-legged suitors look distinctly down at the mouth. They continue to arrive days after she's gone. Despite what their noses tell them, they have fetched up at the pub with no beer. At least Peter, the cat, is no longer here to suffer the influx of deep-breathing, odoriferous pooches. She always had a sniffy disdain for dogs.

The 'holiday weather' of 2002 was dismal and in late August I wrote, 'With only ten days left before they return to school, Fin and his pals deserve some good weather. In the summer-camp of our house, boys come and go, sleeping in heaps in rooms, often having arrived back from their forest redoubt at daybreak, wet to the skin and smelling of wood smoke. With them, they drag drenched tents, sleeping bags and blackened pots and pans, their breakfast attempts abandoned after yet another dawn downpour following upon a night of sleeping in rain-filled pools. One cannot but admire their good spirits in the face of meteorological adversity. "Hope springs eternal ...", as the poet said.' In 2002 September happily brought summer with it and, joy of joys, they were able to enjoy dry camping on the two last weekends before school.

One of their camping venues was Sherkin, an island one hour west of Courtmacsherry, in Roaringwater Bay, and we went to collect them in the car. The 'major' route west, the R592, is a winding two-lane road, more 'mean' than 'main'; they sound the same in the West Cork vernacular. It has the usual bad surfaces, blind bends, and stunning off-road scenery. Twenty miles from Courtmacsherry, the land changes dramatically. The green sward of agri-biz abruptly stops at the Roaringwater River. Beyond it, the ground is riven by bedrock, and there is more gorse than grazing. The fields are small patchworks, rock-rent and bockety, joined by seams of hedge. Here, the land is 'free', even if owned, undomesticated, even if farmed. It's a skipping land, up and down and lively as a fiddle air, jigging and reeling as it goes. Much is not worth 'developing', for you can't grow grass on rocks or spuds in bogs. It offers little sustenance, and that little is hard won.

Of food for the spirit, there is a feast, and if we could live on scenery we'd be satiated. Here, like the sea or sky, the land is nature's domain and humans pass but leave no mark. Beyond the roadside fields, the bog stretches like a brown mantle to the hills or sea. In winter it is drab as sackcloth; in summer it is softened with heather and bright with gorse. Walking there, the views are always of uplands and islands. On the outward leg, low, brown hills fill the horizon and beyond them the mountains of Caha and Kerry rise. On the return, the wide Atlantic is below us, with the small and big islands of Roaringwater Bay.

Little is changed in this part of Ireland. Here and there are farmhouses, holiday homes and shoe-box bungalows but, off the laneways, few feet have ever walked the rough land. No longer is most of the view changed in some way by man; now, most is unchanged, altered only by time and nature. Four thousand years ago, paths crossed these bogs to reach the copper (some say, the gold) workings on Mount Gabriel, the first copper mines in Western Europe. These paths have long since been subsumed beneath the brown blanket, but without doubt the back roads often follow these routes.

Ballydehob and Schull are character-full and pretty settlements. Ballydehob, the smaller, has its strong West Cork 'feel', its imposing twelve-arched bridge – last and finest remnant of the West Cork Tramway – its pubs and eating places. Schull has its pier which serves the islands, its holiday cottages, restaurants, bookshops and boutiques. Ballydehob has for some years been home to a small colony of native and expatriate artists and literati, while Schull is a holiday venue for Dublin glitterati, yachtsmen who launch and ladies who lunch. For all this, the native charm of both villages is undimmed, the *arrivistes* aping the natives, rather than the other way around.

Sherkin is only fifteen minutes by ferry from the mainland at Baltimore but the sense of place is quite different. A steep road leads up from the small pier, past a ruined abbey. Visitors set off, carrying their luggage; no cars come to meet them. The near absence of cars doesn't alone explain the change of atmosphere and pace; new sounds surround one immediately – not silence but bird song and bee-hum, the only sounds in the island air. That afternoon swallows twitted on the wires and we met friendliness everywhere. When my bike tyre went soft, the woman at the shop produced a half dozen different pump connections to get me mobile. We saw butterflies we don't commonly see.

At the O'Driscoll castle, now a few ivy-covered walls and a stumpy tower looking across at Baltimore, we found yellow-flowering plants of black mustard and a green, celery-looking species, which was wild parsley. These ancient culinary plants are no accident at such sites. We imagined the last O'Driscoll chief, old Fineen, the rover and pirate, picking himself a bit of black mustard to go with his haddock and sack back in 1537. Sir Fineen, as he later briefly became, had had a good year. The O'Driscolls could still levy a fee for any boat, from anywhere, fishing between the Stags and the Fastnet Rock, and he had lately seized a Portuguese ship, bound for English merchants in Waterford, with a hundred tuns of wine.

From early times O'Driscolls ruled West Cork between Kinsale and the Kenmare River. The castles of the Baltimore O'Driscolls included *Dún na Séad*, the Fort of the Jewels; *Dún na Long*, on Sherkin, the Fort of the Ships; *Dún an Óir*, on Cape Clear, the Fort of Gold; *Dún na nGall*, on Ringarogy, and others. Much O'Driscoll land was confiscated when they supported the Geraldine Rebellion of 1534, but some was later restored and Fineen the Rover, for swearing allegiance to England and impounding passing Spanish ships, became Sir Fineen, High Sheriff of Cork, and was granted all the O'Driscoll lands as his personal property. His son left for Spain in disgust. However, when in 1601 the Spaniards came in force to aid the Irish, Fineen sided with the Gaelic cause. After the tragic defeat at Kinsale, the Flight of the Wild Geese and the end of the old Irish order, his lands were again confiscated. He was left with *Dún na Séad* and Baltimore village, which he leased to English settlers.

On June 20th 1631, Algerian corsairs, the human salee rovers, arrived out of the night and the sea and sacked Baltimore, carrying off one hundred and ten of these unfortunate settlers to the slave markets and seraglios of the Barbary Coast. The remainder, in terror, moved inland and founded Skibbereen town. Eighteen years later, an emissary from the English parliament, sent to North Africa to ransom captives, could find only two of the Baltimore slaves.

There was something not quite right about the bundle of black fur we saw on the road as we drove home. I turned the car and went back to take a look. It was a young mink, a fresh road kill, sinuous and beautiful in death as it must have been in life. I approached it cautiously; a spark of life left, a quick turn of the head and I might lose a typing finger, and I have only two. But it was defunct all right; no more killing left in that mink. I picked it up; the coat was black as night, soft and thick. The little body – eighteen inches long from snout to tail, was plump and well fed, and perfect; it had been struck on the head. To throw it in the hedge would seem a sin, so I took it home to show to Fintan and our Japanese visitors, a fierce denizen of the Irish ditches, close up. I considered skinning it to make Marie a mink collar, but dismissed the idea. When I was a child, I tried to make my mother mouse-skin gloves with disastrous results. So I took it away, not knowing quite what to do with it, knowing only that it was too perfect to leave to the worms. In the event I presented it to a friend who has made a collection of Ireland's fauna, stuffed and mounted. I will see it again, on his mantelpiece, no doubt.

September 1995 was dry for weeks and fish-watchers said that when there was rain, so many salmon and sea trout would run up the rivers that angling would be like slaughter. The rivers would be packed with fish that had been queuing in the bays for weeks. No depth on the weirs had stopped their progress from the deep Atlantic to the river pools of home. With rain, there would be an almighty rush. Some authorities might close the rivers, altogether, to give the fish a chance but the conscientious anglers, in any case, would restrict themselves to one salmon a day.

Apropos such enlightened behaviour, I heard an ironic tale of an angler who arrived at the pub to tell his friends that he had hooked and landed the mother-or-father of all salmon but, because he had earlier caught and killed a ten-pound fish, he had had no alternative but to throw the monster back. It had weighed, he estimated, seventy-five pounds. A sixty-four-pound salmon was the largest ever landed in these islands – caught by a woman, in 1922 – so, as he put it back in the water, our angler must have been ready to eat his hat, flies and all. But fishermen are fishermen: they are prone to exaggeration. So his friends – no mistrust intended – decided to check out the size of the alleged monster for themselves. Donning masks and snorkels, they entered the pool. Yes, the salmon was there and it was indeed bigger than any fish ever landed. But – here comes the rub – there wasn't just one monster in the pool, but two.

I am told that women have a certain feel for salmon, which men do not. Witness the Big Fish record books. Of the ten largest salmon ever caught, women caught eight. Macho male anglers will tell you that salmon are attracted to women, that it is not only skill but pheromones. If a woman puts her hand into a weir up which salmon are running, the fish will continue to run. If a male hand dips in the water, they stop. As the tortured Hamlet put it: 'There are more things in heaven and earth, Horatio/ Than are dreamt of in your philosophy.'

In September each year, as the summer season closes, Courtmacsherry puts on a story-telling weekend. *Seanachaís*, raconteurs and yarners arrive from all over Ireland, performing for their keep and modest expenses. It is well known that if one gives an Irish man or woman any event of consequence or inconsequence – a car breaking down, a trip to town, or a mouse under the bed – they will make drama and poetry out of it. In the love song *The Rose of Tralee* the tenor tells us, 'The cool shades of evening their mantle were spreading/ And Mary, all smiling, stood listening to me …' Mary may, indeed, have been smiling – and quite why, we cannot know – but it is also possible she was simply politely waiting for him to finish so that she could begin. For three nights, in the Courtmac pubs, the story-tellers weave spells in which one could hear a feather drop. Yet, so relaxed is the ambience that one might think they are at their own firesides, reminiscing with a group of domestic friends.

In Ireland the rider that '… he (or she) tells a great story!' is extenuation for almost any sin. The centuries of oppression, which saw rebels, musicians, pamphleteers and priests on the run, strengthened rather than weakened the oral tradition. Musicians could not afford or carry pianos; they composed for fiddle, tin whistle, harp or *uilleann* pipes instead. For the word-musicians, the gifts of eloquence and memory required not even pockets to carry them, so these gifts survived, preserving the history, language and pride of a people sorely suppressed. *Seanachaí*s [pron. 'shan-a-keys'] were traditional story-tellers, male or female, local unpaid practitioners of the ancient art. They would come to a house at night, settle in the chimney corner, and tell their tales. 'Fadó, fadó …', 'Long ago, long ago …', the tale began.

That they were exceptional narrators cannot be doubted. From the fifty souls that still lived on the Blasket Islands in the 1920s, Robin Flower elicited three classic books, written in Irish, translated into English; Ó Crohan's *The Islandman*, young Maurice O'Sullivan's *Twenty Years a-Growing* and Peig Sayers' *An Old Woman Remembers*. Ó Crohan's was the most remarkable. His ironic description of the Blaskets as 'the last parish before America' has become clichéd, but his style and his personal character, the poignancy with which he describes the death of his sons and his beloved wife, will remain forever in the reader's mind, a testament to the faith, stoicism and sagacity of the simple Irish; one would want to quote the whole book. Courtmacsherry had native Irish speakers within living memory; indeed a local fisherman, now in his forties, Doney O'Brien, still uses the Irish names of the coves and creatures; I'm sure he knows the English names but he prefers the Irish.

As the weeks pass, blithe days slip gently into mellow evenings. There is a hint of autumn, a sharpness and a stillness in the air. In West Cork, now, the noontime sea is blue and shimmering and the fields green and gold. As we walk cliff paths, the slopes above us are mats of yellow and purple, with dwarf gorse and heather brilliant in the sun. Whales are passing on migration, and their 'blows' can be seen from Narry's Cross and all along the Seven Heads.

Whooley the Whale Watcher assures me that no whale sight he has ever witnessed equalled that enjoyed by himself and marine biologist Simon Berrow, off the Seven Heads last Sunday morning. On a perfect day, two humpback whales rolled and blew around Colin Barnes' whale-watch boat, one of them so close beneath it in the crystal clear water that Colin said, '… you could count the barnacles on its head, and see its white flukes extended out for twelve or fifteen feet on either side of the boat as it hung suspended below us.' Again and again, the pair breached only yards from the large catamaran and showed their tails in classical whale fashion. I have seen the slides and, yes, one can see every dimple in their skin and various distinctive marks which confirm that one of the pair was also here last year.

To add to the thrills, a big leatherback turtle from the Gulf of Mexico passed by the boat, drifting lazily until it saw it, and dived. It is heartening to hear of a healthy leatherback encountered at sea; every year a few are washed up, usually dead, on local shores. 'Big-winged New Englanders', humpback whales were called back in the days when they were slaughtered, named no doubt for their flukes which indeed seem like giant wings. How exhilarating it must have been to see them between the Galley Head and the Old Head of Kinsale. And, as always in winter, the sea was alive with dolphins.

On September nights, whimbrels, elegant cousins of the curlew, fly over Ireland on their 3,000-mile trek from the Arctic to Africa. Listen for seven repeated twittering notes, their distinctive call. On the coast, albatrosses are seen, three black-browed, off Mizen Head, with a passage of sooty shearwaters, also from the South Atlantic, and many cory shearwaters from the Med.; our south coast is a regular highway of oceanic birds, blown inshore because of fortuitous winds. Last week an amazing passage of more than six hundred great shearwaters per hour was spotted at Clear Island as dedicated birders, perched on cliff tops, peered through telescopes in biting winds and driving rain. The fearless feather-lovers counted some five thousand of these magnificent, long-distance birds which skim the waves on a 7,000-mile circuit of the Atlantic from nesting homes on remote

Tristan da Cunha and the Falklands Group. Like the birds, the 'sea watchers' are a tough breed. Years ago one of my sons, an *aficionado*, lived for two days and nights in a cliff-top toilet in Caithness subsisting on four cans of cold baked beans – but that weekend he saw his first albatross.

On the rough ride home from Clear Island, the doughty watchers stood on deck, scanning the broken sea. Far from the misty headlands, in that element of chaos, gannets dived on mackerel shoals amongst the bucking breakers, and small kittiwakes beat over the white caps, besting the wind. Storm or no storm, it was business as usual for the birds, no stoppages for bad weather; three cormorants on a spray-flung rock looked like the lost lighthouse men of Flannan Isle. Closer to shore terns, with tails flared, rode the wind and plummeted into the sprat-fat sea. On the deck, not only the birders but various island-visiting foreigners stood, rain-slicked and dripping, including a baby in a perspex-house push chair, rocked by a mother facing into the wind. What a holiday, what a world away from downtown Düsseldorf or Île de France! In the two minutes it took to disembark at Baltimore, so fierce was the rain that they were as wet as if they'd swum from the island. But they ran in gales of laughter to the pub.

Our avian summer visitors now are leaving. The swallows nesting above the heads of customers in Fahey's Bar, Clonakilty, have left the fledglings to take care of themselves. It was a good roost, where the parents could hunt until all hours, the yard light attracting all sorts of late-night lepidoptera. They would whizz out, centimetres above the customers' heads, and whizz back in, five minutes later, with a beak full of flies. After hatching, the fledglings sat at first in the nest, pink gapes opening wide as soon as they heard the swish of wings. Foreign visitors could hardly believe that swallows would so trust people as to nest a mere metre above their heads. On summer nights, when it is light until eleven, the clientele could closely observe the process of nest-building, hatching and rearing as they meditatively sipped their pints. At last the fledglings would emerge and sit in a row on an electric light flex, still as statues, with their impeccable and motionless parents, like a clever taxidermic display. The illusion was quite potent until, with a graceful sweep, one or the other would take wing.

Year after year, swallows have nested in Fahey's pub. Male swallows are 'site faithful' and return from South Africa to the Irish barn or building where they were born. This is a good survival strategy; if the nest site was safe for you, it is likely to be safe for your offspring. However, 200,000 migrating swallows are regularly popped into cooking pots in Nigeria where they stop to rest in reed beds, and this may have been the fate of the Fahey's swallows, which now come no more. Their roost under the roof beams was a fine one; indeed many humans also like to spend the day perched in Fahey's bar. The rafter corner has a distinctive character, with the soft buzz of talk and the sweet smells of porter and old malt rising from below. A fibre-glass beam in an 'Inne' in the English Home Counties, with Hurrah Henrys hooting amongst the horse brasses, wouldn't be the same at all.

On being told that swallows were assembling in the village, as they do before they set off out to sea, I went for a late stroll but saw only our parish priest, wearing a baseball cap as he sat on a ride-on mower cutting his own lawns. He waved happily to me; there is always an edifying sight to be seen in the great outdoors. Next morning there were twenty birds on the wires, all juveniles, without a long tail or a red *smig* between them. One adult did then alight – was he/she the navigator, staying behind to lead the young south, to the sun? Most adults have now departed. The young, left with the lepidoptera to themselves, have had a better chance to fatten but they too must go now. They shuffle and crowd on the wires, making short sallies. 'There is no staying/ and no second chance/ the flock moves on/ the winds push/ the moon beckons/ the young dash out/ splitting the sky.'

Two thousand or more hirundines were gathered over the reed beds behind Long Strand, one evening last week, like swarms of flies. Behind them Castlefreke, the vast, windowless, one-time home of the Freke family, stood gaunt and ghostly in the dying light. In Kerry, a week ago, we saw a swallow still feeding its young in a nest high on the wall inside the Gallarus Oratory. The oratory was built more than thirteen centuries ago, the only material unmortared stones. It not only still stands but, despite the legendary Kerry rain, is dust dry inside. Perhaps swallows twittered above the old saint's head as he prayed, and dashed back and forth through the open door or shafted window. The proportions of the simple building are awesomely beautiful. And it is as enduring as the stones of which it is made.

Nearer home, on the Barryroe road, above the village, a six-yard swathe of ivy catching the autumn sun seemed of little consequence as I walked towards it, but for bees, bugs and butterflies, it was a Bacchanalia. Winged creatures of every buzz and hum swarmed over it, thousands of them. When a car passed, they rose in a melodious cloud, then alighted again and browsed on. Hours could be whiled away observing them. In the sunlight, honey bees with tiny rugby balls of pollen under their back legs buzzed and laboured. Drone flies droned. Bumbles bumbled and one large bee, asleep in a curled yellow leaf, scratched itself like a dog in front of a fire. The green ivy flowers, barely recognisable as flowers – the petals are tight as buds – are an immensely rich source of nectar. Miner bees, carder bees, cuckoo bees, don't-ask-me-which-bees clambered over every bloom. Hover flies, soldier flies, sawflies fumbled in every flower. A painted lady butterfly landed on a leaf close by me and opened her wings as if to be admired. Speckled wood butterflies, red admirals and small tortoiseshells came and went. Jaw-dropped and fascinated, I stood, staring into the hedge; my neighbours, passing in cars, must have thought my mind had gone astray altogether. Iridescent greenbottles, brilliant bluebottles, gall wasps and wall wasps – for examples of Nature's construction, industry and artistry that stretch of humble ivy was an education.

When one gets to know an area well – a privilege I have rarely enjoyed, having been, all my life, nomadic – one gets to know the local wild life as well as the local people. One misses a song thrush no longer singing, or martins that nested under certain eaves. Progress is necessary, but I am saddened to realise that a pair of local stonechats will be gone any day now when their strip of habitat, already half taken away, is finally removed. I'm sure they have occupied that rough hedge for generations; they have chirped and bobbed each time I've passed, for years. Now the hedge unfortunately blocks the view for some new houses. It is indeed a pity to level it; but I suppose everyone, except the stonechats, deserves their view of the bay.

As the month ends there is not a puff of air, not so much as would stir a single hair of one's head. The sun was so hot yesterday that, as I stood speaking to a man through his car window, I found myself automatically placing my hand on the top of my head to protect my patch of naked dome from sunburn. In the Canary Islands, it is common to see balding men, caught in the open with an urgent need to communicate, conduct conversation each wearing a hand on his head. Last night, a light heat mist hung over the bay and it was as warm and romantic as any tropic shore. Walking with my udder-flapping dog, Sally, I looked across at Courtmac, where the lights of the pier made candles on the oil-still water. The dog thought it strange to keep stopping. I believe it was the loveliest night of the year.

This morning that follows is lovely too, the air smoky and pellucid. The bay is flat calm. Near the shore, cut-out cormorants sit on a rock, still as statues. There is an almost blinding luminescence further out, where sea meets sky. In the higher reaches of the bay, below Timoleague Abbey, the water is infinitely still, although broken now and then by the snout-wave of a mullet as it pushes against the shining surface or rises in a lazy flop for who knows what, since mullet do not take flies. Sometimes there is an otter, a brown head moving across the channel. One has to be very early or very lucky to see the otters. But they are there, as they have been for generations, slipping into the tidal waters below the bridge, or higher up in the fresh water of the Argideen.

The red boats in Courtmac Harbour catch the sunlight. Nothing stirs. It is marvellous to be here to see it. As Wordsworth once said of London, on some long-ago, miraculous morning, 'Ne'er saw I, never felt, a calm so deep!'

October

'And summer's lease hath all too short a date …'

October is the lees of summer; nature moves towards winter, but slowly, like the holiday sailor hauling his craft ashore. These are the last weekends. Now, it's farewell to the land of summer, and off to the city until the boat is put back in the water on next Saint Patrick's Day. There is a snap in the air at morning and evening, but flowers continue to bloom, bees to hum, butterflies to fly and, on warm days, a drowsy lassitude overcomes the land. There are hazel nuts and sweet chestnuts, mushrooms and windfall apples, sloes and haws. The sea is at its warmest now, and hardy children still swim.

~

Sloe poitín: a benison of the hedgerow gods.

orse was flaming high in the Cork and Kerry mountains when we crossed into the Kingdom one glorious afternoon last week. Fallen fuchsia turned the roadsides purple. Our American friends of many years, mother and daughter from chic Manhattan, ooo-ed and aww-ed. New England, Vermont and upstate New York are stunning in autumn, with areas of forest half the size of an Irish county burnished red. But where they have woods, we have mountains, with purple heather, yellow furze and red, dead ferns. Ours is a starker kind of beauty, and a novelty to them. But here or there, almost any landscape looks lovely in the slanting autumn sun.

Out walking with the lady, we came upon an ivy bush as big as a cow byre, covered in butterflies and bees. A resounding buzz filled the near air. 'Bees!' cried my lady. 'I don't like bees!' I hustled her away. In fairness, she and her daughter, on their first visit to Ireland, were remarkably brave in the untamed reaches of the Caha Mountains, hitching up skirts to negotiate barbed wire fences, crossing fields full of feisty young beeves, later standing on wild cliffs with gales howling past them and, later still, sitting in singing pubs with Gaels howling all around them. Unfazed by anything the landscape, weather or society could throw at them, they declared themselves enchanted by it all.

The evenings have been beautiful, with the sun golden on the sea and the bay full of mackerel. We swam, up to a week ago. Timoleague never looked more colourful than in the autumn sunlight, the multi-coloured house fronts that line the single street almost blinding the eyes with fresh paint. Over the bay, the morning skies are deep blue from horizon to horizon, the night skies bright with silver stars, unmisted, clear and cold.

Sunsets too were resplendent last week. Some Japanese students went Atlantic sunset-watching and were rewarded with magnificent displays. At this time of the year there will be much autumn-watching in Tokyo. Small parties, like pilgrims, will be visiting the slopes of Mount Fuji to admire the fires and quenchings of the autumn leaves.

The moon is full and rides a clear sky. We can see Jupiter and its three moons through the telescope. Our Japanese students gasp in wonder at the close-up landscapes of the moon. They do not see any rabbits. Japanese believe the moon is the home of rabbits, and so, being holy aliens, one would not eat them. To see rabbits on the moon seems silly; but then they are amazed when we point out the Man in the Moon, which we always see. Upon identifying the eyes, the overhanging eyebrows, the bridge of the nose, the laconic mouth, they are awestruck. Every time they see the moon in future, they will see the Man.

October 7th, it is still shirt-sleeve weather during the day, and bees still fumbling the flowers. It must have been such weather when Keats wrote that Autumn conspires 'to set budding more,/ And still more, later flowers for the bees,/ Until they think warm days will never cease. ...' Autumn 1819 must have been like autumn now.

It has been a week of phenomena, seeming to indicate that, despite sometime evidence to the contrary, West Cork is entering the tropics. As a rural sage once told me, 'All we need is to tow it a bit-een south'. He was right. So often a magic ring of high pressure is tantalisingly just to the south of here, over the Bay of Biscay, where the gannets fly to every day. But last week a tropic sunfish was caught in the shallows of Courtmacsherry Bay by a young man trolling for mackerel. Presumably it was looking for the sun but was hungry at the same time. A very amateur angler, he was surprised to hook anything, let alone such a strange item. He had spotted its tall fin, circling in three feet of water, and could hardly believe it when he found himself battling to land the extraordinary thing. It is indeed extraordinary, a denizen of much warmer seas where it sometimes grows to eleven feet and weighs a ton.

Mr Hunt's specimen was a modest eighteen inches; I saw it yesterday, fresh from the freezer. It resembled a disc, having no tail whatsoever, but a rounded stern. Two long, narrow fins, three-quarters way back from the head, point one towards the sand, the other towards the sky. I asked the young man's mother how she intended to cook it. She said she didn't think she'd chance it, at all. I intimated that I would be only too happy to eat it, should she be giving it to the cat.

Most fish can, I think, be eaten. They may, in some cases, be too bony or coarse to make them worthwhile but I cannot imagine many of them poisoning one, except for the famous *fugu*, a poisonous fish of Japan which costs a fortune to sample. Cooks preparing it for the table need a government licence, certifying competence to identify and cut away the poisonous parts. Either the rest is delicious or the Japanese like living dangerously. 'Licensed to kill', one might plead, if things go wrong. I believe they seldom do.

It is a decent man who will tell you about his mushroom field, but I was let into a secret last Sunday morning and taken to a field where, effortlessly, I picked two kilos of perfect specimens in half an hour. There is always an ethical question with newly sprouted mushrooms. The caps are no larger than one's thumbnail: it is a sin to pick them so tiny; they deserve time to grow. However, should one pick them before someone else does, or leave them, thereby taking the risk they'll be gone when one returns next day? Twenty hours a-growing will better ease the conscience and fill the pan. Like my decent friend, let us not be covetous; let them grow, and take the chance.

Picking white mushrooms in a green field is a delight to be savoured as much as the aroma of the caps sizzling in the pan. New-born mushrooms, with their shiny skin and salmon pink gills, are truly lovely creations. There is always something beautiful about the young; even a baby naked mole rat is beautiful. The mushrooms not only look good but taste much better than the shop-bought kind. Also, they take one out into the fields early in the morning, when the grass is bright with dew, and the air fresh and clean. The morning heat coaxes them out, and the light rain drives them. They burst into the world with what must be an audible 'Pop!'. I imagine if one was in the field at the right time, there would be small 'Pops!' all around one. So are things born. Perhaps if one watched a square metre of short sheep grass for an hour of a humid morning, one could catch the birth of a mushroom. All things that grow must make a noise, if we have the ears to hear them. In the countryside, there is always a background of sound, a discordant or harmonious orchestra changing tune by the minute. Even in winter there must be the dying sighs of the falling leaves, the drip of deliquescence from ink caps, ragwort screeching as it curls up.

As the leaves begin to fall, the dappled walks of Courtmacsherry give way to sunlit clearings and the fuchsia hedges are resplendent with painted ladys enjoying the sun. A pair of red admirals chase one another, rising in an aerial dance even as autumn leaves fall in dying spirals around them. On Tuesday last, heat waves shimmered over the fields and the sun sparkled and danced on the sea as I walked west from Broad Strand. The countryside is blood-red with haws. This was the colour given to me by Fintan, dismissing my 'wine red' and 'carmine' as insipid. If we could harvest the haws this year, we'd be millionaires. Sweet, meaty haws are a treat enjoyed by country children from generation to generation. The blackberries go, the haws come. They are even floury when they are very swollen. No wonder the birds flock to the hawthorns, and redwings fly all the way from Scandinavia to feast on Irish haws.

Haws were associated with Druids, and the whitethorn, or May blossom, bedecked pagan revellers. Anything was, no doubt, a relief after a winter in smelly skins, and what more pleasantly perfumed that a sprig of May flower strategically attached to the person when cavorting around the old standing stones in the light of a spring dawn. The thorns were removed, I imagine, otherwise the revellers would quickly be as blood-red as the fruits soon to burgeon on the bushes. Hawthorns were set along field margins before the advent of barbed wire, making impenetrable barriers between fields. Cows may browse the fresh shoots but nothing ate the thorny, haw-laden branches except perhaps asses; hence, 'Hee-haw …'

Six o'clock on a beautiful evening, with the sun yellow on the field beyond the trees across the stream that edges our garden. As I watch rabbits chase one another about on the grass, I cannot but think that they are lucky bunnies. If my father was alive and here, he would be singling out tender young 'graziers' for conversion into rabbit stew. A retired bank manager, he had acquired a taste for rabbit as a boy on the family farm and thought nothing of shooting his dinner with the old point-twenty-two rifle he still carried in the boot of the car when he was ninety-one. Field sports were the fashion of his time.

By the grace of the Great Creator, I have never had to kill to eat or live. Not everyone is so fortunate; we who are must try to provide similar security for those who are not. However, to do this requires that we regularly crank up food production to feed the new millions. Far better if fair distribution of resources could achieve this; however distant this goal may seem, the righteous must never lose sight of it. It may be that it is our greed that kills us. Goldsmith said, 'Ill fares the land, to hastening ills a prey,/ Where wealth accumulates, and men decay. …' Should we not be grateful for nature's natural bounty and ask no more than that it sustains us and we sustain it?

We demand extra at our peril. From now on, if we produce more, it must be production without destruction. We must not kill the earth cow. Like the herdsmen in Kenya, we may bleed her, but we must not kill her. All things that have nurtured her, however humble or obscure – the things under stones, the lichens, the flowers, the things that live deep in the ocean, that fly high in the sky, the bunnies in the fields – must be sustained. Some may have already saved us from unknown disasters. No death is an island: in losing any living thing, we risk the whole; it may be the unknown soldier upon whom our survival one day depends. Barry Lopez, one of the twentieth-century's greatest naturalists said, 'The earth is a living animal upon which all other life depends.' Obliterate a species, and it is our blood also on the ground.

In October 1995, perhaps after a warming drop, I wrote, 'In this blessed autumn everything in the natural world is at its most productive. The hedges are slicked red with haws, and sloes are as big as grapes in the blackthorn bushes. Now indeed is the time to pull out that bottle of country-made lip-numbing *poteen* – kept in the shed for sick calves and emergencies – and transform it into a benison of the hedgerow gods. Fill a third of an air-tight jar with punctured sloes; the stones need not be removed. Pour an equal amount of sugar on top of them, and then fill the jar to the lid with the said "calf embrocation" or, if it is unavailable, Cork Dry gin. Leave for six months, and then begin to drink it. Your mountain dew with a kick like a jennet will now be a divine nectar. And the whole process will make a stirring after-dinner tale.'

Picking parasol mushrooms under a sunlit fuchsia hedge, I thought of our ex-neighbours in London and how much they would give for a free hour on this idyllic coast, on this idyllic day. When we were locked in the city, I often saw, in my mind's eye, an empty, northern strand, in golden light, with waves breaking on the shore. Now, below me as I emerged from the hedge, I could see that strand. After ten years back in the 'sticks', I cannot say I miss the city. I cannot say I am in the least bored. I have enjoyed watching nature since childhood and have never had better opportunities than now. In Penal times when Irish teachers were hanged and schools proscribed, one who got the rudiments of an education in a 'hedge school' was called a 'hedge scholar'. This term describes my vocation and my prowess perfectly. I have learned volumes since we came to West Cork but still know only the rudiments. I meet something new every few yards and every day.

Last week many lawns were decorated with slim ink caps, like pure white candles set upright in the grass. They make a good meal if picked while still pink, but quickly begin to turn to inky liquid at the edges. The flavour is subtle; they are good mixed with scrambled egg. However, being the source of the alcohol rejection-therapy drug 'Antiabuse', they are best avoided on the morning after a wedding, wake or 21st, or serious tummy tumblings will ensue.

The white mushrooms of early October are gone, but just as the fields delivered a bumper crop, so now do the woods. Our friends' daughter Holly sent us a bag of chanterelles. If ceps are the kings of mushrooms, then delicate chanterelles are the princesses. A Frenchman would have kissed Holly on both cheeks, an Italian would have kissed the hand that picked them, a Pole would have kissed the ground. We thanked her profusely and sent some giant puffball in return. The giant puffballs were found – once again – by Dara, our then teenage son. I came home with my humble parasols, only to be downstaged by two pure white footballs on the kitchen table. They were firm and fat and good – no yellowing in the centre, which would automatically disqualify them for the pan. After distributing the surplus amongst friends, we cut the remainder into large steaks, like marshmallow slabs. Then we wrapped them in bread crumbs and lightly fried them, with a touch of garlic, in bacon fat. Puffballs can reach four feet in diameter, and the largest ever was as big as a sheep. Even with small ones, like ours – merely the size of World Cup footballs – it is as well to have mushroom-eating friends.

Showers punctuate long hours of yellow sunshine and the trees shine like a thousand mirrors. The leaves are falling. Keeping the leaves out of our back yard, and out of the kitchen, is an on-going chore. The foliage of a single, mature beech must weigh tons; the weight of a whole forest's foliage is incalculable. Happily, nature, unaided, recycles all this tonnage, and dead leaves – no more than windfall apples – do not blight nature's beauty, as would human dross. On still autumn evenings, the blue smoke of leaf fires rises from cottage gardens. The floors of the old walled orchards at Kincragie are littered with fallen apples and the blackbirds and red admirals are having a feast.

In October 2001 letters from worried friends in New York and London told me how their lives had changed after the September 11th atrocity. One felt guilty saying that here there was no dislocation. We live in a village of no importance, where the wind blows in off two thousand miles of sea. I would not like, however, to be living on the east coast of Ireland opposite Sellafield where, just over a hundred miles across the sea, British Nuclear Fuels reprocesses the world's toxic rubbish for gain, storing radioactive material with ten times the destructive capacity of Chernobyl. It is the British public's own choice if they want to accept such risks, but it is unacceptable that the people of Dublin should be forced to share the hazards and that the life of the Irish Sea is endangered. I am amongst those who agitate for censure of the UK until this potential dirty bomb is dismantled.

As we reach mid-October, it is pleasant to have a nip in the air, a nip but not a bite. Walking abroad these evenings, one quickly warms. As I walk along the cliffs, flights of curlews rise from the fields with lonely cries and mixed groups of oystercatchers and godwits fly in small squadrons over the sea, heading for the roost up the estuary. The black and white plumage of the oystercatchers catches the yellow evening light and makes them easy to see against the blue of the ocean. Later a soft mist rises from the fields, hazing out the distance. Sounds hang in the air. The bay is mirror-calm, with white birds and bright boats set in the stillness. Smoke rises straight from the village chimneys, blue against the tall, dark trees. Autumn, thought by many to be the loveliest of seasons, descends with its deep and perfect peace.

There is no hard edge to the light in autumn. Perhaps the mistiness is water vapour, rising from the wet earth beneath the grass. The view is in soft focus, the most romantic light. See us by the soft flame of a burning candle, and we all look beautiful; thank God for the light in Ireland that doesn't even require a flame! Even a nuclear plant would look lovely in the grainy distance but, happily, no such installations mar the view.

There is hardly a square mile of Ireland that doesn't bear witness to a human past. Stop by the roadside in the remotest place, and leave the car. Walk a short distance and you are sure to find a fallen cottage, the trace of potato drills, the runnels of ancient cart wheels, a standing stone, a burial mound. Sometimes one can almost hear whispers.

Our early history, not surprisingly in a land of shifting light, is veiled in mystery. In the Christian period, the pagan poets and the freshly frocked priests came together to create a history for us. In the *Lebor Gabala*, the poets won. The first Irish, they said, were the Firbolg, who came eight thousand years ago and carried hundredweights of soil on their shoulders to build the earthworks that still rise above the plain. Later came the Tuatha dé Danann who – every Irish school child knows – vanished into the clear air when the Celts came, changing themselves into leprechauns and fairies that still live, in an invisible dimension, alongside us today. In fact the Tuatha were probably not a people but the gods worshipped by the pagan Irish. In time, the early settlers, visible and invisible, were absorbed by the Celts, or vice versa. They left their testimony of dolmens and standing stones, as surely etched on the Irish retina as the ruined cashels and castles that came after. The simple stones survive unchanged; even the castles and broken churches change little, fingerposts of history stark on the horizon or ivy-clad, just as we saw them as children. They crumble almost imperceptibly, unlike ourselves.

For the Celts, the already ancient Newgrange burial mound, in what is now County Meath, was the tomb of no mortal man but of Aengus, the Celtic love god, and the river Boyne below it was revered as his goddess. Older than the pyramids of Egypt, Newgrange is the finest passage grave in all Europe, built with Neolithic energy by the Firbolg almost three thousand years before the Celts set foot in Ireland, using two hundred thousand tons of stone. At dawn on winter solstice day, the sun, at the moment of rising over the horizon, throws a beam down the dark inner passage of the Newgrange tomb, reaching the furthest recess. I wrote earlier of the science in the stones. Newgrange is not only dramatic but a scientific wonder to behold.

The Celts cremated their dead and buried them beneath huge boulders. After the coming of Patrick, druidic cathedrals, like Drombeg in West Cork, worship-circles open to the sky, were abandoned. Builder monks raised oratories and priories, still of unhewn stone, but roofed now and closed in. In 'The Blackbird of Derrycairn', a modern poem expressing the transformation, Austin Clarke stridently calls on the monks to go out under God's own sky and listen to the pagan blackbird singing. After them, and their robust Celtic church, came the Norman invaders, and foreign orders raising abbeys and edifices to the more universal Roman Christ. The ruins of these great monasteries remain. They throw time's shadows on green fields and brown lakes, haunting and magical.

When it rains, it can do so in deluges. These days I often see West Cork youth, boys and girls, tramping along in downpours, intent on maintaining their social life come what may. They hardly even bother to wrap up for it, while carrying an umbrella would be terminally _déclassé_. Likewise I have never seen a West Cork farmer with an umbrella, except at a funeral. His father or grandfather, who went to the creamery with an ass and cart, insulated himself against the vagaries of the heavens with a thick woollen overcoat and slightly greasy flat cap. Little rain permeated the oxter or the headgear. Beneath the outer layer, which could weigh a hundredweight when well soaked, the man remained dry and warm.

Walking outside Schull last Sunday, only a mile from the smart coffee shops and pubs of Dublin weekenders, we came upon a group of hardy men and boys throwing a 'score', or game, of bowls. 'Bowls' rhymes with 'fowls', and 'bowling' with 'fowling'. When veils of rain drifted in off the sea, they lay back against the high, sheltering ditches, not a rain-coat or brolly amongst them. When it stopped, they again crowded the road, twenty euro notes changing hands and the soft weather heightening their complexions. Mount Gabriel loomed above, black beneath cloud one minute, variegated with sunlight the next.

Road bowling is played mainly in two Irish counties. 'In weather fair, or weather foul/ The West Cork man goes out to bowl ...'; so also does the South Armagh man, hundreds of miles away in Ulster. Bowling is a sport of rural back roads, selected for their bends, diversity and privacy because bowling, into the twentieth century, was 'agin' the law'. The *Irish Examiner* newspaper lists the West Cork venues but, if seeking some excitement of a Sunday, one need only look out for 'sops' on the road. These are lumps of grass carefully positioned by the bowler's 'second' to mark the spots where the bowler should contrive to bounce the tennis-ball-size iron bowl so it will travel 'true' or use of the road's camber to steer it around a corner.

The 'score' is a two-man contest of strength and skill. The bowler 'lofts' the 28 ounce (787g) ball to take it 100 yards or more before it hits the tarmac and skitters away. The longest throw ever was 510 yards (466 metres) by an Armagh man. As many as 10,000 spectators may attend the All Ireland Championships, but the usual 'score' is a few dozen men and boys on a Sunday afternoon. Women's scores are sometimes played but the usual crowd is almost entirely male. Lining the route ahead of the bowler, they allow a narrow corridor for the first hundred yards, after which they densely crowd the road, ready to jump as the flying bowl hops and skitters through them at 60 miles an hour. It is a testament to the jig-dancing agility of West Cork farmers that there are rarely broken ankles. Also, the man whose ankle stopped a throw might well find himself the subject of acrimony, not sympathy – the 'stake' money on a match often runs to thousands of euro.

Side bets follow the action throw by throw. Will he loft the next corner, will he be ahead at the next bowl? 'Travellers', so called Irish tinkers, are 'mad' on the bowling, wild-looking coves in suits, some even sporting incongruous golf umbrellas against the showers. Some fine bowlers have been Travellers and here they are the equal of any citizen, their money as good as the next. Games of 'Pitch-and-toss' are a favourite diversion while bowlers and their 'seconds' confer and measure. Two old copper pennies, laid flat on a pocket comb, are tossed spinning skyward and land on two heads or two tails or one-and-one. More bank notes change hands.

Now a hush falls and the pennies are pocketed as the bowler paces back, then sprints forward, arm rotating in a blurred circle, the bowl released at hip-height, his two feet off the ground. 'Hai, hai, hai!' goes the cry as it hits the tarmac and the crowd scatters. At the end of the course, if it is a 'listed' event, stands the ubiquitous chip van. Appetites are sharp after four hours in the country air. Then the pub, the pints, shouts and red faces, and the lore of 'scores' going back to long ago.

Meanwhile at the seashore on sunny October days, the rock pools are clear as crystal and beautiful as jewels. I spent many summers of my childhood falling into such pools, so absorbed that I'd slip and find myself amongst the fishes. These days, when I'm stooped over a pool, children often approach, wondering what a grown man is doing in this adult-exclusion zone. 'Catch us a crab, please, sir,' they say, in West Cork accents, 'Aah, go on. ...'

Sometimes, at a local teacher's request, I take a shoreline walk with a group of small children. It is mightily enjoyable; their enthusiasm is boundless and one feels like a magician as one fingers the weed along the side of a pool and – Hey presto! – produces a fish. They all recognise the shannies but are wide-eyed and open-mouthed to hear they can live in pools so warm they could cook in summer, or freeze in winter, or be battered to bits in a storm. My plastic-bag-temporary-aquarium trick works wonderfully; a four-inch shanny swimming up and down inside elicits appreciative squeals. The baby shannies are like cartoon fish, their fins, like wings, the biggest part of them. As adults, these fins can be used to make suction discs to hold onto rocks when waves smash down on them and, also, as feet to crawl from pool to pool as the tide goes out. Having no scales, they can worm into small, moist crevices, thus not drying up if 'stranded' between tides.

Why scorpion-fish are also called father-lashers, I can't explain. They are not at all as ferocious, although the head is big and ugly. Adults can be five inches long and very fat. Hiding in the weed, their large fins propel them like torpedoes to engulf, with their big mouths, fish or prawns silhouetted against the surface. Rock gobies, another common species, live under stones, and go black when pursued or captured; just as we go pale with fear, they go black. The males are model fathers, fiercely guarding the eggs.

For the children, and indeed myself, the wonders of the local sea-shore are endless, its inhabitants revealing themselves to be every bit as exotic as the captives in a tropical aquarium, but free and at our front door. Butterfish, sideways-flattened and sinuous as eels, are chestnut-brown with bright, white semicircles along the back; maybe they are so called because catching one is like trying to catch a fast streak of butter. In the shallow pools, we find dark brown rocklings, with whiskers like cat fish; they find their food via a 'taste' groove under the dorsal fin, which shimmers as they move. These, and the others, are all eaten by larger, commercial species, and so are part of the food chain that leads to the children's fish fingers.

Perhaps most amazing of all are the bootlace-thin pipefish, cousins of the sea horse, a few inches long. Sometimes they swim in the shape of a crescent or a question mark, the male carrying the eggs or babies in a slit down his belly; the young swim in and out for a short time after they are hatched. There are neon-pink two-spot gobies and black-and-white flatfish and long, pike-like sea stickle-backs. There are all the non-fishy wonders, shellfish, starfish, brittle stars and cushion stars, anemones and urchins, sea slugs and sponges, shore crabs and hermit crabs, prawns and shrimps. How lucky we are that few places in Ireland are no further than a Sunday drive from the coast! Nowhere is more fun for children, young and old, with birds on the surface, fish and futuristic crustacea below it and teeming life – cockles, clams, razorfish and Virgin Mary shells – beneath the sands. No wonder Edmund Spenser, the poet of *The Fairie Queene*, stood on the shores of Cork four centuries ago and told himself, 'Oh, what

an endless worke have I in hand, To count the Sea's abundant progeny.'
Poor Spenser! I wouldn't begin to try it myself!

Now, in the last half of October, swallows are still with us, and late
clutches are still being fed. A furniture-maker in Charleville tells me
his workshop is a-twitter with birds, frantically trying to fatten up the
late hatch for the early flight. As many as seven adults are dashing back
and forth from dawn to dusk, greeting their landlord with chirps,
swoops and dances in front of his window. While older swallows have
left the local skies, these final providers still labour; they are young
birds from an earlier clutch now feeding their siblings, for some
swallows rear three clutches in a good year. On warm days, becoming
rarer, butterflies still flit about the garden and bees hum in the eaves.
The virginia creeper is purple red. Leaves fall and carpet the ground
beneath. I am reminded of Dylan Thomas's vivid line, 'The town
below lay leaved in October blood'.

On the cold days I begin to put out food for the birds. With luck,
I will entice the best local selection — one can become covetous of
birds — and when the fieldfares and redwing thrushes, hungry from
frozen Russia, pass overhead, they will see the local birds looking fat
and secure and decide to enhance the garden with their twitterings.
Last year we had bramblings and vagrant chaffinches. The dog may
miss out on a few kitchen scraps but she's already well upholstered. It
is a sign of the times and increased affluence that we may consider
feeding the redwings whereas, in the past, the redwings fed us.

Sixty years ago it was common, in West Cork and elsewhere, for
young men, on a windy, winter night, to go lamping thrushes. I am
told they could be picked off the bushes, where they roosted, head
under wing. The blackbird was the main impediment to a successful
harvest. Sentinel of the woods, the blackbird was easily disturbed and,
if alerted, went shrieking through the trees, raising an awful racket
and sending the thrushes scattering like leaves in the wind. Once taken,
the thrushes, no doubt plump on Irish berries, were carried home to
the kitchen. There they had their little necks wrung and their feathers
plucked before being barbecued over the embers of the fire.

One day last week the estuary shores were white with frost and a mist hung over the water, like smoke drifting. The scene was straight from a fairy tale, with the water still as mercury, and the village woods rising behind. I walked west from Courtmacsherry, using the new path that runs along the water, following the route of the railway that once came from Timoleague and Cork. It was early. For long intervals no traffic passed. The bay was full, the tide just ebbing. No shoals were yet uncovered and, therefore, I saw no wading birds. On the opposite shore soft, white fields flowed down to the water.

Rounding a bend by the Abbeymahon, the ruin of a Cistercian church of *circa* 1250, I found dozens of shelduck out on the water, their white breasts and chestnut collars brilliant in the yellow sun. A mile farther, at the head of the bay, the banks of the small creek running west from Timoleague Abbey were densely packed with curlews, lapwing, godwits, redshank, greenshank and dunlin, huddling on the frosty margins, waiting for some heat to come into the day. This precious creek, running alongside the road, is roost to thousands of migrants. We may tame the land, but theirs is another dimension. Their mansions are the vaults of the sky, and these we have not colonised. They know no frontiers. Birds weighing barely an ounce cross countless miles of ocean, deserts and forests, teeming cities, ice floes and mountains. How far they travel, in what flocks, catching what winds, how high they fly or where they rest, we know not but, increasingly, we threaten their survival. They have been following their routes for millions of years, as continents have shifted and oceans filled and ebbed. They are still with us; they are the best testament to wildness we have left.

These autumn evenings, over Courtmacsherry bridge, the air rings with the cries of rooks, strident and clashing in the dying light. From the trees overhead they foray forth in packs over the water, clouds and curtains of rooks, cawing, crying, swirling, filling the sky. At high and low and middle-air, they come and go, in bands and gangs, three thousand at once, all moving, calling. Such sights or sounds one will not find in downtown Düsseldorf, Douglas, or Dublin 4; it is wildness at our doorstep, available for viewing, against the backdrop of Timoleague Abbey, every evening at fall of light. It is elemental and stirs the soul; indeed surely only the irrevocably urbanised or utterly unimaginative do not respond to the wild, are not stirred by the wind, by the sailing moon, by the power of the sea, by skeins of wild birds against a night sky.

The rookery wood is a mere six or seven acres, but what a difference it makes for the birds of the bay! Herons nest there too and bicker high in the branches in spring. *Rucach*, the rooks are called in Irish, an onomatopoeic echo of their jangling call. Black and ragged-feathered, so it seems, up close they shine a wonderful magenta. They are a part of the old Ireland, the hard edge, the scrawny survivors that caw defiance at the manicured hedgerows, the golf courses and would-be Surrey lawns. I count myself blessed to live in a place where such wild birds fill the sky.

On these days between summer and winter, the interludes of mini-weather systems are exotic, to be savoured like brief holidays in other climes. There are infinite gradations. Last week I climbed out of the car and found myself standing in a warm wind, in bright sunlight. It was balmy as the Bahamas in Barryroe. A hour earlier I'd walked the cliffs over a storm-driven sea. Great, long waves rolled in, grey and viscous with sand, curdling in the big pools, foamy and yellow as the heads on old basins of stout. Towards the horizon, the view failed entirely, lost in mist, the bulk of the Old Head of Kinsale like a smudge in the distance, cloud patterns scudding over the green-grey, Buck Mulligan sea.

Today the wind was at it again, buffeting my ears as I walked into the sun, the headlands black as jet against the sea's shimmer. Below me the waves cracked off the rock, spray flew and froth balls chased one another across shiny pastures that trembled and shook like green, ground-hugging versions of Van Gogh's corn fields at Arles. The spaniel's ears blew horizontal to her head, like flapping air balloons; it seemed she might at any minute be swept off the ground. Winter is slow in coming, so far so good, but summer's lease had all too short a time. It's my intention to savour to the full the last drop of summer. If I can get myself out each day for an hour or so, I'll be adding value to my tenure. It's too soon to be drawing in for the cold and dark. But however long the halcyon days last, winter will always come too soon.

The sun still shines and the wind from the south-west is warm and strong, scattering the rain heads and leaving intervals of sheer blue. We set off to imbibe the sweet air between the showers. Leaving home with our jackets buttoned, we return with them slung over our shoulders, in a lather of October heat. The wind whistles softly above the high ditches of the bohreens, but between them it might be summer with bees buzzing and butterflies fluttering as they would on a good August day. Out walking, I see two painted ladys feeding on bramble flowers in a sheltered lane. Sadly, as the north winds do blow – which inevitably they will – such creatures, for all their beauty, will expire.

October is the month for 'conkers', a game provided by nature, older than time. For each new generation, horse chestnuts are an autumn bounty. Stone Age children may have gathered them beneath Stone Age trees. It is little wonder that children can't resist; even if they never string them for 'battle', simply to hoard them is enough. For the child, a new chestnut, gleaming in its freshly opened shell, is surely a thing of wonder, so lovely and polished, brilliant russet and shining white, set cosy and secret and safe in its soft, cream bed. Never mind that it encloses the germ of a tree wide enough to shelter a blacksmith, his forge and his horses, no human technique could manufacture a bead or a gewgaw as beautiful as a fresh conker.

It is no surprise that children, with their newly opened eyes, should treasure them. I remember, years ago, a small boy, now grown, who neither knew nor cared for the value of coins and would exchange a pound for a tenpence, but was heartbroken when he lost the bag of conkers he'd collected, certain he'd never find such bounty again. When he did find another tree, he wouldn't leave it until he'd collected a bushel. There he was, shaking its municipal branches while his poor mother scurried around beneath, filling her handbag and shopping bag, terrified they would both be arrested.

On the estuary, drifts of golden plover rise and ascend to a great height, where they swirl about like wind-blown prairie 'twisters' straight from *The Wizard of Oz*. After the dark deluges of the weekend, Monday morning is bright and shining as a new pin; this is Murphy's weekend weather law. Saturday and Sunday-long, the Atlantic rained down on us from on high and the wind whipped the water into madcaps on the bay. Fintan, along with our local sports mistress, went 'body boarding' on the waves. The air temperature was warm under the drizzle, but sooner they than I. Then Monday October 31st brings shirt-sleeve weather again, like a Mediterranean winter day.

November

When beeches drip in browns and duns,
And thresh, and ply ...

Thomas Hardy

~

*Five minutes after the flare went up, the
lifeboat was surging down the channel …*

Outside an autumn gust sends the leaves flying, swirling high over the mother trees like a flock of mad, late swallows. Marie throws a winged sycamore seed to the wind and it rises and soars over our rooftop like a helicopter. Later, on a country lane, we find some sizeable wild strawberries. She tells me that, as a child, walking to school on the bohreens west of here, she and her sisters would gather 'hurts' – whortleberries – on the ditches. They are still to be found, plentifully in some places.

Yesterday I picked a bag of wood blewits. When my father was alive, he once complained that shop mushrooms lacked the flavour he had enjoyed from field mushrooms as a boy. I packed some blewits in a cardboard box and dispatched them by An Post. Pony Express could not have delivered them sooner; they arrived at his Kilkenny doorstep, in perfect condition, twenty-four hours after they left me. He had never tried blewits before, and it was an act of trust to do so: blue mushrooms, delicate of flavour, growing in Ireland for millennia, appreciated even in heathen England but never eaten here.

While autumn remains the season of mellow fruitfulness, the mists are lately absent, as are crisp autumn days. It rains regularly. Autumn leaves are plastered on the footpaths; they make treacherous the woodland ways. There is not even the schoolchild's fun of leaf-stomping; the cold hasn't yet come and the land hasn't yet 'set'. Thomas Hood wrote a poem about November. It went, 'No sun – no moon – no morn – no noon', no-this, no-that, etcetera. No-torious No-vember, indeed! If it continues like this, I will emigrate back to the bananas. Will it never lift, I sometimes ask myself, the grey army-blanket of a sky, with fields beneath as bleak as Flanders? Are we forever more to wade through mud when we go walking, to drive through rain-filled road gullies when we go driving, to have water dripping off the gutters down our necks when we go out to bring in the coal?

We are blessed, in this part of Ireland, with a mild and aqueous climate – rarely frost, seldom snow – but we pay the price in mud. Farmers, drawing beet from the fields, cannot avoid leaving 'long acres' of mud on the highways; there is also mud pouring off the ploughed, hedgeless fields. Added to this, we have extensive building in the village, extensive pipe laying on the roads. We wonder will Ireland ever be 'finished', will we ever again see a time when we don't have to negotiate truck-gouged potholes of brown water, slippery pavements, diversions and diggers, men in yellow oilskins, mud on the windscreen, mud on our shoes?

'Spain will be great when it's finished!' we used to joke when the 1970s 'costas' resorts were going up, the white skyscrapers of apart-ments, the marinas, the new roads, the promenades. We might say the same about Ireland now. Roads are dug up for improvement, mains services are reaching remote hamlets, house-building is burgeoning in every town. All praise to the burrowers and builders, working in inclement weather; the services are welcome and the house-building will, hopefully, ensure that before long everybody has a decent home, hopefully with a view of Ireland's beauty from the windows. But Lord, give us a few dry weeks of sharp, cold, eastern weather, where things dry out, where we can drive without non-stop wipers and misted-up windows, where we can walk hard paths where leaves rustle underfoot, rather than rot!

The birds sit out on the slob, in the cold wind, seeming to love it. 'Mud, mud, glorious mud!' goes the old Flanders and Swann song. I suppose it's better than Iceland or Siberia. Flocks of golden plover stand two thousand strong on the mudflats in front of Timoleague petrol station. Lapwing and black-tailed godwit dip and ruffle their feathers in the channel. Brrr, brrr! Our dog loves the mud and charges into every ditch and dike available. While dry dogs are only mildly odoriferous, soggy Springers stink. Pretty, she may indeed be, but after a walk her pong pervades the car. At home, muddy paw prints follow her progress over carpets. 'Defenistrate the hound!' I cry, but Marie prevails upon me, 'Suffer the poor creature. She must walk somewhere. You know she cannot fly!' Odourless, self-levitating house-hounds are, to my mind, the only answer. Fancy dog breeders, please note.

As I write, ragged caw-cophonies of rooks fly over the grey bay and a flotilla of fishing cormorants moves in convoy down the channel between the mud slicks; things are so dismal, they have taken to hunting in packs. Should I, I ask myself in autumn's reflective mood, try to rear a cormorant from the nest and have it fish for me? The Japanese, before they invented sixty-mile-long, monofilament fish traps, cultivated cormorants. They put rings around their necks, tethered them to a line and set them to work. From the prows of their skiffs, the cormorants would dive and, catching a fish, would surface and be pulled aboard. Unable to swallow their catch, they would disgorge it and be rewarded with a tit-bit. The boatman – he could hardly be called the fisherman – meanwhile added another fish to his basket. Cormorant fishing off Ireland might indeed be a profitable side-line. There are cormorants and shags in plenty. I may review my brainwave, come the spring of the year.

I see mixed flocks of finches and tits foraging along the roadside hedges, and thrushes from Scandinavia, tremulous as the wind-tossed trees on which they perch. Happily, there are fat berries for all-comers; red clusters hang amongst the holly; will they still be there when Christmas comes? On Halloween night, as local young fellas stoutly tended a huge bonfire in the teeth of the rain driving in off the bay, I heard, I believe, the thin, reedy calls of a flock of redwings blown overhead and fancied, for a moment, that I saw the small, dark shapes pass over the walls of Timoleague Abbey behind us. It could well have been; redwings arrive from Scandinavia about this time, along with fieldfares, their larger cousins. The other morning I woke to the raucous clattering of a band of Viking thrushes in a tree.

The berries will now be getting scarce on the mountain ash along the Baltic, but there are still rich pickings here. Even the song thrushes on the lawn may be Russian, stopping to gorge on their way to over-winter in Spain. Other Irish thrushes are blackbirds, ring-ouzels and mistle thrushes; a friend said she heard a nightingale – also a thrush – sing in Merrion Square, but I think she had had one too many. The song thrush is as good a singer as we get, but what about the poor worms? 'Terrifying are the attent sleek thrushes on the lawn ... Nothing but bounce and stab/ And a ravening second,' said the poet Ted Hughes, giving the worm's-eye view.

Hearing that a winter bird walk was afoot at the weekend, we met our friends, the eminent word-botchers and ornithological quare-hawks, Higgins and Hopkin. These days, Higgins' eyesight is grievously impaired so that the poor man cannot tell a godwit from a gobshite at a hundred paces, at least until it opens its gob. His consort, Alannah, no relation of the prodigious word-botcher, holy Manley Hopkins (he who gave us the definitive field notes on a wind-hover in flight) has a keen eye for nature. The twitchers of the West Cork Bird Group duly mounted their telescopes and aimed them at the mud-banks, offering everyone the opportunity to view.

Birds seem to like County Cork, with its long coastline and huge estuaries. They may even like Cork bird watchers, a harmless bunch which includes red-cheeked, GAA-looking types, local cabinet ministers, scholarly coves and various Sweeneys-amongst-the-Nightingales. The latter look like they might live in nests rather than houses. Emerging from the miasma of a bog, telescopes big as bazookas across their shoulders, beards birds could nest in and wearing camouflage jackets and serious boots, they could double for a band of South American revolutionaries. Guerrillas in the mist? Possibly. An Italian tourist, upon seeing them, looked a little anxious until we gave her a reassuring smile.

Fintan, now fourteen, does not come on bird-walks, but has been doing some nature study while at school. Sitting in a classroom during break – he insists it wasn't during lessons – he spotted some jackdaws digging energetically underneath a conker tree outside. Soon, one of them, with a conker in its beak, flew into a tree where it hopped from branch to branch until it found a flat one, there to lodge the conker between its feet and chisel it open with its beak. Jackdaws, it seems, are very partial to conker kernels, after letting them age in the soil for a spell, perhaps even sprout.

Fintan's nature study reminds me of my own when, at about the same age, I studied chaffinches and mayflies. 'Mitching' from school one warm June day in Mayo, I lay alone on the banks of the river Robe, idly whiling away my stolen time by counting the average number of mayflies taken by chaffinches as they hatched and rose from the water. I was appalled at the decimation. That afternoon of illicit nature-study was a watershed, habituating me to such outrage and time-wasting ever since.

'Bass fishing in the surf' is one of those 'legendary' experiences macho moguls and movie stars aspire to. 'Surf' is a word charged with meaning, evocative of all that is exciting, healthy and ozone-fresh. 'Surf fishing' on a western Atlantic beach in the grey, pearly light of November would sell anything from cars to cosmetics; it epitomises the 'quality of life' of urban dreams. These autumn days, 'surf bass' are running along the south coast and the shores of Courtmacsherry Bay. Certain fish, like birds, migrate. Last week, with two experienced friends, I tried shore-angling. I caught nothing of course, although my lugworm bait was in the same place as theirs, exactly at the breaking of the third wave.

However, just to be there, and then, was glorious. Out in the sea and the wind, we three stood facing into the opalescent afternoon and the spray of the white horses. Two kestrels hung in the up-draught on the hill behind us. Nowhere better to be. The lugworms of course would not have enjoyed the experience. I did not enjoy putting them on the hook; it is not nice to run a barb through the soft body of a blameless lugworm. Lugworms aren't very pretty, but if poor looks deserved hooking, we'd all be gaffed long ago.

Unlovely lugworms are the staple diet of many a fish and fowl, burrowing away in the estuary substrata, ingesting sand, moving it through their bodies, extracting nutrition, growing fat and succulent. Indirectly, as fish food, they feed us, the great predators. What have we got that they haven't got? Brains and mobility, we say. I imagine they were here before we were; maybe they'll be here after us, given our brains. While some are skewered by anglers, most survive to die naturally. For the unfortunate, being hooked by a fisherman can't be much worse than being speared by a wader or nipped by a flounder. Like ourselves, they are here to serve.

The surf bass caught by my companions were reeled in, very gently. Two fish are allowed the fisherman, in a day. Those shorter than sixteen inches are put back. Anglers are often conservationists; their sport – 'sport' is always a strange word when it is predicated upon killing – depends on quarry. I tell myself that the smart fish know free lunches don't exist and, so, survive. Their naïve cousins take what is easy and, so, are landed, not having had the chance to spawn ongoing stupidity. I watch my rod, stuck in the sand, leaning on a tripod. The day is cold, the wind seeks out the fissures in my clothes; the water too has somehow found its way into my waders. On the hill the hanging kestrel drops. It rises, something in its talons. The sea beats in, with many voices. Nothing is won easily, from land or sea.

The alertness of my friends can be seen in their faces. They hardly have to speak. They know the curl of the wave to cast into, they know the behaviour of the line, their tenuous extension into a world where we cannot go. Although they have never been there, in the rolling see-saw of surf, it is as if they are with the bass, nosing about the bait. They know how a bass sees, how a bass thinks, how a bass feeds, how to present a bass with irresistible temptation.

I cannot catch bass. They can. They deserve it; perhaps the bass do, too. On the beach, on the Atlantic littoral, this November Irish afternoon, the age-old game plays on. In the grey light, things die, things live. The kestrel swoops, sometimes successful, sometimes not. I have the feeling we learned all this a long time ago. Now it is 'sport', but it is of an older nature. We are drawn back to the haunts of bass, the breaking surf, the wind-blown littoral, to cast our lines into the ancestral sea.

Every fourth or fifth year, good weather continues into November and there is a rare and poignant beauty to the dying year. In 1992, I wrote, 'St Martin's Summer, November 11th, brings blithe days and the world shines. Everything is dying back but nature is not depress-ing in death. There is great beauty in the trees and, when it is dry, great music in the rustle of dried leaves. Sound carries better for the absent foliage; we hear a raven croak and are amazed to see how far away it is. Bats flit overhead as we walk the lanes, even though temperatures have dropped, with cold, clear nights full of stars, and blue, still days, with the sea calm as glass. One morning last week I came across a red admiral floating over an ivy bush in a hedge, with a bumble bee still bumbling about in November. Never say die, I suppose, as long as the nectar lasts!'

In 1995, on November 1st, I looked up from my computer and was amazed to see six or eight boys in swimming trunks running in and out of the sea. Later I went down to the beach and the sun was so warm that two families were picnicking. Teenies dug sand castles, while the six-year-olds splashed in the waves; thus, November half-term on the Irish Riviera. The weather was so fair in November 2001 that I wrote, 'A scientist predicts that, within a few decades, Ireland may have a Mediterranean climate. Girls in skimpy skirts dancing at the cross-roads and farmers, in straw hats, sipping Rosscarbery red or Dunworley white instead of black porter – a climate, perfect, in a land, fecund. With autumns like this one, will the Irish eat in the garden, drink in the street, sit in the shade and snooze in the afternoon?'

To strangers who think Irish winters are like those of Britain and Northern Europe, lying face down on an Irish beach of a mid-November noon may seem eccentric or penitential, or both. However, given some sun, a West Cork beach in November is a most pleasant place to be and while my neighbours may conclude I am irrefutably mad, at least they know I'm harmless. It is the essence of good sense to soak up winter sunlight in the micro-climate found low down on the white sand, where one is hardly touched by the breeze. Meantime I occupy myself usefully with pencil and paper while watching tiny, shiny sandhoppers leap and turn somersaults on and off the page. Thomas Hardy wrote a poem about being visited by various insects as he sat writing by lamplight. He had no objection. What was good enough for Hardy is certainly good enough for me.

Below the breeze, the sun, where it touches the skin, seems warm enough to tan, although I have not cast a clout but in fact enjoy the insulation of stout corduroys, a sweater and waistcoat. But now, the dog, sitting on a tussock above me, growls. The voice of a concerned person calls out, 'Are you all right, there, Enright?' Like a good citizen and good neighbour, our hotel keeper has climbed out of his car to investigate a prone body on an Irish beach on a November day. I thank and reassure him. Acquainted with my unorthodoxy, he laughs and drives away. We settle down again, the dog and I. The tide is flat out. Just below the white sand, the beach is still wet from the last tide and dotted with cockleshells. Beyond, the sand is still covered in a slick of water and furrowed by the small waves, now withdrawn. The calls of the estuary birds are the only sound here. Nearest me is a party of black and white oystercatchers, shrilling and twittering and crying 'Meep, meep, meep!', as if outraged. Smoke rises from some village chimneys. High above, the white contrail of an aircraft crosses the heavenly blue.

On November 15th, a quite different kind of day, I am surprised to see three swallows thrown about a wintry sky, along with leaves flying off the high trees above our garden. Through binoculars, I can tell they are young birds; their tails are short, not yet grown to the needle-points of adults. Back and forth they hawk for insects which must be few and far between in this cold snap. There is no sign of an adult bird to lead them south, no veterans of the mile-high club to guide them down the latitudes. Will they make it to far Botswana, where Irish swallows go? I fear they've left it late. The wind blows from the south-west, not the way they're going. Lone swallows in an empty sky, a party of three tiny birds, just six weeks hatched, setting off to fly three thousand miles. God speed the swallows!

Otters can be very tame. For half an hour, a sleek, full-grown otter cruised up and down along the sea wall below our house last weekend, with walkers and cars passing only a few feet away. It sometimes came ashore but, it seemed, was afraid, not of people but of dogs. Our neighbour, who walks in every weather – and from her complexion and limber stride, obviously profits from the exercise – sees it regularly. Women tell me the moisturised climate of West Cork is great for the skin and keeps it young. You can tell this from the youthful blush of all the old-young farmers.

An amateur archaeologist informs me his small-holder neighbour found buried walls when cutting turf in a bog near Drinagh. He will report it to University College Cork, which will investigate. At Céide Fields, in north Mayo, the work of turf cutters and then, archaeologists, revealed miles of stone walls buried beneath the bog, the stones untouched since their builders left them some six thousand years ago. Once, they divided lush meadows, surrounded by forests. There a settlement of between one and two thousand Irish men, women and children lived in harmony with their herds and nature. No defensive walls have been found.

In Egypt the pyramids had not yet been built. A thousand years before the first block was laid, the Céide Fields had already been abandoned. To find the walls, archaeologists employ a method traditionally used for locating trees buried under deep bog. An iron probe is pushed deep down into the turf. Where it strikes a hard object, it is withdrawn and replaced by a rod of the same length. In time the track of the subsumed stones is marked, with their varying heights, providing a profile of the ancient wall beneath.

Pottery shards have indicated dwellings and revealed that these people were descendants of a farming/ herding culture that had migrated out of the Near East. They had taken, perhaps, a hundred generations to reach this western margin of Europe, as far as they could go. Céide Fields covers tens of square miles; it is the most extensive Stone-Age monument on earth, the oldest enclosed landscape in Europe. However, a few centuries after the trees were cleared and pastures made, the bog invaded. Bog is formed where the ground is so sodden that the process of decay stops. Plants normally grow, fall over, rot and become humus, but if the ground is too wet, the organisms of decay drown and the dead vegetation builds up in layers, generation upon generation. The farmers moved on. It is likely they didn't move far and that, today, there are few natives of our western seaboard who do not have the blood of these people in their veins.

These Céide farmers were in Ireland 3,500 years before the Celts; they did not speak Gaelic. According to the latest findings, most Irish people today still carry their DNA. We are, in blood and probably in nature, aboriginal Firbolgs with possibly a tincture of Milesian. We have dressed ourselves in the flowing robes of the Celts, with harps and hounds and myths and bards but, in fact, the Celts were johnny-come-latelys when the Irish were already old. They greatly influenced our culture, but little influenced our blood.

In our DNA, we are of the 'old stock', particularly if we have come out of the west and have Irish names. More than 98 per cent of Connacht males have a gene that was common to all Europe ten thousand years ago, but elsewhere in Europe has thinned as new migrants arrived from the east. The last redoubt of these ancient bloodlines is Ireland – especially the west – and the Basque country. Distinctive Y chromosome 'markers', passed from father to son, continue unchanged in Irish blood. In France these markers were detected in 50 per cent of males, in Italy, in 33 per cent, in Turkey, in 1.8 per cent. The Irish, on the farthest edge of Europe, appear to have been hardly reached by invaders, and were little affected by inward migrations of Celts, Vikings, Normans, English, Scots or mythical Spaniards who swam ashore from the wrecked Spanish Armada. A secondary, surprising discovery was that those with native names were most likely to have the genes. But even if you are called Fotherington Fitzthomas and your people are from the west, you are likely to be more Firbolg than Plantagenet.

Year after year, the big beech trees outside my window withstand whatever the weather can throw at them. One squally night, they will no doubt fall, but not in my time. I see the high tops redden in spring and later, in the space of a single day, green over. What magnificent vegetables they are, rising to nearly a hundred feet, stalwart-boled, vigorous, sturdy. Rooks and jackdaws use them as lookout posts, and mating pigeons bill and coo in high branches of golden evenings, enraptured out of their pigeon brains with sap and love.

The vista of mixed forest I see from my window is full of colour these yellow winter mornings. On the east side of the bay are four or five fine old houses, each with its tree-lined drive. Austin Clarke, in 'The Planter's Daughter', makes the observation '… the house of the planter/ Is known by the trees'. After the defeat of the Irish and Spanish at Kinsale in 1601, lands confiscated from the Irish were awarded to English 'planters'. They made trees a feature of their fine houses. The turf-roofed *botháns* of the Irish peasantry did not have trees; poverty may have dictated that what grew was used for firewood, or the poor quality of the land left to them would support little else but *sceacs* and sycamores. Hedges too are often remnants of the old planters' demesnes. Last week, killing time in Dunmanway town while my car was having its annual road-worthiness test, I feasted on late blackberries and tried to identify the trees and shrubs in a hedge skirting a laneway along a nearby lakeshore.

M.D. Hopper, the British botanist and historian, studied hedges around old UK estates which could be dated by historical record. He discovered that in every thirty yards of old hedge, there will be one tree or shrub species for every one hundred years of its age. According to Hopper's Hypothesis, the lakeshore hedge I studied is older than any building in Dunmanway.

In the first thirty yards I found sycamore, ash, hawthorn, holly, wild privet and hornbeam. In the second, all were present except hornbeam; there was oak instead. In another stretch I found the first five, along with crab apple. In five sections, I found, in addition to the above, some alders, a shrub I couldn't identify and a tree with small, black fruits, damsons or bullace, perhaps; I ate one and didn't expire. I found no blackthorn, strangely but, in all, eleven tree or shrub species. Applying Hopper's rule, sections of the hedge seem to be six hundred years old, or older. The lady at the garage told me that the oldest house in Dunmanway was Jacobean, built between 1603 and 1625. It stands at the east end of the town and, significantly, these hedges are behind it; they were quite probably once part of its estate. They may even have pre-dated its construction, perhaps, the edge of an old forest. The wild plum, and the spiky plant I can't name, may have been ancient garden escapees.

Old hedges in Britain are often forest edges, like Wordsworth's hedges beside the Wye. The ancient uses and claims of hedgerows are, these days, not valued. For centuries they protected stock, broke the force of floods that would otherwise sweep away soil, nurtured wild creatures and produced fruit for wild life and ourselves. Without the haws, would the winter thrushes arrive from Europe, and wouldn't it be a drab land without the white blossom on blackthorn and whitethorn in spring?

November 20th, and the millpond-still sea reflects a clear blue sky, and the mudflats and birds are swept by yellow sunlight. In this light, everything is sharp, crisp, clear, all colours brightened – the yellow flash on a drake teal's tail, the creamy flash on a drake widgeon's forehead. The eyes of cormorants are deep, dark emerald, lit from inside, and the eyes of oystercatchers are ruby red. Lapwings' faces are orange, or lime, depending on the light, and their feathers are glossy green and magenta.

From noon to 4pm, a roosting flock of golden plover carpets the mud at Timoleague creek with an acre of gold. Amongst them, tiny dunlin and ringed plover scurry, and redshanks preen on the saltmarsh margins beyond. A tall egret, pure white and graceful, fishes a muddy channel; behind, a leery-looking grey heron stands half-concealed in a reed break, wings wrapped around him like an ad for Sandeman port. I saw a barn owl again the other night, sitting on telegraph wires. Although on 'taxi service' for my kids – country parents know all about that! – I thought, let them wait, and turned the car and drove slowly back. I made three passes before the owl left. I think it got tired of watching me.

On these darkening evenings, the wildness of old Ireland begins at the sea's edge. As night draws in, waders whistle and cheep on the mudbanks in front of ancient Abbeymahon. Rooks, in hundreds, caw and clatter homeward against the sky. History is behind one, timelessness before one. Night comes down, and time now is a small cluster of lights, faintly winking on the hill.

The weather continues mild. Marie and I walk in the late afternoon, the best time. The leaves of autumn match her hair. Yesterday, in a blast of sunlight, I picked the last blackberries from a briar and gallantly gave them to her, a late birthday present. She declared them sweet as the donor: as the poet might have said, 'Gather ye blackberries while ye may. ...' Domestic bliss: at night, we gather around the fire and roast chestnuts. Sweet chestnuts are ignored in Ireland. The 'Spanish' chestnut, an imported tree, grows wild almost everywhere in West Cork and most years the nuts are fat enough to be worth the gathering. The green husks, spikier than horse chestnuts, split and lie open, like white rosettes, on the forest floor. In rural Spain and the Canary Islands, the nuts are boiled in salt water and peeled when they are soft. They are a common offering in the autumn – a bowl of boiled *castañas* and a jug of red wine from the home *bodega*. In the woods we also find the three-faced nuts called 'beech mast'. Once, their oil was made into beechnut butter. Some years, they are swollen enough to be worth peeling, and provide a sweet morsel as we go.

The storms last week were spectacular, the bay brown with the issue of rivers, streams and gullies that ran down hedgeless fields, leapt ditches, crossed roads and made for the sea. Beyond the shelter of the headland, waves tossed and the sea's face was so broken that even a six-foot punt could not have enjoyed an even keel for a minute without being pitched high and low. Three sailors, two men and a woman, snatched from the maw of death by the Courtmacsherry lifeboat, were brought to our door at 4am, seeking warm beds, hot showers and refuge. Twenty miles off the Old Head, they had abandoned their mast-less yacht, climbed into a tiny life-raft and committed themselves to the black of the night and the rage of the sea.

It had taken six hours to find them. At 10pm we heard the loud bang of the Verey gun ring out over the village and saw the flare arch skyward, summoning the lifeboat crew. From household hearths and television couches, from behind the counter of the quiet pub, they ran or drove pell-mell to the pier. Five minutes after the flare went up, the lifeboat was surging down the channel, headed for the vast dark and the bucking sea. Those who manned it were ordinary men, our neighbours. Their courage cannot be doubted; how, otherwise, could they plough twenty miles into the screaming wind and towering waves to save utter strangers, knowing nothing of them but that they were fellow men?

Next day and the next, the rescue was on the local radio news. The yacht, stripped to the bare hull by the sea, was found by a trawler and towed in to Helvick. Valued at €120,000, it was, perhaps, the best catch the fishermen had had all year. A search, launched by the owners the previous day, had failed to find the almost-submerged carcass. The personal belongings of the owners were saved, but sodden. For the loss of the boat, the insurers would pay.

In November 2001, after the brilliant weather early in the month, the sea washed over the walls of the bay and wrecked the hard work of the Walk Committee who had set up a lovely, and much enjoyed, pathway along the track of the old railway line that skirted the bay shore between Timoleague and Courtmac. The power of the sea, driven by the wind, is awesome. It threw itself over the road and gouged under the tarmacadam, lifting whole sections of roadway behind the beach. It inundated and undermined the walk route that had been so carefully and expensively created. It cast sizeable rocks ashore. Only perhaps once in a year, or once in every three or four years, does it lash the shore with such ferocity – only when the highest of tides is driven by the strongest of winds – but what destruction it can do! The bridge at the mouth of the Argideen river, below Timoleague House, normally clearing the water by some ten feet, was overrun but survived. All traffic had to take to the high roads. Happily, when the moon waned, the tides dropped and calmed.

The floods that laid waste human endeavour covered the salt marshes with silt and built more land. In its own realm, nature doesn't so much destroy, as recycles or replenishes. Leaves turn to earth, shells to sand, flesh to humus. Does anything, once born on this earth, ever disappear from it? Even rocks burnt in volcanoes leave ash. Even the Pharaoh's cat, and the Pharaoh's cat's rats, still lie in the dust of Egypt. And, when I come to think of it, my poor old goldfish is still feeding the roots of a tree.

On the coast the storms roared on for half the week. For us, in this sheltered village, in the lee of the wind, its force was manifest only in the tossing white caps out beyond the sand bar. It could be heard in the woods behind our house, like express trains passing through tunnels. No boats went to sea; anxious owners and skippers were seen adjusting ropes and buoys. The village, one might say, was battened down, and the storm passed over it.

When the storm goes, the bay is beautiful. The sky seems full of clean new clouds, drifting sedately in the blue. Everything appears new and shining, the gulls, the boats, the beach, the sand flats. All are imbued with a scrubbed, fresh-faced look. The roads are slicked with leaves, and raindrops twinkle on the grass where horses stand knee-deep in mist. Dylan Thomas's lines about a child's vision upon waking in a Welsh farm spring to mind; the same lines might apply to our landscape after the gales: 'So it must have been after the birth of the simple light/ In the first, spinning place, the spellbound horses walking warm/ Out of the whinnying green stable/ On to the fields of praise.'

At the weekend, seals-on-wheels was the urgent business as a network of previously unacquainted people mobilised to get a small white seal from a storm beach on the Seven Heads to a swimming pool in Dublin. A woman living in a remote farmhouse on Broad Strand alerted us to its presence. As soon as we came upon the bundle of white fluff, it raised its head and uttered pathetic cries. The sound – 'Maw, maw, maw!' – was so uncannily like a human child that one could understand the old stories of folk falling off cliffs while searching for children stolen by the fairies. As beach walkers stopped to look, it may have thought they were seals in trousers, as it lifted its woolly white head and cried 'Maw!' Few mammals are more endearing than a white-coated baby seal.

Our first plan was to guide it back into the surf. In refusing this option, it was smarter than we were. The 'baby fur' has little oil and easily becomes water-logged; besides, it hadn't 'lost' the sea – it simply had had enough of battering and near-drowning. Its knees were raw, and a long wound ran down its nose and under the chin. Grey seals have a tough cradling. They have just three weeks with mother before she abandons them in the waves. Armed with two weeks' supply of life-sustaining blubber, they must learn to survive storm and starvation. In bad years, up to 80 per cent of pups die. This 'white-coat' would not have been abandoned; rather, huge waves had washed it away from its mother.

Leaving some boys to keep the dogs off, I phoned Brendan Price, founder member and sole full-time worker at the Irish Seal Sanctuary in Dublin, a dilapidated swimming pool and pens ten miles from the sea. He and his wife have saved many an orphaned seal from death by dehydration and starvation, feeding them until they weigh about a hundredweight and then returning them to the sea where they came ashore. 'Stay well away from the teeth,' Mr Price told me. 'Hold it by the back flippers and ease it into a fish box, then get it to Cork station and put it on a train …' With hands wrapped in thick gloves, the transfer from beach to box was smoothly effected. Another box was upended on top and the handles of both tied tightly together. We were too late for the Dublin train, so we took the orphan home, created a small cave in an outhouse and settled it for the night. Village children came to view – it's not every day you see a seal in a fish box.

On Sunday, as crow-cawing, curlew-whistling dawn broke in fiery clouds above the bay, a young couple, members of the Cork Regional Museum Sub-Aqua Club, and I loaded the foundling, in his box, into the back of their van. At Cork station, Iarnród Éireann was most obliging; it wasn't the first time they had transported Price seals. It arrived safely in Dublin. We hope to see it again one day, as an adult, on Horse Rock, perhaps as 800 lbs of rutting male, with a ten-female hareem and white pups.

This evening, out on the beach, with the yellow sun behind me and my shadow thirty foot long, Ireland was another country, rich and rare. The bay was lake-calm, the green-blue colour of Tibetan turquoise. That was when one looked away from the sun: looking into the setting sun was impossible. It pierced through the trees above the village and spilled onto the shadowy waters in front of it in a river of gold. The houses behind were lost in shade. Smoke rose in straight columns from the chimneys. Swans swam on the golden river, cut out in black. A sky of clouds like fish scales soared over the trees, more a mullet than a mackerel sky. The peace was palpable, the air thick and still.

Later, as I returned from walking, the street lights lit up along the shore, the longest electricity bill in Ireland, as I call it. Their reflections shivered like orange candles on the black sea. The pier light then came on, brightest of all, and a green glow showed on one of the moored, small fishing boats. On the beach in front of the hotel, two boys, with hurleys, pucked a ball to one another in the fading light. Not a word was said. The sky was white now, with grey clouds drifting. Last sallies of rooks cawed and cruised, in ragged skeins across it, making for the home roost at Timoleague. Could we live anywhere more lovely, more tranquil – the Greek islands, the Canaries, the shores of the Arabian Sea? I think not; I have tried them. But it takes far-travelled eyes to see home.

December

In December, the channels between the sandflats,
lit by winter light, shine like gold. Our local woods
are far from leafless or drab. Beeches and oaks are
bare but the winter sun flashes like a million tiny
mirrors on the waxy leaves of holly, ivy and myrtle.
Then, there is the warmth of pubs with open fires
and the sort of spontaneous singing that starts in
a corner and spreads. And there is Christmas,
the families who have had homes here for generations
reuniting, midnight mass, bonhomie and goodwill.

~

Sally, mother of pups claimed to have the highest IQ in Dogdom.

The month began with the tide so high and the run-off from the fields so prodigious that young Fintan and his friends had to be taken home from school on a tractor when the bus, a full-size, Bus Éireann, long distance charabanc, broke down in a lagoon that had overtaken the road along our bay. The boys and girls waded to the shore – actually the verge – while the doughty driver remained stoutly in command of his vessel. A recovery vehicle was sent for and the omnibus rescued.

In the morning, when the deluge stopped and the sun shone, it was wonderful to walk out on the tide flats in the winter light, a strong wind scouring the banks and sending sand devils, with long tails, racing across the beach like things alive. Out at the bay mouth, the crests of the incoming waves were caught and flung back like plumes on the heads of creatures fighting to come ashore. The low tides last week exposed casts of thousands of peacock worms, ragged tubes of beach debris glued with mucus and standing half an inch out of the sand. Hidden in the lower tube at low water, the worms emerge as the tide covers them, spreading gorgeous feathery fans to filter the sea. Why these gills or food rakes should have colours as beautiful as a peacock one wonders but, as we know, dazzling displays in nature often occur where they will never be seen by a human eye. Patently, such artistry wasn't put there for our delectation, any more than were the amazing geometric shapes of krill or the wondrous lights of the denizens of the deep oceans.

As we walked, we cast long shadows ahead of us. The beauty of the furrowed sand was finer than any moody black-and-white photograph and couldn't be created by all the ingenuity of man. Across the estuary, gulls flew and flashed in great white curtains; perhaps sprats were trapped in the tide pools. Soon now we will have the annual sprat spectacular, when millions are trapped in the local bays and thousands of birds, along with amorous seals, arrive to feast on them. Remembering that some small grandchildren would be with us for Christmas, I trawled a rock pool with frozen fingers and was pleased to find a young shanny still in residence, although most rock pool life makes for deeper water once temperatures fall. So when the children arrive from London and we make the usual seashore expedition, we'll likely find not only shannies but brown, sinuous rocklings with whiskers, butterfish, crabs and perhaps brittle stars. Also there will be beadlet anemones, with their necklets of iridescent blue, strawberry anemones with green pips, and the various periwinkles and whelks.

On the estuary the mudflats and sandbanks shine like wet gold in the sun, and there are thousands of birds. On this beautiful and blessèd day in early December, it's so mild it could be spring and I am not at all surprised that the birds come here. In my garden there are nine blackbirds, seven of them probably from Scandinavia. They are feeding on the last wind-fall apples on the lawn. Last week I came upon a flock of Nordic thrushes, redwings and fieldfares, during a storm. They perch on the topmost branches of the trees, as if delighting in the blast. Quite unlike our garden song thrush, they are very wild and not easy to close in on. As the weather hardens, they arrive in dense flocks from Scandinavia and Russia and can strip the berries from a haw or holly tree in minutes. Then they are off, in a blur of wings, thrown on the gale like scattered leaves.

Fieldfares are immensely elegant birds, almost blue in outline, with cheddar yellow breasts and jet black tails. The smaller redwings, with rust-red sides and white eye-stripes, often travel with them, along with migrant mistle and song thrushes. Lost American birds arrive on this coast regularly, swirled aloft by hurricanes as they cross the Caribbean en route from breeding sites on the Canadian tundra to winter quarters in South America. Jet streams in the high atmosphere can move at 200 mph and a bird, like it or not, may reach West Cork from Florida in eighteen hours. Cape Clear Island, an hour west of here, has a famous bird observatory and is the southernmost place in Ireland, except for the Fastnet rock. Wherever American vagrants show up, the word goes out and bird-watchers from all over Ireland and the UK descend on the lucky spot, contributing welcome winter income to the local pubs and B&Bs.

If migrants are flying high enough, they may, in a sense, be falling for most of their journey. Some years ago a squadron of RAF jets was scrambled when a mysterious object appeared on radar screens over Derry city in Northern Ireland. It turned out to be a flock of whooper swans flying at 31,000 feet! A modified haemoglobin, capable of storing more air than ours, equips birds to survive and function at altitudes where we would perish. Some species migrate over Everest. Dunlin, no bigger than thrushes, have been recorded more than four miles high on migration from Scandinavia, although there is a 3°F drop for every 1,000 feet of the 23,000 feet at which they fly. Migrant birds know no frontiers. The imagination leaps to think that small creatures, fine-boned enough to be crushed in a human hand, tread the night sky miles above the icy poles and candlelit cities, each tiny body guided by the stars.

After storms, we often find our sheltered strands littered with the narrow, scabbard-like shells of razorfish. A native of these shores, the razorfish lives vertically beneath the sand and is rarely seen. The clean brown and white half-shell, up to eight inches long, is like the blade of a cut-throat razor: as kids, we thought shipwrecked sailors could shave with them. Recently I went fishing for bass with razorfish I had caught when, one day, while I walked along the surf as the tide came in, they literally shot up all round me out of the sand. Some stood upright, some fell over; why this extraordinary behaviour, I don't know. Picking them was like pulling carrots, except that the 'meat' was already out of the ground. I took a dozen home and kept them in the freezer. Next day I set off with a bagful to the shore, to see if they would attract bass, as I had been told. After an hour of seeing my bait taken by crabs but not by bass, I became bored and, what with the sea air, a trifle peckish too. I decided to sample a razorfish – we eat cockles, after all. Having discarded the siphon, I popped it in my mouth and chewed tentatively. Delicious – tender, oyster-flavoured and tanging of the sea! Deciding that bites in the hand were better than notional bites in the channel, I reeled in my line and made a meal of the bait. Bass have good taste in shellfish; I suppose they ought to know.

To gourmet readers desiring a fine dish of *fruits de mer*, I will reveal an arcane and esoteric method of catching razorfish, called 'razor-shells' in some places. First you should find an estuary of clean sand and go there at very low tide. Then you stalk stealthily along the sea's very edge, carrying a loaded salt cellar. If you like your sea-food *al fresco*, you might bring pepper and a slice of lemon too. When you find two small holes set in a keyhole-shaped depression in the sand, you have found the razorshell's lair. It may be filled with water; no matter. Into each hole, decant a teaspoon of salt. Shortly the razor will appear, the shell rising rampant, an inch at a time, until it stands on end, entirely exposed, and falls over. Alternatively, after a third of its length appears, you can grip it very firmly and pull.

Some say the tang of the salt makes the razorfish think the tide's come in and it's time for lunch (which, in a profound sense, is true). Others believe the concentrated salt is an irritant. In any case, remove the tube, then cook, freeze or, if you dare, simply open the shell, discard the siphon, add pepper and lemon and enjoy the poor man's oyster.

Along the bay margin, seashore and woodland run side by side. On good days the sea is dazzling in the clear, sharp light and in the woods the sheen of the winter sun on ivy gilds the tree trunks. Ivy cleverly displaces its leaves to ensure that each catches the maximum of sun. It is as if the leaves can see, and indeed some plants, during darkness, turn their leaves to be ready for the first light of dawn. Ivy is a vigorous old pagan, associated with druids, and with Bacchus and booze. It comes with the decorative holly at Christmas, possibly because it was considered a protection against a malevolent *pookeen* invading the old turf-roofed cabin. It has the last flowers of the year, offering a final drop of nectar to superannuated butterflies and bees.

Berries were all over our local holly until a couple of weeks ago, but I notice that the most accessible trees have now been stripped by holly hunters or birds. Happily, however, Fintan tells me he knows a secret bush, so off with him (when he comes back from school on the tractor) before someone else finds it. We should of course have harvested earlier, and stuck the sprays in the earth floor of a garden shed; this keeps the leaves bright and the berries fat and glowing right into the new year. In lore, the red berries are associated with Christ's blood, the leaves with the crown of thorns. Perhaps this is why cutting down a holly tree was considered bad luck, but it seems odd that lopping off branches at Christmas is acceptable.

It is no wonder mistletoe was considered magical in pre-Christian times, mysteriously sprouting, as it does, from the bare limbs of deciduous trees, especially oaks and apples. Oaks were sacred to the druids; mistletoe berries were thought to be the seeds of the oak god. At the winter solstice it was cut with a golden sickle to symbolise the death of the old year and the birth of the new. Kissing underneath it was the modest Christian substitute for robust fertility rites. Mistletoe itself has some funny habits – not our mistletoe, where only the people beneath it do funny things – but an American cousin. The seeds of our mistletoe are dispersed by getting stuck to birds' bills and then being rubbed off, ideally into the bark of the next tree. In the fruit pods of the dwarf mistletoe of the USA, the seeds lie in liquid. As they grow bigger the pressure builds until at last the pods burst and sends the seeds flying at up to sixty miles per hour to reach the next tree. Maybe better not kiss under the American variety. A seed travelling at that velocity could have a more knock-out effect than a kiss.

After four days of high winds and dramatic storms, there is suddenly an ominous stillness. As I dress, I look out my bedroom window. The sky is dirty yellow and two rooks flap between the trees like pterodactyls. They are never, normally, so low in the branches. As I watch, they glide to the broken-off top of a tall pine which, two nights ago, the gale snapped like a pencil. Nothing stirs in the garden except the rooks. Here, by the sea, there is often a small breeze, but not now. As I set off for a walk, I notice that no birds are feeding in the garden. The rooks hop aimlessly amongst the splintered branches, as if killing time. The air is dead and my movements and those of the dog seem muffled. At the pond, mallard and teal skulk along the reedy edges. The sky grows darker, night overtaking day. The wind hasn't risen yet but there is a short, vicious gust as I set off along the foreshore. The fields of the dark green hill behind me are dotted with *pilibíns* (lapwing) and curlew. They are not feeding or preening. They stand in ranks, shoulders hunched against the cold.

Out on the estuary, dense, white wedges of gulls crowd the sandbanks, beaks facing north-west, from where the wind will come. Along the tide wrack, thousands of rubbery, brown stalks of oarweed lie piled like flattened hurdles or staves. Everywhere are shells, particularly the 'Virgin Mary shell', the grey, fragile shell of the sea-potato, a spined urchin-like creature that burrows in the sand. As children, we pointed to the 'M' shape of tiny perforations on the upper surface, and said it symbolised Mary, the Mother of God. Nuns, I am told, say that, counted, these dots number the beads of the Rosary. And on the reverse side some see the Sacred Heart. People come from far and wide to collect them at Inchydoney Island, near Clonakilty, and a local hotelier tells me she has had letters from America asking her to send 'Virgin Mary shells'.

On the sand spits, empty clams and cockles bear witness to the ferocity of the seas which, forty-eight hours ago, ripped them from their beds and left them to the mercy of the birds. During these exhilarating but violent days, sprats, in their thousands, were thrown ashore at Rosscarbery. All the south coast bays have been full of sprat and herring and for the past week the gannets have been plummeting and diving very close inshore. As we watched, a huge wash of sprats ended on the sand opposite Rosscarbery pier. I wished I had had a bucket to hand. As a child, I remember a man in shirt-sleeves and a soft hat, with a horse and cart, selling fresh sprats at sixpence a bucket in Clonakilty. He stood in the back of his cart and simply scooped up a bucket of sprats as one might scoop up a bucket of water. A shovel stood buried in the small sprat mountain; he had shovelled them up on the beach and presumably washed them with bucketloads of the sea. This was nature's bounty as it used to be. There used to be more of every living creature, except ourselves.

One mid-December week, some years ago, marked the departure from this life of Sally, our liver-and-white Springer spaniel, mother of pups which their owners claimed to have the highest IQ in Dogdom. I wrote about her at the time, recounting her history with us and the place she had won in our hearts. I wrote that, the night she departed life '... a small boy sobbed himself to sleep and in the morning told us he had used up an entire box of tissues. She was thin as a lath but full of life and in good coat until a week before her death. We had taken her to a vet, concerned that, although she ate a bucket of food a day, she put on not an ounce of weight and had ribs like the ridges on a washboard. He – like everyone else – adjudged that it was probably because she had been feeding pups.

'She was a marvellous and beloved dog. We will sadly miss her as a companion on our walks and she is a great loss to the children. She was given to us by a hunter because she was "gun shy" and, for him, useless. But she raised game, providing us sight of woodcock and snipe we mightn't otherwise have seen and, while harming nothing, sometimes brought us closer to nature. I remember one warm January day when she was lazing on the lawn below my work-room window. A magpie, gleaming iridescent blue, alighted nearby. She stood, and gave chase for the fun of it, like she often gave hopeless chase to gulls on the beach. As if on cue, a second magpie swooped from the trees and hovered over her. She sprang up at it. It rose like a helicopter, teasing her, just out of reach. Then, it too alighted. She dashed at one, then the other, with not a hope of success.

'At first, I thought something edible near her might have attracted the birds. But no; it seemed the exercise was sheer mischief, no more or less. After a series of mad dashes and frantic sallies, the unfortunate dog gave up and sat, suddenly busying herself with her fleas. Now, the magpies glided softly down and alighted, one on each side of her. They strutted closer, wearing that chest-puffed, self-important air that magpies often have. Next, they began marching around her, left-right, left-right, one behind the other, in circular progress. Clearly, they had nothing in mind but devilment. "Here's a dumb dog," they seemed to have decided. "Let's get a rise out of her!" Poor dog! All she could do was to ignominiously leave the lawn or remain and pretend she didn't notice. Meanwhile, like toreros around a befuddled bull, they arrogantly circled her, no more than a foot away. It was heartening to see that, in nature, not all is hard work and grubbing, that there's time for fun too, even if at the expense of our poor distracted dog!

'Up to only a week before her death, she still walked enthusiastically and begged for the chance to retrieve stones. But, for some time, I had noticed that when I threw them, she ran only a short way, then returned. Usually she would retrieve from the very farthest distance of one's throw. On a beach of a million pebbles, she could find a stone one had touched for only a second. Then, one day, following Dara down the drive, she walked straight into a parked car. We looked into her eyes. They were as clouded as moonstones. She was totally, irreversibly blind.

'She was not an old dog – only 6, or 42 years old in human terms. A second vet was consulted. He asked if she drank water by the gallon and ate insatiably. When we confirmed this, he diagnosed diabetes. Hoping against hope, we sent her to a small animal hospital in Cork. There she stayed two nights, while tests were done, in the hope that her ketones might be adjusted. Forlorn hope. She would be blind forever and her chances of survival, even with daily insulin injections, were poor. As long as she lived, her diet would have to be carefully monitored. A square of chocolate offered by a child would put her into coma from which she would likely never return. An active, outdoor dog, her life wouldn't be worth living. Professionals advised that the best home was the great kennel in the sky. …'

At Christmas, music abounds in West Cork homes and pubs. Since coming back to Ireland, we've often said that every community on this island seems replete with musical talent but that we would likely find the same if we examined remote communities anywhere in the world. Music and story are the Irish arts, alive, robust and practised in every townland. It is said that we never became concert pianists because pianos were too big to carry around and, for many centuries, the Irish who retained and nurtured the culture were often on the run. Our music is of the fiddle and flute, the *bodhrán* and *uillean* pipes, and, just as important, the music of the voice. Voice music is not only song but story. In the first years of the twentieth century, Kuno Meyer discovered and recorded great music in far-flung places all over Ireland, while, as I mentioned earlier, Robin Flower, when he went to the Blasket Islands in the 1920s, found three great story-tellers in the then population of only fifty souls.

Those Blasket story-tellers, Tomas Ó Crohan, Peig Sayers and young Maurice O'Sullivan, might well have written plays as good as Synge's had they been born into a world with a theatre. The famous, it seems, were often 'discovered' by chance. They are fine exponents of their art, but others, as good, may elsewhere exist unsung. I've heard farm boys with the stamp of greatness fiddle in cottages, and heard lines worthy of Wilde written for local pantomimes. Take a small population anywhere and you will likely find a poet amongst them, a singer, an instrumentalist, a character actor, a comic, a storyteller. Long before we could turn on the television, we were adept at entertaining ourselves. In West Cork this is still the case. Walking into a country pub at eleven or twelve on a weekend night, it is not unusual to find a hushed audience and a voice rising clear and pure, full of a warmth and freshness not found in professional shows. At Christmas there is hardly a pub in the countryside or small towns of Munster where one can't find such unaffected gatherings of 'ordinary' Irish people and, in West Cork, almost certainly a sprinkling of expatriates too.

The old Irish Tourist Board slogan claimed, 'The most interesting people come to Ireland.' Indeed, there is hardly a parish along the south-west coast that isn't host to some 'blow-in's, as West Cork people call the strangers who come and settle in their midst. It is not an offensive term; the 'blow-in' can be a farmer who married-in from the next parish, or a foreigner from the far end of the earth. Both are welcomed by an easy-going people. Of the expatriates, some buy a ruin and an acre and struggle for a back-to-the-earth life; many of the organic producers who created the 'country markets' are ex-pats. Others are writers, painters, musicians and chancers; they contribute to the diversity and the *craic*. Artisans, chefs and potters create fine furniture, exotic food and fine ware. Some are, or were, international stars, seeking anonymity and peace and quiet in West Cork. The rich come and buy castles and paint them pink; the poor buy *bothán*s and dig over old acres. New Age 'crusties' live in caravans and benders on Cool Mountain, make fine baskets and entertain us at the famous *Craic na Coillte* summer street festival in Clonakilty. Like the first Normans, as the well-worn saying has it, it isn't long before they, and their school-going children, 'become more Irish than the Irish themselves'.

I, like the married-in farmer, am myself a 'blow-in', but not an 'expat'. Marie is a daughter of West Cork, born on a farm on a lovely coast twenty miles west of here. I spent some years of my childhood in a fine Georgian house in Emmet Square, Clonakilty, as did Michael Collins, the revolutionary, although he was dead long before I saw the light of day. My family moved on; I lived in every province in Ireland. Later, while I set up house by tropic seas, expatriates settled on my home shores. I returned, after thirty years, to an Ireland entirely changed, and knew I must stay. It wasn't simply that the society had 'liberalised'. No, the elements I found compelling had always been there, but I had failed to see them before I left. It was this older Ireland, the Ireland of which I have written every week for over twelve years, that brought me home, not the new-come dispensation, the cosmopolitan identity, the *à la carte* Catholicism, divorce and cohabitation – one can find all these elsewhere. T.S. Eliot made a wise observation, 'And the end of all our exploring/ Will be to arrive where we started/ And know the place for the first time.'

When I left Ireland in the 1950s, a parochial, inward-looking ignorance stalked the land; Gaelic culture was rammed down our throats, *fáinne*-wearing, GAA gobshites and priest-panderers sneered at or banned, with self-serving zeal, all 'foreign' and 'pollutant' influences. They banned O'Casey, they banned James Joyce. This narrow Catholic-nationalism eclipsed, for me and many others, the true nature of my fellow citizens, their quick intelligence, self-effacing humour, soaring poetry and irrepressible souls. In my youth and blindness I even failed to see the unique beauty of the land. Beauty was everywhere and commonplace; it was no compensation for immurement. Ireland was a gilded cage. The only hope was the boat to England and beyond.

When I returned in the 1980s all had changed, immeasurably, for the better; those who had stayed and rung in the social changes were the cause. Returnees and blow-ins helped, but it was the home-bound Irish themselves who had made the opportunity. In-comers added spice to local life and, paying high prices for scenic views, copper-fastened the value of an unspoiled environment. In 2002 I wrote and presented a series of TV programme for RTÉ, the national station, and in-comers, and their input, was the theme of one. My interviewees were a diverse and entertaining crew of blow-in salmon-smokers, boat skippers, sexy-sculpture makers, guest-house owners, environmental activists and artichoke farmers; all had been part of West Cork life for going-on thirty years.

I remember a brief return visit to Clonakilty in the 1960s, then a dusty country town, with the biggest news the unfortunate holiday-caravan horse that had dropped dead in the street. Today it is still as peaceful, but its attractions have burgeoned. Musicians abound, some of them internationally known. The environment and social life is entirely Irish, the population only six thousand; yet one can dine French, Italian, Thai, Pakistani, Hungarian or Chinese. One can shop at health food stores, attend a homeopath or alternative healing centre, buy French, Italian, German and American newspapers. Is the culture not diluted? is the town not tourisised? does one not hear blow-ins braying in strident American, Sloane Ranger English, or Australian 'strine' in the pubs? No: the buzz in the streets and the pubs is Irish: that is what the strangers came for: that is why they stay.

Today, as I write, a small tortoiseshell butterfly alights on my desk and is now fluttering at the window, looking very bright in the late December sun. Tortoiseshells suddenly appear like this during the winter or we find them on curtains and pelmets, wings folded, dry as if dead, which they sometimes are. Flutter, it may, but it would be unwise to release it into the elements. Perhaps it will go back to sleep until spring.

Outside it is a crisp, dry day, warm in sheltered corners. Colours are bright as new paint. This morning, below the cliffs, I crossed some rocks splashed with lichens as orange as the yolks of seagulls' eggs. Nearby, other lichens were red and others white, the rocks like artists' palettes. Medieval artists used the white of eggs for binding pigments. The lichens, as vibrant as the colours they made, stir old memories of magical December light, making me wonder if there is a recurring theme in Irish weather. I remember, as a child, the Christmas morning walk, to get us out of the house while my mother prepared the dinner. The day always seemed to be shining – yellow sun and frost along the verges and the bare branches of hedgerows hoary with crystals which sparkled against a sky so intensely bright that we could look at it only with slit eyes. It all seemed to fit very well with what we had been told about the glory of the day.

That was in inland Tipperary. There, of course, the winter air is sharper and crisper than in these soft, coastal climes. But during those childhood years, while I remember few white Christmases (one in Mayo, one in Donegal), I cannot remember the weather ever being wet. I cannot remember a Good Friday that was otherwise. These are the general impressions that colour a life and we probably all entertain them. Statistically, they may be wrong and reflect more a state of mind than a history of climate. All the summers of our childhood were sunny, we know.

Having spent many years and Christmases away from Ireland, I was overjoyed this year to have my memories confirmed. Christmas Day was wild and windy and there was little sun, but it didn't rain. St Stephen's, however, was a pet day, the air mild, with the landscape and seascape gilded with sunlight all the way west from the Galley Head. St Stephen's Day here – 'Boxing Day' elsewhere – is a traditional day for walking and visiting. Before settling down at warm hearths over hot whiskeys or mulled wine, we drove to Castlefreke, near Clonakilty, and set off down the mile-long stretch of Long Strand. The sun lit up the dunes and the beach was a promenade of delighted people. Smiling and chatting, they strolled arm-in-arm, accompanied by children, walking stick or dog. It seemed the whole world was out, red-faced and hearty as the jolly burghers of the old Dutch paintings, greeting one another on the frozen canals of old Amsterdam.

The mildness of the weather was wonderful, warm as summer in sheltered places. Before we'd gone five minutes into the Monterey pines behind the lake, behind the beach, we already had our jackets off and were depositing them, to be collected later, deep in the ferns. Here I saw my traditional Stephen's Day wren, hopping and churring and happily not 'caught in the furze' as the old mummer's song puts it. When I was a child 'Wran Boys', in rags and soot-blackened faces, would come to our door and sing the song and ask for money, some-times displaying a dead wren hanging in a bush. The pagan rite of dressing up and carrying the bush still prevails but, happily, nowadays they no longer murder a poor 'wran'.

On our walk today we remember Sally and talk of how she loved to race across this very strand, chasing gulls that she had no hope of catching. Sally is long gone; the children who played with her are grown; life, for Marie and myself, continues. This is a blessèd place, and we are blessed to walk here. At ruined Rathbarry Castle, two cock robins are conducting a barney about territory. It is the only dissent we have come across all day but is purely vocal, the pulse of life stirring, negotiating space to raise a new brood in a new year.

Index